GENESIS AND FALL OUT OF US-UK MILITARY ACTION IN IRAQ

Editor
V.D. Chopra

Publications

KALPAZ PUBLICATIONS
DELHI - 110 052

On Behalf of
International Institute for Asia–Pacific Studies, New Delhi

Genesis and Fall Out of US-UK
Military Action in Iraq

Rs. 790/-

ISBN : 81-7835-292-3

Published in 2004 in India by
Kalpaz Publication,
C-30, Satyawati Nagar,
New Delhi-110 052
Email : kalpaz@hotmail.com

Lasertype Setting by: Tact Computer Graphics, Delhi
Printed at: Chawla Offset Press, Delhi

Contents

Preface

In this volume entitled "Genesis and Fall Out of U.S.-U.K. Military Action in Iraq" outstanding scholars of India have examined objectively and in totality the recent military operation of U.S. and U.K. in Iraq, which began sometime in March 2003. Before this unprecedented military offensive was launched on Iraq, both Washington and London wanted the world public opinion to believe that this military operation was being organised to destroy stockpiles of weapons of mass destruction in Iraq. However, for eight long months no weapons of mass destruction in Iraq were found. As a matter of fact right from the beginning U.S.-U.K. ruling circles took the position that this military attack on Iraq was being launched for restoration of democracy and destruction of dictatorial regime of Iraq.

As the U.S. war on Iraq, "Operation Iraqi Freedom" entered the second week, some unexpected developments had taken place. The week-long military operations had proved some of the U.S. assumptions incorrect. Foremost among them was the supposition that the Iraqi people would invite the U.S. forces in with open arms and look to them as liberators from the "oppressive" regime of their President, Saddam Hussein. Even the U.S. military commanders had to admit that they were surprised at the stiff resistance offered by their adversary. This shows that the common people of Iraq considered this military operation as an occupation of their country by foreign military powers. With passage of time the opposition to this military occupation went on increasing causing serious damage both to the military might of the United States and its image in the entire world, in the Arab world in particular. It is, therefore, not surprising that not a single Arab country has supported this military adventure. On the contrary the militant and radical forces in the Arab world have been actively participating in opposing this military operation both physically and morally. The fact that this military operation has been opposed throughout the world, including in the United States and Great Britain is a clear manifestation of the growing opposition to this military venture.

To understand and analyse this development one has to bear in mind certain basic factors.

Firstly, although divided into thirteen sovereign states, more than a hundred million inhabitants of the Arab East are remarkably homogeneous. They share a common language, culture and excepting parts of Lebanon-religion. They believe in the concept of the Arab nation (Umma al Arabiya), and are proud of the predominance enjoyed by the Arabs in Islam and Islamic history. The principal dimensions of Arab nationhood appear to be a collective awareness of a common history, a distinctive language and culture - literature, art and folkways, a degree of similarity in appearance which is not racial since the Arabs are an amalgam of races and do not practise racial exclusivity.

Arabic is a major unifying factor; and all those who speak it are regarded as part of the Arab nation. Spoken Arabic varies widely from area to area, but the literary language is more or less the same throughout the Arab Middle East. 'Arabic is the holy language of Islam, and specifically - in its classical form - the language of the Koran', according to David Holden, a British author and journalist. 'Its meanings and symbols are woven into the entire fabric of Arab life, providing, as it were, a common nervous system through a complex inheritance of linguistic and religious cross - references'. This shows how deep rooted is the consciousness of the Arab nation in the psyche of the Arab people. The U.S.-U.K. military attack on Iraq is considered by the Arab people as an offensive on their nationhood. This is the crux of the problem but there is something more to it.

Secondly, the American stand on creation of an independent sovereign state of Palestine and its policy towards Israeli aggression on various Arab states, on Syria, Lebanon in particular has led the Arab people to believe that both Washington and London are using Israel as an instrument to subjugate them and control their oil resources. The Palestinian factor has played a key role in anti-American and anti-British feeling among the Arab people.

Seen in the context of these two factors the military operation in Iraq has unleashed a new ferment in the Arab world and this in turn has consolidated the extremist elements in the Arab world. To say this does not mean that the democratic, liberal, socialist and radical forces are not active in the Arab world. Nevertheless, American aggression in Iraq is being opposed by all the forces in the Arab world.

It is also relevant to mention here that though many western scholars had emphasised on the religious composition of Iraq - Shias, Sunnis and Kurds - saying that Saddam Hussein, belonging to the Sunni sect of Islam, which constitutes around 20 per cent of the Iraqi population, is hated, there is little evidence of this so far. In fact, they underestimated the hold of Arab nationhood on the consciousness of the people. They ignored the fact that even during the height of the Iran-Iraq war from 1980 to 1988 when a spiritual leader appealed to the Shiites in Iraq to revolt against the regime in Baghdad, they did not heed the appeal. This shows that despite authoritarian regime, the Iraqi people are not willing to accept the occupation of their land by American forces. The growing resistance against American armed forces should be seen in this context. In this sense no one can predict the outcome of the conflict in Iraq. However, from whatever angle you look at the recent developments in Iraq, one thing is certain that it is leading to growing alienation of the ruling circles of Washington and London. This is confirmed by the massive demonstration in London when President Bush visited this city in the third week of November, 2003. American President George W. Bush should have known by now how the rage against him from initiating the Iraq war and more generally at U.S. foreign policy have been unfolding itself and that too not just anywhere but in the country that counts itself as America's closest international ally.

In the end, it should be mentioned here that scholars and academics from Jawaharlal Nehru University, Institute of Defence Studies and Analyses, Jamia Millia Islamia University, Strategic Experts including retired Army Officers and Political Leaders have made rich contributions in this book. I profusely express my gratitude to them in making it possible to bring out this book which is the first of its kind since U.S.-U.K. military operation in Iraq, which began in the third week of March, 2003. But for their cooperation it would not have been possible to undertake this comprehensive study. I hope this book will serve as a source of information to the scholars, academics, researchers and policy makers. I must also compliment the senior members of the staff of the Kalpaz Publication, Delhi for their cooperation.

V.D. Chopra

List of Contributors

1. **V.P. Dutt** — Former Pro-Vice Chancellor of Delhi University and Former Member of Parliament.
2. **B.K. Shrivastava** — Former Professor, Centre for American Studies, Jawaharlal Nehru University, New Delhi and an outstanding Expert on the United States.
3. **K.R. Singh** — Former Professor, School of International Studies, Jawaharlal Nehru University, New Delhi.
4. **Rakesh Gupta** — Professor, Centre for Political Studies, School of Social Science, Jawaharlal Nehru University, New Delhi.
5. **Maj. Gen. (Retd.) Afsir Karim** — Security Expert and Editor, *Aakrosh,* Journal on Terrorism.
6. **Prakash Karat** — Member of Politbureau CPI(M) and an Author.
7. **V.D. Chopra** — Former Head of Economics Department in D.A.V. College, Rawalpindi, Former Chief Editor, *Patriot* Daily and *Link* Weekly, Vice-President for International

			Institute of Asia-Pacific Studies, New Delhi and a wellknown author.
8.	**Asghar Ali Engineer**	—	Chairman, Centre for Study of Society and Secularism, Mumbai, and Editor, *Islam and Modern Age.*
9.	**Manohar Singh Batra**	—	Deputy Director General (Retd.), All India Radio.
10.	**Justice Rajindea Sachar**	—	Chief Justice (Retd.) High Court of Delhi, UN Special Rapporteur on Housing, Member, U.N. Sub-Commission on Prevention of Discrimination and Protection of Minorities (Ex.) President, Peoples Union for Civil Liberties (PUCL) India (Ex.).
11.	**Shri Prakash**	—	Professor, Academy of Third World Studies, Jamia Millia Islamia University, New Delhi.
12.	**Brig. Chandra B. Khanduri**	—	AVSM, Senior Fellow ICHR, ABI and USI.
13.	**R.R. Subramanian**	—	Senior Research Associate, Institute for Defence Studies and Analyses.
14.	**Kalim Bahadur**	—	Former Professor, Jawaharlal Nehru University and an Expert on Pakistan.
15.	**A.K. Pasha**	—	Chairman, Centre for West Asian and African Studies (CWAAS), School of International Studies, Jawaharlal Nehru University, New Delhi. A leading Expert on the Gulf Countries.

16. **Jagdish P. Sharma** — Arab-Africa Specialist, Associate Professor, Deptt. of African Studies, University of Delhi.

17. **R.K. Wadhwa** — Asstt. Professor, Indian Institute of Foreign Trade.

18. **Girish Mishra** — Leading Economist.

19. **Manorma Dewan** — Editor, Press Asia International.

1
The Iraq War : An Overview

V.P. Dutt

We have to look at the broader picture than merely the attack on Iraq. We must take into account the framework within which the war against Iraq took place. There has been a paradigm shift in the analyses and objectives of many sections of the American foreign policy elite, after the end of the cold war, particularly after the gulf war and the disintegration of the Soviet Union. It is a new view of how America should wield its power and organize the world order.

The new thinking was first revealed in 1991-92 in a document prepared by Paul A. Wolfowitz, Trotskyite turned neoconservative, then defence aide and now Deputy Defence Secretary to Dick Cheney, then Defence Secretary and now Vice President. The 46-paged Defence Planning Guidance was the first to lay down the doctrine of preemptive strikes and adhoc assemblies in place of present international system, but also that America shall brook no rival on this planet, no matter whether friend or foe. It made a case for a world dominated by one superpower with sufficient military might to deter any nation or group of nations from challenging US supremacy. Four potential rivals were identified: Germany, Japan, Russia and India. China did not find a place but it is asserted that it was added to the list subsequently. The document also discussed India's "hegemonistic aspirations over the other states in South Asia and the Indian Ocean". The document was leaked and had to be disowned.

At another level was Richard Perle, until recently Chairman of the Pentagon's Defense Advisory Board, who has had to resign under the shadow of a scandal involving the dispensation of military contracts. It should be noted parenthetically that Richard Perle was representing Global Crossing, a telecommunications company seeking Defence Department approval to be sold to a firm controlled by Chinese investors. Indeed, Perle was not the only member of the Advisory Board with corporatise to the Pentagon. In all, atleast nine of the Board's thirty members were reported to be linked to companies that won more than $76 billion in contracts with the Defence Department over the past two years. This picture reflected what was described as incestuousness between the defence industry and the Pentagon. To take another example, former CIA director, James Woolsey, was the main partner in a firm that was soliciting investment for homeland security companies. Similarly, retired Admiral William Oeens, former vice-chairman of the Joint Chiefs of Staff was a director on the boards of five companies that won more than $60 million in defence contracts in 2002. These men were defending themselves on the plea that since they were unpaid for their service, there was no ethical conflict. Whether this argument cuts any ice may be left to the judgment of the reader.

To get back to the issue of the neo-conservative philosophy, Richard Perle was writing obituaries of the international system that was "outdated" and did not serve the security interests of the United Nations. He told the *Washington Post:* "we have to take the war against them (the terrorists) often to other people's territory" and "we could not have our hands tied by an antiquated institution", that is the traditional international system and the UN.

George Bush enthusiastically embraced these ideas which were further refined and defined by Donald Rumsfeld and Condoleeza Rice. These ideas found ample expression first in George Bush's State of the Union address in January 2002 mentioning the axis of evil, then his commencement speech at West Point in May rejecting deterrence and containment as outdated and finally on 20 September 2002 with his pronouncement of the policy of preemption when the national security doctrine was proclaimed.

As a significant aside, it should be noted that the United States grew faster than the other major states during the 1990s and dominated investment in the technological advancement of its armed forces (revolution in military affairs—RMA) so that the US moved so quickly in high-tech warfare that no state or coalition could challenge US hegemony, and now with a new security doctrine, none would be allowed to do so in future either.

The doctrine of preemption, however, would be available only to the US because of the indefinable nature of the threat to US security. Rumsfeld articulated the new thinking: "there are things we know that we know. These are known unknowns. But there are also unknown unknowns. These are things we do not know that we do not know. Each year we discover some more unknown unknowns". Therefore, the United States should have the right to preemptive strike at these unknown unknowns. Again Rumsfeld: "the absence of evidence is not evidence of absence of weapons of mass destruction". The US should have the right to decide. "It is the mission that must decide the coalition, not the coalition that decides the mission". Ipsofacto America must not be bound by the constraints of the international system to ensure its security against such elusive threats.

Or take another statement by Richard Haas who until recently was Director of Planning in the State Department: "What you are seeing in this administration is the emergence of a new principle or body of ideas... about what you might call the limits of sovereignty entails obligations. One is not to massacre your own people. Another is not to support terrorism in any way. If a government fails to meet these obligations, then it forfeits some of the normal advantages of sovereignty, including the right to be left alone inside your own territory. Other governments, including the United States, gain the right to intervene. In the case of terrorism, this can even lead to a right to preventive...self-defense. You essentially can act in anticipation if you have grounds to think it's a question of when, and not if, you're going to be attacked."

Let us consider the situation as it prevails on the ground today in the world. Almost the entire globe is ringed with US bases. So far as Asia is concerned, the Americans now have military presence in Afghanistan, Pakistan, the Philippines, Japan, South Korea, Central Asia, Saudi Arabia, Kuwait, Oman, Bahrain and Qatar - some 50,000 troops in these bases. Afghanistan has some 8,000 US troops; Pakistan an unspecified number; atleast 3,000-5,000 troops in Central Asia; some 18,000 US personnel and 84 combat aircrafts in Japan which is also home to the 7th fleet and 20,000 marines; 29,000 in South Korea; naval and air bases in Guam and Diego Garcia; about 108 in Thailand; the Philippines still has 7,500 US troops and in the last couple of years, America quietly built 13 air bases in Central Asia and towards the Middle East.

Let us not forget the 98,000 US personnel in Europe (50,000 troops and 60 combat aircrafts in Germany; 12,400 in Italy; 9,200 in U.K.; some 8,000 in Belgium, Greece, Netherlands, Norway, Portugal, Spain and Turkey). The Mediterranean is patrolled by US 6th fleet, the Balkans boast presence of some 2,000, Kosovo 5,000 and 840 army and airforce personnel in Hungary and Macedonia. The 5th fleet navigates between the Gulf and the Arabian sea and the least 370 army, airforce and marine personnel in Columbia and Honduras. Just as in the Pacific, there is a large naval presence in the Atlantic.

The significance of American dominance from Central Asia to the Gulf region has wider dimensions. The Gulf has two-third of the proven oil reserves of the world with Saudi Arabia presently holding 269 billion barrels and Iraq 112 billion barrels of proven reserves. Central Asia has proven reserves of some 30 billion barrels and potentially could hold around 104 billion barrels.

The figures for consumption and import of oil by major oil consuming countries make a telling picture. Let us first note the consumption pattern and then the import pattern. North America consumes 24 million barrels daily, Europe 14 million barrels, and the Asia-Pacific region 20 million barrels. As for imports, the United States, the European Union (EU) and Japan import 60, 75 and 80 per cent respectively of their oil consumption. The import of crude oil from the Middle East accounts for a high percentage of the total import of oil by these countries or their formations, for example, the United States 22 per cent, the EU 36 per cent, Japan 80 per cent, China 44 per cent and other Asia-Pacific countries 73 per cent.

What does all this add upto: that oil is one vital factor but not the only one; that hegemony is another factor, but it goes well beyond hegemony and aims at dominance over the world order. American imperialism has become coterminus with American nationalism. There is a widespread belief about American exceptionalism and uniqueness. Robert Kagan, a former State Department official and in the American context a liberal, for instance, compares USA with Mars and Europe with Venus. America has the power and has to use it. Europe no longer has the power and is, therefore, an exponent of the rule of law and the international system. Kagan adds: "Americans have always been internationalists, therefore, but their internationalism has always been a by-product of their nationalism.. That is why it was always so easy for so many Americans to believe, as so many still believe today, that by advancing their own interests they advance the interests of humanity. As Benjamin Franklin put it, America's cause is the cause of all mankind...It is reasonable to assume that we have only just entered a long era of American hegemony...Americans seek to defend the advance of a liberal international order. But the only stable and successful international order Americans can imagine is one that has the United States as its centre. Nor can Americans conceive of an international order that is not defended by power, and specifically by American power" .

So, the issue was not just Saddam Hussein and a brutal dictatorship. The issue has been and still is what kind of international system we wish to see established. The Iraq issue was before the United Nations. The UN inspectors had been sent to Iraq under a UN mandate. They had submitted two reports. They wanted more time to complete their assignments. But the US decided to have no more of it. It could not get a majority in the UN and so decided to act unilaterally. What could have been achieved through peaceful means became the subject of a brutal war.

So where are the weapons of mass destruction that Saddam Hussein was supposed to possess? Or the chemical and biological weapons against which the American troops had worn masks in the early stages of Iraq war? The Bush and Blair teams continue to insist that they would some day find these weapons. No one else believes so. The blame game is on and both Bush and Blair are looking for fall guys. Bush has already found one in George Tenet, the CIA head. In perhaps the most detailed description of the trail that led to the deliberate exaggeration of the threat from Saddam Hussein, Barton Gellman and Walter Pincus of the *Washington Post* brought out the story of the rhetoric on the threat outgrowing the supporting evidence (*Washington Post*, 10 August 2003).

A CIA analyst presented on 22 January "evidence" about Iraq's efforts to buy high-strength aluminium tubes to be used for centrifuges to enrich uranium for a nuclear bomb before the United Nations' nuclear inspectors who had been skeptical about Saddam Hussein's possession of the nuclear hardware. But the IAEA, UN's nuclear watchdog was unimpressed as it had uncovered strong evidence that Iraq was using the tubes for conventional rockets. Nevertheless, a danger of a nuclear-armed Saddam Hussein, "more potent as an argument for war, began with weaker evidence and grew weaker still in the three months before war". Thus, began a pattern in which President Bush, Vice President Cheney and their subordinates - in public and behind the scenes – made allegations depicting Iraq's nuclear weapons programme as more active, more certain and more imminent in its threat than the data they had would support. On occasions, *Washington*

Post writers discovered, administration advocates withheld evidence that did not conform to their views. The White House seldom corrected mis-statement or acknowledged loss of confidence in information upon which it had previously relied. They slurred over or fudged the fact that what Saddam Hussein did not have was the principal requirement for a nuclear weapon, a sufficient quantity of highly enriched uranium or plutonium. The administration had no real evidence that Iraq was trying to obtain those materials.

In fact, the US administration began as early as last August systematic coordination for propagating the view about Saddam's possession of nuclear weapons, when Bush's Chief of Staff Andrew Card formed a White House Iraq Group (known as WHIG) to set the strategy for an escalating confrontation with Baghdad. The rhetoric on Saddam Hussein's nuclear weapons and the imminent threat became louder by the day. To cut the story short, the White House, the Vice President's Office and the National Security Adviser and her aides mounted a systematic campaign not supported by the evidence produced by the intelligence agencies and about which there were serious doubts within the agencies themselves.

Many knowledgeable analysts believe that the Bush administration actually wanted to make a statement and establish a point for which Iraq was the most convenient spot. The point was that USA was the top guy and no one should be in doubt, least of all the terrorists. The world should know that USA had the capacity to inflict "shock and awe" through its high-tech weapons of mass destruction at its adversaries, be they be one, or two or three simultaneously.

President Bush and his teammates are brazening it out with matter of fact statements that even if no weapons of mass destruction were found, Saddam Hussein had to be ousted in continuation of the war against terrorism. Deputy Defence Secretary, Paul D. Wolfowitz, put new emphasis on the current fighting's in Iraq calling it "the central battle" in the post-September II, 2001 war on terrorism. He told Fox News that "it is the sacrifice that is going to make our children and our grand children safer because the battle to win peace in Iraq now is the central battle in the war on terrorism", without providing any evidence of a link between Saddam Hussein and Al Qaeda. In fact, Wolfowitz admitted that "nature of terrorism intelligence" was "intrinsically murky", but went on to link Iraq to the September 11 attacks on the World Trade Centre and the Pentagon. This elicited a retort from Senator Levin, "Boy, it sure didn't sound murky before the war. There were clear connections we were told between Al Qaeda and Iraq. There was no murkiness, no nuance, no uncertainty about it all".

President Bush has also accused those asking awkward questions about the whereabouts of Saddam Hussein's weapons of mass destruction of re-writing history. In a speech he said in the middle of June: "we made it clear to the dictator of Iraq that he must disarm. He chose not to do so, so we disarmed him. And I know there's a lot of revisionist history now going on, but one thing is certain. He is no longer a threat to the free world and the people of Iraq are free" . But as two senior American scholars have pointed out, if anyone is revising history, it is the US President. Mr. Bush had made the Iraq's WMD programme as a test case for his doctrine of preemption. He had said before the start of the war that the threat from Iraq was "grave and growing". "Intelligence gathered by this and other governments leaves no doubt that the Iraqi regime continues to possess and conceal some of the most lethal weapons ever devised," he warned on the eve of war. "We know where they are," said Donald Rumsfeld, the defence secretary, as US and British forces advanced into Iraq. But 90 days after the main fighting ended, US forces have yet to find a single chemical artillery shell, litre of anthrax or uranium enrichment facility.

The US administration was certainly hoping to utilize the Iraq oil resources as well as massive re-building contracts to be sold out to US companies for boosting the economy. The media reported prominently how Kallogg Brown and Root (KBR) and the Bechtel Corporation were rewarded contracts in the region of $1 billion for reconstruction in Iraq, that included rehabilitation of oil supplies from Iraq. The media also pointed out that KBR was the construction side of Halliburton that had been doing big business with the US military in the last two decades and that the Vice President, Dick Cheney, had been a chief executive of this company from 1995 to 2000. The former Secretary of State, George Schultz, is not only on the board of Bechtel, but is also chairman of the advisory board of the Committee for the Liberation of Iraq, a group with close ties with the White House and engaged in reconstructing the Iraqi economy through war. The company also hired Kenneth J. Oscar who had been acting Assistant Secretary of the Army associated with the Pentagon's $35 billion-a-year procurement budget.

It is another matter that as events unfolded in Iraq after the war, the Iraq victory failed to oil the world economy. The US had planned for a quick resumption of the production of 2 million barrels a day, but three months since the end of the war, the refineries have been plagued by power cuts, sabotage, and some of them are at a standstill. The target of 2 million barrels a day appears to be far from achievement immediately. Indeed, the post-war destabilization is contributing to the high price of oil around $28-29, which suits the OPEC but is detrimental to the growth of many countries in the world. The anti-US guerrillas have taken to economic terrorism as a senior official of Standard Chartered bank quipped, "a prolonged period of $30-a-barrel price is not the prescription central bankers and finance ministers would have written for the world economy right now".

The war has not gone the way the United States expected. Firstly, the US administration has unleashed forces that it may not be able to control, Washington has gone out there not as a shining example of democracy but as an imperial power. This has also resulted in a fairly violent struggle between various Shia clerics for control in the wake of overthrow of the Saddam regime. It raises disconcerting questions whether a secular state, that Iraq was, would give way to a theocratic regime or even whether Iraq may degenerate into mutually feuding regions under the domination of either tribal chiefs, warlords or "fundamentalist" clerics. All this may not happen and while hoping for the best, it would be prudent to expect the worst.

Secondly, the war has not gone Washington's way in a real financial sense too. Washington did not anticipate the ballooning expenditure that it would have to incur in Iraq and that too for a long time. The current expenditure comes to around $4 billion-a-month and estimated at $50 billion every year for how long, no one knows. Neo—Conservatives in the United States are already a worried lot. Some of them are calling for "do what it takes in Iraq" - more troops, more money and more civilian workers to avoid a possible disaster, They, perhaps correctly, anticipate that President Bush's "vision" could die in Iraq with a resultant consequence for the future course of American foreign policy, world leadership and American security. They are, therefore, asking for a huge augmentation in US troop strength in Iraq as well as massive increase in the "necessary down payment". They no longer seem to hope - which has been the official Washington line - that reconstruction in Iraq would be funded by Iraq's oil revenues.

The administration is still averse to follow this course which could lead to fateful consequence for itself as well as for the doctrines that they have espoused. Both Rumsfeld and Washington's man in Iraq, Bremer, still insist that there was no need for extra troops for they believe that it was preferable to tolerate the current level of casualties and sabotage than to expand the security forces and the expenditure of capital in Iraq because of its incalculable consequences. They are also gambling on a gradual reduction in violence hoping that the people would tire out. This might happen gradually but there is the danger that it might not turn out like that. Although much of the trouble until recently had come from Sunni Arabs, the evidence is very clear that the Shia communities, who formed the majority, are increasingly restive and could prove to be a highly destabilizing element.

Yet another factor in Iraq influencing domestic politics in the United States is the mounting casualties of the so-called coalition forces. In fact, more American soldiers have died since the end of the war than during it. Daily, US soldiers are becoming fatal targets of guerrillas and snipers. So, it is not only the Iraqi public which is becoming restive but the American public too. We need not dwell on this aspect but it should be kept in focus while considering the international implications of the Iraq war. Yet another disquieting dimension is the harmful impact the Iraq war has had on the international struggle against terrorism.

As Senator Graham, former chairman of the Senate Intelligence Committee and now a candidate for the Democratic presidential nomination, pointed out recently that the decision to go to war against Iraq had actually harmed the war on terrorism. "It took our focus off our number one enemy, Al Qaeda and refocused it on Iraq and has, therefore, allowed Al Qaeda to regenerate", the Senator said on Fox TV.

Unfortunately, the US and British administrations have given almost a fatal blow to the international order. They have arrogated to themselves the right to change governments in the world and have thereby pushed the world to the edges of disorder. Their actions have disrupted the United Nations and have gravely damaged their own alliance system. They have sown the seeds of disaffection throughout the world. There was a great deal of sympathy for the United States after the September 11 attacks on the World Trade Centre and the Pentagon but this fellow feeling has been rapidly dissipated. As former President Jimmy Carter put it aptly: it is *just_war*-not a just war.

The Bush administration believed that by throwing out Saddam and occupying Iraq, it would "transform the Middle East". Once Saddam was gone, there would be a liberal democracy transplanted in the pliable soil of Iraq, far–reaching changes in Saudi Arabia and the political map of the whole of West Asia would be redrawn in the image of the United States. Those assumptions proved to be more a case of wish being the father of thought than rooted in history and sociology.

It is apparent even to the foreign policy elite in the United States that those assumptions have gone awry. They have induced new tensions and divisions both within the administration and the foreign policy elite. One section wants that the United States should put in more troops and pour in more money in order to secure its objectives while the other wishes to turn to the U.N. body for assistance. As an instance of the first line of thought, Robert Kagan and William Kristol have written recently in a conservative magazine that "the danger that the resources the administration is devoting to Iraq right now are insufficient and the speed with which they are being deployed is insufficiently urgent. These failings, if not corrected soon, could over time lead to disorder". This is at the heart of the problem that the U.S. is facing.

On the other side, Senator Biden points out that the administration is saying publicly that they do not need any more troops, but they are trying to get the Indians, the Turks and the Bangladeshis to contribute 40,000 additional troops as early as possible. Henry Kissinger has added: "it will not be possible to keep asking for assistance without giving them some role. Big countries which participate have to be given some sense of political participation". As yet many foreign policy experts continue to believe that there was no exit now without causing a catastrophe for the West in the Islamic world and that USA might have to go alone but should try to involve the world community.

It is, of course, easier said than done. The U.S. wants to eat its cake and still have it. They would like U.N. members to contribute troops and help stabilize the situation in Iraq but they still want it all under U.S. command and control. But as the *New York Times* pointed out in its editorial on 27 August (2003): "The United States will pay a high price in blood and treasure if the Bush administration persists in its misguided effort to pacify and rebuild Iraq without extensive international support... Mr. Bush needs to enlist help from more experienced officials in Washington and at the United Nations. That will not be easy for an administration that openly advertises its contempt for the UN... The administration should also be honest about the investment - American and international - required to rebuild Iraq. A stable peace in Iraq cannot be won on the cheap or absent foreign partners. With the death count mounting daily, it is time for Mr. Bush to stop pretending otherwise".

Similarly, the *Washington Post* in its editorial of 28 August referred to the US administrator in Iraq, Paul Bremer's skeptical statement: "how does the situation on the ground get better" if the UN is given a slice of his authority. With equal sarcasm, the editorial retorted: "Here's one answer: It would facilitate the arrival of tens of thousands of capable troops from Turkey, India and Pakistan and spring billions in reconstruction donations from European and Arab governments. But for too many in the administration, unilateral US control, rather than stability or democracy, has somehow become the paramount objective in Iraq, even as painful American casualties increase."

India has had ancient historical ties with the region now called Iraq as well as political and economic relations with the modern state of Iraq. India's policy should be clear. It should take steps where it can help, like sending health workers or setting up of hospitals, assisting with teachers and utilizing the NGOs for reconstruction of Iraq and for improving living conditions to the extent that it can feasibly do so within its limits. But India cannot and must not be seen as a occupying power or as a part of a coalition of occupiers. This should not mean any policy of confrontation with the United States. It should be seen only as actions in pursuit of India's national interests. By sending a few thousand troops (17,000 in all) against a US troop force of 150,000 cannot mean that India necessarily starts playing a big role in world affairs. Certainly the arrival of 5,000 Police troops in Iraq does not signify that Poland has now become a world power. We should keep aligned with the world community, but not necessarily with any particular country.

Indeed we should keep reaching out to the democratic impulses of the American people. The United States is not a monolith and a particular administration's policy cannot be equated with the opinion of the entire country. We continue to develop economic linkages with the United States without sacrificing our own interests. Our interests demand that Iraq should emerge as an independent entity - the sooner the better. We can help the international community in healing the wounds but not in imposing upon the people of Iraq or suppressing them. We are certainly a part of the world-wide coalition against terrorism, but the Iraq conflict should be delinked from the war against terrorism, for the conflict in Iraq has in no way been a struggle against terrorism.

2
The New Trends in World View of the United States

B.K. Shrivastava

During the long decades of the Cold War the United States perceived itself as the leader of the West that was engaged in a war for freedom and democracy against totalitarianism and expansionism of its adversaries. It viewed the world as divided between friends, non-aligned, and adversaries. With all its flaws the world was still an interdependent world. Even economically and militarily the most powerful country in the world needed the cooperation of other countries for the realization of its foreign policy agenda. In its competition and conflict with adversaries, the United States sought the cooperation from friends and allies. This American worldview began to change with the end of the Cold War. There was no power that had the capacity to threaten the security of the United States. It could, if it so decided move its armed forces in any crisis situation without worrying about the conflict escalating into a wider war with the Soviet Union. The United States saw itself at the center of this new world order. Nothing could be done without its cooperation. It was the terrorist attack on 9/11 by Al Qaeda that shattered the complacency of the United States. It found itself vulnerable despite its formidable military capability. A non–state actor breached its security with an unimaginable and non-conventional weapon. The terrorist organization that stunned the world by its audacious attack against the United States had spread its network in more than sixty countries. The United States alone could not counter the threat without the cooperation of other countries. It sought international cooperation to meet the new challenge by threats and blandishments. There were, however, many that willingly joined the war against international terrorism under the leadership of the United States because they themselves had been waging their own struggle against international terrorism. While these countries no longer faced criticism for the violation of human rights and carried out their own little wars, it was the United States that ran the global war against international terrorism.

In the early seventies the US conceded that the Soviet Union had achieved nuclear parity with it and Germany and Japan posed a challenge to its economic leadership. In nearly two decades after that, the United States had moved far ahead of its rivals in economic and strategic areas. It emerged after the end of the Cold War as the sole superpower, with a high tech army, and occupied the top slot in the global economy. The co-relation of forces had changed. The economy of the Soviet Union, in contrast, had been declining throughout the eighties. With its limited economic resources it was in no position to sustain its policy of military parity with the United States. China had turned inward in search of higher economic and strategic capability. The German and the Japanese economies were mired in difficulties. The United States, in the nineties was in a happier position to carry out its unilateral foreign policy agenda and reconstruct the world in its own image.

In the emerging world order, the United States did not perceive its freedom to pursue its own policy goals restricted in any way. This became evident during the Kuwait crisis in 1990-91. Brent Scowcroft, President George Bush's National Security Advisor wrote in the context of the Gulf War: " ... we had sought United Nations support from the outset of the crisis... **not because we thought we required its mandate. The UN provided another cloak of political cover. Never did we think that without its blessing we could not or would not intervene."** (Emphasis added.)[1] And in November 1990, President Bush wrote, "when the

French Foreign Minister Roland Dumas again proposed that we tell the Iraqis that if they pull out, we would agree to a conference on the Middle East." There was no way the United States could support the proposal. An exasperated George Bush, concluded: " It was clear to me that it was going to be the United States **alone** that have to pull the trigger." (Emphasis added). The United States sought the Security Council resolution authorizing the use of force only "as a political measure to seal the international solidarity and strengthen its domestic support by spelling out that we could use force."[2] Before intervening in Panama the US did not seek authorization for the use of force from the UN. And in case of intervention in Haiti, it achieved its objective without firing a single shot. But during the entire crisis it paid scant attention either to OAS (Organization of American States), or, overwhelming public opinion against intervention in Latin America. [3]

In the1991 Gulf war, the United States succeeded in getting the endorsement of the United Nations Security Council and support of more than thirty countries that included several Arab countries and four non– Arab Muslim countries. It could therefore present its action as multilateral effort to liberate Kuwait, an occupied country. US politicians of all shades thereafter swore by multilateralism but none of them ever renounced unilateralism. The United States set its own policy agenda and then consulted with the allies and sought the endorsement of the United Nations. Consultation did not mean acceptance of their views. In the Kosovo crisis, the United States deliberately bypassed the United Nations because Russia had asserted that it would veto the resolution authorizing armed intervention. It used NATO as a substitute of the UN to give its intervention a multilateral character. That such disregard weakened the UN was evident but there was no serious protest then either by France and Germany who are now protesting so vigorously. In fact, just a few days before leaving office in January 1993 George Bush declared that while the United States should strive for international support of its action that can not be a prerequisite... sometime a great nation has to act alone." This accurately summed up the US position.

The United States concedes that it is not possible to intervene in all crises in the world. George Bush, Sr. repeatedly argued that the Bosnia crisis was in Europe and therefore it was Europe's responsibility to solve it. Only when Europe could not solve it, the United States intervened, justifying it on the basis of national interest. The US emphatically renounced the role of a global policeman but claimed to lead the world. The role of the US as the leader was the theme that was constantly emphasized by President Clinton to rationalize the unequal burden that the US had to bear. The US also proudly declared that no problem could be solved without its assistance. Germany and Japan had no capacity to solve any problem. And countries wanting to assist in international intervention on humanitarian concerns could not do things on their own. In support of the contention it pointed out that it had to ferry the French forces to Somalia and the British forces to Bosnia.

During the last presidential campaign, George Bush did not reveal any grasp of international affairs or an exciting new vision of a world order. Indeed, it turned out that he had very limited exposure to the outside world. It was rightly presumed that he would be heavily dependent on his foreign policy advisors. He is a fervent Christian and had empathy with some, if not all the ideas of the Christian right that had emerged as an influential group within the Republican Party. It often adopted extremely conservative positions and expressed them aggressively. Within the larger entity of this group there were number of smaller groups with their own different favourite agenda. The Christian right had become for the Republicans what the trade unions were once for the Democrats. During the Cold War it had strongly assailed the "evil empire" and supported assertive and aggressive foreign policy stance of the Reagan Administration. After the disappearance of "evil empire", it found a new focus on cultural degeneration in the United States. Its emphasis on "family values" had won for the Christian right a big following. President Bush himself was a strong supporter of "family values" and stood squarely with the Christian right on such social issues as abortion and the rights of the homosexuals. In foreign policy, it wanted to aggressively advance the value of freedom and democracy. The Christian right opposed giving MFN status to China before the Congress, pleaded for sanctions against countries that prosecute or limit the freedom of the Christians, opposed funding to the IMF and the United Nations, and supported the anti–communist forces in El Salvador, Honduras and Nicaragua. It supported Israel. Some fundamentalist Christians within the group believe that the Second Coming of the Christ would occur only after Israel rebuilds God's temple in Jerusalem. They support Israel's full control over the land - not ceding to the Muslims any of it.[4] Historically; there has been tension in the relations between Christians and the Jews. But the Christian right reversed the trend. Its newfound "enemy" was the Islamic world that was antipathetic to western values and supported terrorism. Rev. Franklin Graham and Jerry Falwell went to the extreme of suggesting that Islam is "evil" and that Prophet Muhammad was a terrorist.[5] The President leaned towards Christian right even though he did not share their antipathy towards Muslims and Islam.

Besides the Christian right, the neo-conservatives (neocons) have profoundly influenced the worldview of the Bush Administration. Like the Christian right, the neocons are opposed to liberal worldview. Indeed, many of their leading lights claimed that they had moved from left to right in the American political spectrum. It was said about the neocons that they ran away with the foreign policy agenda of the United Sates and the first item on their own agenda was war.

In the eighties, the neocons became an intellectual force to reckon with. They derived great comfort from Reagan's aggressive foreign policy because opposing the "evil empire" was on the top of their agenda. But Reagan himself moved away from his aggressive stance during his second term. During the eight years of the Clinton Administration they lost much of their shine but with the election of George Bush, Jr. in 2000, especially after September 2001 terrorist attack, infused a new life in them. Richard Perle, a leading neocon figure, was the chairman of the Defense Policy Board, a non-official organization, which advised US Defense department. Irvine Kristol, one of the neocon *Gurus*, once observed that neocons were liberals who were mugged by reality. They believed that the United States should be militarily strong. They had strong commitment to human rights and promotion of freedom and democracy was central to their ideological position. Some analysts argued that promotion of democracy was impossible in an Islamic country. The neocons responded by pointing to Turkey, which was Islamic as well as democratic. They contended that people basically want freedom and on that premise unrealistically predicted that there would be reaction to extremity of *sheria.* The critics of neocon mocked them by calling them "chicken hawks" as many of the neocons (Perle himself) had not served in the military. A large number of their leading lights were Jewish and would not agree to anything that would be against Israel's interest. This would partially explain their attack on Islam and the Islamic world.[6] Norman Podhoretz, the founder of *the Commentary* argued in that journal in February 2002 that "Islam has become an especially fertile breeding ground of terrorism in our time. This can only mean that there is something in the religion itself that legitimizes the likes of Osama Bin Laden, and indeed there is obligation imposed in the Koran to wage holy war..." Such pernicious and misleading arguments completely ignored the fact that there were terrorists who belonged to other religions as well but those religions were never linked with terrorism.

The Administration was divided on its worldview. While the Pentagon and the Department of Defense under Donald Rumsfeld, his deputy Paul Wolfowitz, and National Security Advisor Condeeza Rice reportedly headed the hawks, Secretary of State Colin Powell, a realist, opposed any hasty rush to war. He wanted to work with the allies instead of going alone. Much depended on with whom the President would side. David Frum, another influential neocon, was a speechwriter of the President from January 2001 to February 2002. He was author of the phrase "axis of evil." That the President included the phrase in his speech indicated that the President agreed with this characterization.

The inclusion of Iran in the axis came at a time when its President Muhammad Khatimi was pushing hard for greater freedom for the Iranians. Frum subsequently wrote "much of the American elite out of a combination of guilt and self doubt and the urge to be seen as good fellows "were willing to constrict the freedom of action of the US by accepting such international agreements as Kyoto protocol, International Criminal Court, and Land mines treaty." He added that with his "axis of evil" speech President Bush served notice to the world that he felt no guilt and no self doubt, and he was a lot less eager to be perceived as a good fellow than he was to stand up to the bad fellows." Anthony Lake, National Security Advisor to the President in the Clinton Administration, reviewing books regretted that whereas the Americans had played a prominent role in moving the proposal for the setting up of the International Criminal Court "Bush and his associates arguing that they must guard against the remote possibility of Americans being prosecuted, have carried on a determined drive to destroy the court before it can begin its task of judging those accused of genocide, war crimes and crimes against humanity,"[7] For the neocon the world was divided between the bad and the good guys and the United States stood at the head of the good guys ready to battle against the bad guys for freedom, free market, and the world peace. When they looked around they found Saddam Hussein as the identifiable incarnation of evil that had to be removed.

After 9/11 the nation rallied round the President. The international community sympathized with the United States. It was shocked and itself felt threatened by international terrorism. This was fully exploited by his neocon advisors. Earlier efforts of the US against international terrorism were directed at marshaling support of the international community. It pointed to the common danger that threatened the world. It, however, made no secret of its desire to extend the war beyond Afghanistan. The Pentagon sources suggested that further action against targets and organizations accused of terrorist activities or complicity could include Iraq, Somalia, Sudan and Yemen. Alarmed by such statements, the ED after agreeing to participate in the war against terrorism cautioned the United States that war could not be expanded without prior consultations.[8] The United Nations endorsed the use of force against Afghanistan and many countries particularly Afghanistan's neighbors offered to facilitate the war against international terrorism. But neocons wanted a larger war than limit themselves to the war against Afghanistan.

Iraq was in the gun sight of the Bush Administration from the beginning of the military campaign against the Al Qaeda and the Taliban in Afghanistan. However, before action could be taken against Iraq, the war in Afghanistan had to be won and situation stabilized. Afghanistan then could be presented to the Americans at home as a success story that could be replicated elsewhere. However, there was a big gap between the American perception of the success in Afghanistan and ground reality. After nearly a year and a half after the war in Afghanistan ended and the government of Hamid Karzai was installed in Kabul, the Taiiban forces regrouped and are attacking the stabilization and newly formed Afghan forces. Osama bin Laden, whose capture dead or alive, was one of the main objectives of the war is very much alive. Hamid Karzai is known as "the Mayor of Kabul"(the phrase used by Senator Kennedy) and the authority of his government does not extend beyond the capital. Without pursuing the war against international terrorism to its logical conclusion the Bush Administration decided to take the war to the Middle East.

The decision to remove Saddam Hussein and reconstruct first Iraq and then the Middle East was taken long before the objective was made public. Some analysts have suggested that the President kept his plan secret not only from be rest of the world but from his own top officials. There was no imminent threat to the security of the United States. A case had to be built. On June 1, 2002 addressing the Corps of Cadets at the Defense College Bush argued for a "preemptive strike" strategy than for deterrence. He said: "We can not defend America and our friends by hoping for the best. We cannot put our faith in the words of tyrants, who solemnly sign nonproliferation treaties, and then systematically break them. If we wait for the threat to fully materialize, we will have waited too long." This was a break from the military doctrine that had been followed for more than half a century. A few days later the President again reiterated his doctrine of preemptive action in a speech before the United Nations. The President left no one in doubt against whom he intended to apply his doctrine. The Administration hastened to make it clear that other countries like South Korea or India or Pakistan could not exercise the right of preemptive strike. It insisted that each of these cases was different.

The US gave three reasons for removing Saddam Hussein. He had developed weapons of mass destruction and had failed to comply with the conditions of the cease-fire to which it had agreed in 1991. The defiance had continued for twelve years and could not be allowed to go on any longer. Second, his regime provided shelter to Ansar-al-Islam, a terrorist in northern Iraq. Saddam Hussein was a threat to the peace and security of the region, the United States, and the world. Third, he was a brutal tyrant who had killed thousand of his opponents and used chemical weapons against his own people. The Iraqi people living in fear must be liberated from his tyranny. What was not mentioned was that a friendly government in Iraq would have given the United States control over the second largest deposit of oil in the world and even more importantly put it in a position to command the entire Middle East from Iraq, which has been rightly described as the historic pivot around which Middle Eastern politics has revolved. For more than a decade, the United States had made several attempts to eliminate Saddam Hussein through military coups and uprisings. But Saddam Hussein had survived. Now the ground was being prepared for a direct invasion.

On any issue in public discourse in the United States there are divergent views. But it is the Administration alone that has the capability of implementing its policy preferences. Before run up to the Iraq war, there were sharp differences within the United States on the unilateral use of force against Iraq. Not only the Democrats like former Secretary of State Warren Christopher and former National Security Advisor Zebigniew Brezinski but Republicans like former Secretary of State James Baker, and National Security Advisor Brent Scowcroft, who had served in the Administration of Gorge Bush, Sr. assailed the idea attacking Iraq without the approval of UN. Baker wrote in The *Washington Post* arguing in favor of UN route.[9] Brent Scowcroft considered war against international terrorism a more pressing priority than removing Saddam. Disagreeing with the argument that was being advanced by the Bush Administration, he wrote that there was "scant evidence' to tie Saddam with terrorist organizations" and "even less to September 11 attacks." Furthermore, Iraq was not threatening the security of the United States. He went on to caution that the war was going to be a lot more expensive "with serious consequences for the United States and global economy." And if, indeed, Saddam Hussein had the weapons of mass destruction, driven to desperation he was more likely to use them. He candidly observed: "the shared view in the region is that Iraq is principally an obsession of the United States, the obsession of the region, however, is the Israeli-Palestinian conflict."[10]

A few days before the Iraq war began, Senator Edward Kennedy (D., Mass.) accused President Bush of "single minded rush to war with Iraq." He agreed with Scowcroft that the United States faced "greater and more imminent threat from Al Qaeda and its terrorists," and that the war would only divert attention from this unfinished war. The Administration's policy was weakening the coalition that had been built against international terrorism. He reasoned: "We can have effective relationship with other nations without adopting 'a-chip-on-the shoulder', 'my-way-or-the highway' policy that makes all our other goals in the world more difficult to achieve. We cannot be a bully in the world schoolyard and expect cooperation, friendship, and support from the rest of the world." He firmly asserted that "the Administration has not made a convincing case for war against Iraq or its costs, or its consequences.?" The inspection, he said, still had a chance to work. (A view shared by France, Germany, Russia and China among others and rejected by the Bush Administration.) Kennedy also stressed that the American army was now deployed in Afghanistan, Bosnia, Pakistan and now in Iraq, in the Philippines and Georgia. The United States was thus over-extending itself.[11] The critics of the Administration's policy presented a different worldview. The massive anti–war demonstrations in American cities revealed the depth of feeling against war that was in consonance with this other worldview.

Realizing that American opinion would be more supportive of war if Saddam Hussein could be linked to international terrorism, the Administration leveled charges against him that he was harboring Al Qaeda in northern Iraq. Deputy Secretary of Defense Paul Wolfowitz, a strong advocate of war, wrote: "the war on terror and disarming Saddam Hussein are not merely related, disarming Iraq is a crucial part of winning war on terror."[12] Those who advanced the argument never provided credible evidence to prove the connection.

The Administration's reasoning did not carry conviction. Former Senator George McGovern from South Dakota and the Democratic Presidential candidate in 1972, wrote: " The President and his team building on the trauma of 9/11 have falsely linked Saddam Hussein's Iraq to that tragedy and then falsely built him as a deadly threat to America." He continued: "It has been said that the Iraqi leader is hiding a few weapons of mass destruction which we and eight other countries have long held. But can it be assumed that he would insure his incineration by attacking the United States? Can it be assumed that if we are to save ourselves we must strike before Iraq strikes us?"... "The symphony of falsehood orchestrated by the Bush team had devised to defeat an Iraqi onslaught "that was never threatened and never contemplated."[13] Robin Cook, an important member of British Prime Minister Tony Blair's cabinet, while explaining the reason for resigning in protest against Britain's decision to support the war, raised a few uncomfortable questions. He pointed out that Iraq's military strength was less than half of what it was in the last Gulf War.

That was the reason why some were claiming that the war would be over in days. "We cannot base our military strategy on the basis that Saddam is weak, and at the same time justify preemptive action on the claim that he is a serious threat," he wrote. He pointed out that Iraq probably had biological toxins and battlefield chemical munitions. **"But it had them since the 'eighties. When the US sold Saddam the anthrax."agents and the then British government built his chemical and munitions factories."** He went on to add: "What was the urgency of taking military action now for possession of weapons that Iraq had for more than twenty years, he asked? Why the UN weapons inspectors could not be given more time." That question was never answered. As for Iraq's defiance of UN resolution for twelve years, Robin Cook pointed out that Israel has not complied with the Resolution 242 for more than thirty years but that did arouse the same concern.[14] (Emphasis added)

To win wider support for a course of action he had already decided upon President Bush decided to take the UN route in August 2002 hoping to get the UN endorsement. The UN Security Council passed Resolution 1441 unanimously giving Iraq last chance to reveal its weapons of mass destruction. Iraq denied possessing any prohibited biological or chemical weapons. The weapons inspectors reported that they did not find any stockpile or manufacturing facilities. They wanted more time for inspection. The US persistently argued that the onus of proving beyond doubt that it had destroyed the weapons was on Iraq and therefore the non-discovery of weapons by the UN inspectors did not mean that force should not be used to remove them. France, Russia, China, and Germany disagreed. Britain, Spain and Bulgaria supported the US. The United States reluctantly agreed for the second resolution even though it claimed that "there's more than enough authority for military action, if that is decided upon, in 1441 and previous resolutions." Besides, Secretary Powell claimed authority "in the inherent authority of the President to defend the nation.[15] However, France opposed any war. It insisted that weapons of mass destruction should be removed by giving weapons inspectors more time to find the weapons and destroy them. Undeterred, President Bush repeatedly stressed that if the United Nations would not remove the weapons of mass destruction, the United States would. The United States' insistence on the removal of Saddam Hussein and reconstructing Iraq ruptured the Atlantic alliance that had been the corner stone of its foreign policy for nearly five decades. Rumsfeld ridiculed France and Germany as Old Europe. For hawkish Secretary of Defense, the former communist countries of Eastern and Central Europe like Hungary. Poland, Romania, Bulgaria and others, eager to join EU and because they were willing to support the US became "New Europe". The United States was willing to lead the "coalition of the willing." One humorist called it "coalition of the billing" because the United States offered financial inducements and arms deals to win their support. Once the war began the opposition to the war in the United States declined considerably. This was not surprising. Scholars have noted the existence of "rally round the flag' effect" when a country goes to war.

American success in the war against Iraq, whose capability had been debilitated by the UN sanctions, was never in doubt. Many were, however, surprised when the war ended only in six weeks. The Iraqis hardly offered resistance. Reconstruction of Iraq was much more difficult. In Somalia reconstruction had failed and the US had hastily retreated. But it had much more at stake in Iraq and was willing to commit far greater resources and take hard knocks. The United States continued to repeat that Saddam Hussein's government was allied with terrorists and was in possession of weapons of mass destruction.[16] As weapons of mass destruction were not found the US shifted its justification of war to liberation of Iraqis from Saddam Hussein' tyrannical rule and elimination of terrorist threat. The American occupation met with unexpected resistance. Although Iraqis welcomed the end of the old regime but they also wanted Americans to leave. They wanted to reconstruct their own country. With thousands of innocent civilians dead (according to one estimate more than 7,000 by the end of July) and even a larger number severely wounded, libraries and museums destroyed, and the institutional structure ruined, the

Iraqis are wondering about the price they had to pay for this "liberation". Mounting resistance against the occupying forces led the United States to acknowledge that it was facing a guerrilla war in Iraq that was becoming better organized. The occupation was attracting the *jehadis* from outside who were operating independently of the loyalists of Saddam. This was proved when these elements carried out blasts against the embassy of Jordan in Baghdad. The US had fought the war successfully in Kosovo with zero casualty. With each body bag arriving in the US from Iraq American unease with the occupation has been growing. The war against Iraq and its occupation did not win support from many countries in the region. A few Arab countries that supported the war efforts were under great stress as they were doing so against strong popular opposition. After the US announced the formation of the Governing Council, the countries in the region, the Arab countries did not rush to recognize it. The twenty-two members Arab League meeting in Cairo in the first week of August decided that it would not accept the Governing Council as representing Iraq but would rather wait until an Iraqi government is elected. Many in Iraq and the Arab world dismiss the Governing Council as the puppet of the occupying forces.

The US goal is not restricted to the reconstruction of Iraq. One unnamed US official told the *New York Times*: "We have to make it clear that we did not just come to get rid of Saddam. We came to get rid of the status-quo." The United States was certain that the success in the war would strengthen the governments in the Middle East, which supported the war. Nothing like that seems to have happened. What the US really want is to redraw the political map of the Middle East. It believed that the success in Iraq would convey a message to other countries in the Middle East not to obstruct the reconstruction of the entire region.

The next US objective is the resolution of the Palestinian problem. In cooperation with Russia, EU, and the United Nations, the US had prepared a road map for the creation of a Palestinian state that would exist side by side in security and peace with the state of Israel. Within days of the end of the war the road map was made public. It was the quartet that had prepared the road map but Colin Powell informed the members of the Senate Foreign Relations Committee in February that he believed that "first and foremost, it will be the United States and the United States leadership that will be required to see something happen." It is hard to believe that where vital interests of Israel are involved, the US will be an impartial mediator. Israel is the only party that has not accepted the road map thus far and Colin Powell is trying to convince officials in Cairo that the use of the word "accept" is not necessary.[17] It should be recalled that the United States had demanded a regime change in the Palestine because it believed that Arafat was either unable or unwilling to control the terrorist attacks against Israel and end corruption in the Palestinian authority. It did not matter to it that Arafat had been duly elected. The United States succeeded in forcing Arafat to appoint a more cooperative Mahmoud Abbas as the Prime Minister and share power with him. Undoubtedly some progress has been made but the process of reaching an agreement has far to go.

The United States wanted to pressurize Syria and Iran so that they would end their support for Hamas and Hezbollah. On April 14, Rumsfeld accused Syria of hiding the fugitive from Iraq and developing chemical weapons. He accused it of violating UN sanctions by clandestinely getting oil from Iraq and paying it with goods in a two-way trade. Syria had been for quite a long time on State Department's list of states supporting terrorism. To allay the fear that after Iraq, Syria would be the next target, Secretary Powell declared that "we have no war plan right now." But diplomacy and economic pressure could be used. The use of the word "right now" aroused concern of the countries in the Middle East.[18] The US plan appeared to be working. Syria denied these charges and appeared to be much more restrained and cooperative.

Indeed, the Bush Administration was changing the pattern of US relationship with the countries in the Middle East. It had maintained very close relations with Saudi Arabia that had permitted the use of Prince Sultan air base and allowed the stationing of American troops in the country since the first Gulf War. After 9/11, the United States increasingly became impatient, as it was not receiving expected cooperation in the war against terrorism. Saudi Arabia did not permit the use of the air base in the war in Afghanistan and later against Iraq. The critics were pointing that of the 19 people, who were indicted for the 9/11 attack, fifteen were Saudis. It also turned out that members of the Saudi ruling family had contributed to the Islamic charities which was then used by the terrorist organizations. In May, Rumsfeld traveled to Saudi Arabia and announced that as Saddam Hussein had been removed, the American forces in Saudi Arabia would be drastically reduced. Their presence fueled anger against the United States and the royal family. Although the Secretary of Defense had earlier denied report in the *New York Times* that the United States was seeking access to four Iraqi air bases, it is evident that Iraq would henceforth be more important in American strategy than Saudi Arabia. However, their mutual interests are too important and would keep them together even though relations may not remain as close as before.

The United States approach to the crisis created by North Korea's declaration that it possesses nuclear weapons was in stark contrast to the one it adopted towards Iraq. It has been suggested that it was the inclusion of North Korea in the "axis of evil" speech that triggered North Korea's defiance. The Bush Administration strongly denied the charge. North Korea demands bilateral negotiations with the United States leading to a pledge of non-aggression. The United States has declined to enter into bilateral negotiations. President Bush asserted that the US would not accept North Korea's blackmail. It wants to resolve the crisis in consultation with its allies, South Korea and Japan who are threatened by North Korea's nuclear weapons. It wants China to use its influence over North Korea for reaching some sort of an agreement. An agreement has been reached to hold a six powers (North and South Koreas, China, Japan, United States and

Russia.) meeting. In the meanwhile John Bolton, Assistant Secretary of State for National Security and Nuclear Disarmament traveled to North Korea where he described President Kim-il- Jong as "a tyrannical despot and extortionist who lives "like royalty" while hundreds of his people were locked up and millions more endure a life of 'hellish nightmare... scrounging the ground for food in abject poverty." This most extraordinary characterization of a country and its head, reminiscent of the language used for Saddam, led some analysts to question whether the war party in the Bush Administration was trying to sabotage the forthcoming negotiations and was contemplating another "regime change".[19] With its deep involvement in Iraq, there would be no support for another military adventure. Its regional allies, South Korea and Japan also want the resolution of the problem without the use of force. China and Russia also have taken a similar stance. If the US did not use force against North Korea it was because it was not a feasible option under the circumstances.

The Bush administration distrusts the United Nations. A divided United Nations can frustrate the implementation of an American plan by endless debate. And even if a resolution gets through it can be vetoed. Therefore, while willing to hand over such innocuous function as distribution of humanitarian assistance and some function relating to the maintenance of law and order to the United Nations, it is not going to concede any major political and military role either to it or to the countries which stridently opposed its invasion. In a press conference Ambassador Paul Bremer, Administrator of the Coalition Provisional Authority, categorically rejected the suggestion of a military command under the United Nations in a press conference. He said: "it is important to have unity of command on the military side. And for the time being and for the foreseeable future, the command will be in the coalition, not in the UN."[20]

Bill Kristol of the Weekly Standard and Robert Kegan, the two neocon ideologues argued that the aim of the United States Foreign policy should be "benevolent world hegemony." In the military strategy that the Administration spelled out last year, it emphasized the right of preemptive strike. It also declared that it would not let any other power to overtake the military capability of the United States. Its predominance of the world economy appears to make attainment of these objectives plausible. There are leaders and analysts in other countries who believe that their country's security and economic interests are best served by accepting this reality. However, there are many others who strongly resent the loss of their autonomous space in this worldview. France, Germany, Belgium and Luxembourg revealed their plan to set up a Central European Headquarters of an autonomous defense organization in the year 2004. These four countries are also members of the NATO. Chancellor Schroeder put his finger on the spot when he remarked that there is very little of Europe in NATO's decision making. The United States dominated it. The group also plans to establish a nuclear collective capacity for planning and conducting operation for the European Union. Britain and the United States promptly dismissed the plan as divisive and unconstructive.

The Christian right- neoconservative world view that dominates the Bush Administration is based on the premise that the western values of freedom, democracy, and free market are universal. Any government that does not ensure these values to its citizens is tyrannical and oppressive. The United States has a mission to remove such a regime and liberate the people if possible with the support of the international community. At the annual conference of Organization of American States in Santiago, Chile, Secretary Powell on June 8 asked the organization to "hasten the inevitable democratic transition in Cuba. He argued that it would be consistent with the democratic charter the organization adopted two years ago. But the members did not appear to be convinced. Some argued that a country that was not present in the conference should not be discussed. There were others who wanted to discuss the economic embargo against Cuba along with the issue of democratic transition.[21] When the liberals and the students demonstrated in June against the Khatmi government demanding liberalization, the United States strongly supported the dissidents. Richard Perle in an interview urged European countries to join the United States in pushing "to replace the dictatorial regime in Iran with the help of the opposition inside the country." [22] The present American worldview does not limit itself by unilaterally pursuing its national interest but wants to impose its economic and political values on recalcitrant states. Use of force may not be the only option but that remains the goal. The phrase "regime change" aptly sums up that goal.

This American hegemonic worldview of the United States does not gel with the vision of a multi-polar world of France, Germany, and Russia, which also claim the heritage of western values. Criticizing President Chiraq's frequent allusion to multi-polar world, the British Prime Minister Tony Blair said on April 29, that such a concept could lead to rivalry and instability. He suggested that Europe and the United States must work as "one polar world." Tony Blair was not much concerned either for his country's autonomous space or those of the other European countries. He was satisfied with his country's position as the junior partner of the hegemon. Responding to Blair's comment Chiraq explained: "For balance to exist there will have to be strong Europe and a strong United States linked together by a strong cultural pact. That means relations between the EU and the United States would have to be relations of complementarity and partnership between equals. Otherwise it would be a different world which is not what France observes and wants." [23] It was easy for the United States to demonise Saddam for he was the "perfect target" but difficult to explain the growing estrangement of important European countries which were its former allies.

If the European challenge to American worldview is from within the Christian and Western culture, the challenge of the Islamists comes from outside. The extremists only form the fringe of the Islamists and do not represent its totality. The vast majority feels that the western value system is not compatible with Islamic values. At the same time, there is growing awareness among the Islamists that Taliban type of extremism must be avoided. With many Muslim countries prefixing the word Islamic to their official name and growing influence of the extremists in countries like Indonesia and Bangladesh, it is unlikely that the United States would succeed in making the Islamic world accept secular, democratic, western values in near future. The invasion of Iraq and the ongoing conflict will only further strengthen extremism in the Islamic world. The anti–Americanism draws its sustenance from two sources: nationalism and religion. The neoconservative American worldview has increased this polarization. Abul Magid, a noted Egyptian international lawyer told the correspondent of the *New York Times*: "never have America's friends felt so estranged from the United States, have the sense of being betrayed, misunderstood, taken lightly... to most people in this area, the United States is source of evil on the planet earth. And whether we like it or not, it is the Bush Administration that is to blame."[24] American officials, who were expecting warm endorsement of their effort by the Shia majority in Iraq, were surprised by the outpouring of anti–Americanism and mounting resistance from militant Islamic clerics and Arab nationalists. They view virulent outburst of Shi'ite religious militancy to be a chief threat to American plans for a democratic elected government in Iraq. Instead of reducing the anti-Americanism, the Iraq war has sharpened the contradiction. [25]

As the US and British occupation of Iraq is proving expensive and it appears that it may last longer than had been expected, American approval of the neocon worldview appears to be declining. The Republicans are facing the prospect of a tighter presidential race in 2004. There are strong voices of dissent, which speak for "a more constructive internationalism." It spells out a foreign policy that would support the United Nations, work towards expansion of international trade, while protecting workers and environment. It would also support the Kyoto protocol on global warning, the international criminal court, an international ban on land mines and the anti ballistic treaty. [26]

The United States has opened Pandora's Box by invading Iraq. Each important player in international affairs is drawing its own conclusion and changes its stance towards the United States. Some may draw the conclusion that their security and economic interests would be best served in a unipolar world under the leadership of the US. But the major players in the international arena would strive for creating an autonomous space for themselves. It is not possible that the world would willingly accept "benevolent world hegemony" of the United States. With the falling approval rating of President Bush and sluggish economy, one cannot be certain that the present worldview will not change in the next administration that would take office next year.

References

1. George Bush and Brent Scowcroft, *A World Transformed* (New York: Alfred A. Knopf. 1998), p. 416.

2. *Ibid*. p. 448.

3. See B. K. Shrivastava. "United States and the Sovereignty of Small States in Post-Cold War Era." *Man and Development*. June 1995, pp. 118–33

4. See: "Think Tank with Ben Wattanbarg, The Christian Right in American Politics," Transcript of a radio discussion, July 29, 1994; Abraham Mclaughlin and Gail Russell Chadlock, "Christian Right Steps in On Mideast." *Christian Science Monitor*, April 16, 2002: William Martin, "The Christian Right and American Foreign Policy," *Foreign Policy*, Spring 1999 and Norman Podhoretz, "The Christian Right and Its Demonizers," *National Review*, April 3, 2000.

5. These views have been cited in Augustus Richard Nixon, "America in the Middle East: Statesmanship Vs. Politics," *Current History*, Vol. 102, No. 660, January 2003, pp. 3.

6. Think Tank with Ben Wattenbarg. Transcript of Interview with Richard Perle.

7. Quoted in Anthony Lake in *New York Review*, January 3, 2003.

8. "EU warns US against extending War on Terror." *The Hindu*, December 16. 2001.It stated in the draft conclusion of the meeting "There can be no possible geographical extension of these operations without the prior approval of the international community."

9. James A. Baker, III, "The UN Route." *The Washington Post*, September 15, 2002.

10. Brent Scowcroft, " Don't Attack Saddam," August 15, 2002 *http:// WSJ.com Opinion Journal*

11. Senator Edward M. Kennedy's address to the United Methodist Church annual conference in Washington on March 4, 2003. Official Text, Public Affairs Office of the US Embassy, New Delhi. March 5. 2003.

12. Paul Wolfowitz, " Why Saddam Is a Target in Our War On Terror," Independent's. January 30 2003.

13. George McGovern. "The Reason why." *Nation*. Article posted on the website on April 3, 2003.

14. Robin Cook' article was originally published in *The Guardian* (UK) Reprinted in the *The Hindustan Times*. "Why I had to leave the cabinet," March 19, 2003.

15. See Hearing of the Senate Foreign Relations Committee On State Department Budget. Testimony of Secretary of State Colin Powell on February 6. 2003.

16. Transcript of President Bush's speech on April 24, 2003 in Lima, Ohio. Official Text, Public Affairs Office of the US Embassy, New Delhi.

17. *The New York Times* on the Web. May 12, 2003.

18. David e. Sanger and Thomas Shanker. "Bush says Regime in Iraq No More: victory certain." *ibid.*, April 6, 2003.

19. *The Guardian* (UK). August 10. 2003.

20. See the Press conference by Bremer in Washington on 23 July 2003, Official Text, 24 July 2003, Public Affairs Office. New Delhi.

21. *The Hindu*. June 11, 2003.

22. *The Hindustan Times*. June 18. 2003. printed from the New York Times.

23. *The Hindu*, May 1, 2003.

24. Susan Sacks. " Egyptian Intellectual Speaks of the Arab world' Despair," *The New York Times*, April 8, 2003.

25. Craig S. Smith, " Cleric in Iraq Says Shi'ites Must Act." *ibid.*, April 26, 2003.

26. George McGovern, "A More Constructive Internationalism." *The Washington Post*, May 12, 2003.

3
New Trends in American World View

K.R. Singh

There is need to shift our focus on USA's world view from the Cold War era to the post-Cold War period. There is a major reorientation that needs to be understood. The end of the Cold War had a profound impact upon USA's perception of its role as the sole superpower. During the Cold War era, USA, though a superpower in its own right, was also the leader of an alliance that was formed vis-a-vis a specific adversary - another alliance led by another super power. Europe was the primary focus of global competition. Hence, during the Cold War era, USA's superpower status was conditional upon the unrestrained support of its alliance partners, particularly in Europe.

The end of the Cold War and more particularly the disintegration of USSR, had a two-fold impact upon USA's world view. USA's dependence upon its alliance partners from Europe (NATO allies) for its superpower role at the global level was greatly reduced. Also, its strategic focus began to shift from Europe to Asia-Pacific and the Indian Ocean, USA had, since the Second World War, developed a capability to project forces across the oceans in support of its military operations in Europe and the Asia–Pacific region. This overwhelming long-range force-projection capability was further enhanced during the Cold War era. In the post-Cold War era that capability has enhanced its military and, therefore, its political role as the only superpower capable of operating at the global level. This was reflected during the Gulf crisis of 1990-91, and the subsequent military operations in Yugoslavia, Afghanistan and Iraq.

A debate was going on in USA on the need for a new strategy. Critics believed that USA's military posture was still linked to its Cold War military strategy and needed to be radically transformed. These critics also wished to incorporate in this context, the much debated concept of revolution in military affairs (RMA). The Pentagon was seen as the main stumbling bloc in this transformation. On 10 September 2001, US Secretary of Defence, Donald Rumsfeld, launched a public counter-offensive against the Pentagon's bureaucracy. He contended, "The world has (changed), and we have not yet changed sufficiently. The clearest and most important transformation is from a bipolar Cold War world where threats were visible and predictable to one in which they arise from multiple sources - most of which are difficult to anticipate and many of which are impossible to know today".[1] These threats made themselves known the very next day (9-11) in most terrific term.

The destruction of USSR had left USA as the only Superpower. Over the years, American policy began to transform itself from a superpower to a sole and undisputed leader and finally as a global hegemon. This was clearly reflected in the White Paper on National Security Strategy, October 1998.[2] It said that America's strategic approach recognized that America must lead abroad if it has to be secure at home, "We must have the demonstrated will and capability to continue to exert global leadership and remain the preferred security partner for the community of states that share our interests. The White Paper, however, put limits on US involvement in the world. "We must be selective in the use of our capabilities and the choices we make always must be guided by advancing our objectives of a more secure, prosperous and free America".It continued, "The United States will not allow a hostile power to dominate any region of critical importance to our interest. We will work to protect the spread of nuclear, biological and chemical weapons, and the material for producing them; and to control other potentially destabilizing technologies, such as long-range missiles. We will continue to ensure that we have the effective means for countering and responding to the threats that we cannot deter or otherwise prevent from arising."

The White Paper of 1998 also underlined US desire to act unilaterally if necessary. "We must always be prepared to act alone when that is our most advantageous course". The White Paper also mentioned the desirability of a coalition in support of US policy. "Many of our security objectives are best achieved or can only be achieved through our alliances and other formal security structures or as a leader of an ad hoc coalition formed around a specific objective."[3]

USA had to pay a heavy price to retain its military capability. Despite the breakup of USSR and the absence of any major military threat to US security, USA continues to have a large military expenditure even after the end of the Cold War. Even that began to rise from $253.7 bn in 1996 to $360.7 bn in 2003[4] and is expected to grow to $451 bn by 2007. What impact such a large military expenditure will have upon America's national economy remains to be seen. It is possible that in the near future, like in the USSR during the second half of 1980s, USA too might face domestic pressure to cut down its military expenditure and consequently its overseas military commitments. May be the economic consequences of heavy defence expenditure might bring about an American version of regime change and hence a corresponding change in its foreign and defence policies. The coming years are, therefore, going to be of crucial strategic significance not only for USA but also for the rest of the world.

America's world view has also come under the growing influences of the neo-conservatives (neo-cons). They were an alternate policy group during the eighties. They were vocal but isolated during the Clinton era. But the election of President Bush (Jr.) in 2000 AD has brought them into the forefront of decision making. They constitute the inner core of decision making group like Donald Rumsfeld, Paul Wolfowitz and David Frum. Many of them are Jews and hence are reportedly pro-Israel. The terrorists attack of 11 September 2001 (9-11) has greatly strengthen their role as well as aggressiveness.

Events of 9-11 gave a new thrust and legitimacy to USA's policy towards combating international terrorism, and related topics like countering threats arising from weapons of mass destruction, their delivery systems, doctrine of preemptive measures, winning war decisively and regime change. President Bush, in his speech to the US Congress on 20 September, could offer to the rest of the world the challenge, "either you are with us or you are with the terrorists". Thus, an alternate view was rejected. It reminded one of the statement in 1950s by John Foster Dulles when he had called non-alignment as immoral. The war on terrorism was also sought to be equated with war on Fascism.[5]

The American administration released in December 2002 a truncated version of the National Strategy to combat weapons of mass destruction (WMD) which, probably for the first time, emphasized preemptive actions against WMD shipments and facilities while raising counter-proliferation to a higher level of importance. The document said, "US military forces and appropriate civilian agencies must have the capability to defend against WMD-armed adversaries including, in appropriate cases, through preemptive measures."[6]

According to the *Military Balance, 2002-2003,* an affinity for preemptive action in America's counter-terrorism strategy is broadly compatible with US Secretary of Defence Donald Rumsfeld's view of future American military strategy - to conduce decisive action with rapidly deployable and agile stealth forces that could respond to various contingency requirements with a minimum of logistical support. The new strategy seems to incorporate the concept of RMA. The principle measure of effectiveness would be represented less by the number of weapon platforms that could be brought to bear on the enemy than by the quality of networking between sensors and shooters.[7]

Another concept associated with the new US administration was winning decisively. Though the concept had been in circulation even before the events of 9-11, and was a part of the strategic review conducted by Secretary of Defence, Donald Rumsfeld, after he took over his post, it was subsequently incorporated in the new Quadrennial Defence Review (QDR). Winning decisively has been defined as the ability to march on an enemy capital with the intent of overthrowing its regime. Deputy Defence Secretary, Paul Wolfowitz, in his press conference on 16 August 2001 had qualified the term with unconditional surrender of World War-II.[8]

US policy in South-West Asia since the end of the Second World War has been based upon preserving two main interests; control over its oil resources, and the security of Israel. Of late the security of both has come under the shadow of the new threat of international terrorism based largely upon ethno-nationalism. As far as oil and Jewish interests are concerned, though both goals are inherently contradictory, each President has tried in his own way, to pursue an even-handed policy, if only because he needed both Arab oil and Jewish campaign contributions. Of the two, interest of Israel takes precedence because USA can risk antagonizing an Arab oil producer but not Israel.

Today, Saudi Arabia is allegedly not only the major oil producer and exporter but also an important Arab ally of USA. The firm foundation is reportedly based upon the continuity and stability of the Saudi dynasty. Yet some American experts are prepared to sacrifice the Saudi family. By 1996-97, the Saudi regime was reluctant to wholeheartedly support US policy vis-a-vis Iraq. Americans, though professing democracy, often refuse the coalition partner the right to differ. Such an ally is dispensable. According to Adam Garfinkle, "Chances are that other forms of governments in the Arabian Peninsula would also be eager to sell large amount of oil, so the role of the House of Saud is neither a necessary nor a sufficient condition to safeguard US interest."[10]

By contrast, Israel often occupies and indeed preoccupies more of the US public landscape and political energy than even its oldest allies, Great Britain and France or its nearest neighbour, Canada and Mexico. American presidents of both parties routinely pledge unqualified support for Israel's security as do overwhelming bi-partisan majority in both houses of the US Congress. Yet there is no overall treaty of alliance between the two countries. In that context the so-called Jewish lobby led by the American Israel Public Affairs Committee plays a crucial role.[11]

US policy in the post-Cold War period faced overt and covert opposition from its erstwhile alliance and coalition partners. Yet the overwhelming military successes turned USA's perception of its role from that of the leader of a coalition of like-minded powers to one of an independent actor capable of dictating its terms largely due to its unquestionable military superiority. That also led to political intransigence and intractability. Thus, by the end of 1990s, leadership of a coalition, i.e. policy of multilateralism, was turning into a policy of unilateralism. Several factors made such a role possible; lack of countervailing power like USSR, inability or unwillingness of some major European powers (NATO partners) to challenge USA militarily, capability of USA to influence several regimes of the Third World in support of its policy of unilateralism by providing USA with bases and base facilities etc.

In the nineties, USA was employing political pressure mostly through UN, combined with punitive military strikes mostly by employing air power and Tomahawk cruise missiles. That was the case during the anti-Iraq operations since 1991 as well as in Yugoslavia. However, by the beginning of the 21st century, USA began to bypass and even challenge UN, ignore the wishes of its erstwhile coalition partners who refused to be blind followers of USA, and to use its military power to achieve decisive victory as also regime change. While that stance was visible even during operations against Al-Qaeda and the Taliban regime in Afghanistan in 2001-02, it came out vividly during operations in Iraq in March 2003.

USA had opposed many regimes before and had even worked covertly for regime change as the overthrow of Mossadeq's government in Iran in 1953 or in employing the so-called Iraqi opposition to overthrow Saddam in 1990s. Now regime change by overt military means has become an intrinsic part of US policy. Some Americans had even suggested that the Iraqi state be allowed (perhaps even helped) to fall apart.[12] The policy of regime change was, however, articulated by President Bush during his speech on 1 June 2002 at West Point military academy, in which he had publicly articulated the US desire for regime change in Iraq.[13]

One sees a perceptible change in USA's world view after the victory of President Bush (Jr.), and more so after the events of 11 September 2001. Though the change can be traced even earlier, US policy makers after 9-11 publicly talked of using military power to bring about, even unilaterally, a regime change in states that, directly or indirectly, were capable of harming the interests of USA or Israel. USA also proclaimed war on terrorism. Since non-state actors cannot be easily targeted, attempt was made to link those behind the events of 9-11 to Al Qaeda and hence with the Taliban in Afghanistan. US-led and supported military operation in Afghanistan was aimed at destroying the power base of Al Qaida and the Taliban in Afghanistan. USA succeeded in achieving a 'regime change'. The new regime of Karzai is protected and monitored by USA and its partners including Pakistani regime. Afghanistan was sanitized, at least for the time being. The threat from Al Qaida was reduced. Afghans were, however, left to their own fate and to the traditional tribal and feudal system.

Prompted by the easy success in Afghanistan, the US administration under President Bush decided to target Iraq and the Baath regime under the leadership of President Saddam Hussein. Though the excuse offered was the elimination of WMD and long-range missiles, the real objective was regime change: overthrow of the regime of Saddam Hussein and installation of an Iraqi version of Karzai that would be protected and monitored by USA. Though USA has as yet offered no acceptable Karzai, yet, with the Iraqis divided amongst themselves on ethno-religious and ideological grounds, USA expects that Iraq will not be able to pose a threat at least for some years to come.

How will USA behave in future? Though the success or failure of Bush (Jr.) in the next election may leave its impact upon USA's foreign policy it remains to be seen if the operations in Afghanistan and Iraq have proved to US decision makers about the correctness of their new policy of unilateralism. International response to US policy was nothing more than impotent rage translated into high-sounding righteous rhetoric. No state made any gesture to block US-led military action. Public anger, though visible, also had no impact on US policy. Rather, selective use of information technology through CNN and BBC made Anglo-Americans look like liberators of Iraqi population from the dictatorial regime of Saddam Hussein. Whether Iraqi masses buy that line and allow Anglo-American forces to occupy their land and shape their future is increasingly becoming doubtful. It seems that now USA is about to face liberated Iraqis.

Post-war race for share in the cake of Iraqi spoils of war reconstruction to be shared by using Iraqi oil money may even bring some of those states that had politically opposed US-led coalition's war on Iraq to accept the role of USA in shaping the post-war policy in Iraq. Does the military outcome of the war on Iraq mean that USA has succeeded in imposing its policy of unilateralism even upon its erstwhile critics? Will the military success embolden USA to further flex its muscles and target other 'rogue' states? Or will US policy generate a move to bring other great powers into a stronger coalition to check US designs more effectively. Will the trend give shape to a new Cold War with USA as the leader of the unilateralist camp as opposed to the other great powers coming together under the multilateralist camp? It is still early to comment upon it.

How should India respond to these new developments. Should it join, as some wish, the camp of unilateralists and of benevolent hegemonism or wait for the signs of consolidation of the camp of multilateralists. If India joins the camp of unilateralists it will have to compete with Pakistan for obtaining US favours. They are seldom granted. On the other hand, if India retains its time-tested policy of judging each issue on its merit, the basis of its policy of non-alignment, it retains the option to pursue a more meaningful national policy. As in the fifties, once again Indian leaders are offered the choice of pursuing an independent foreign policy or joining the coalition led by USA. The choice is still open.

References

1. *The Strategic Survey, 2001-2002*, IISS. London. 2002. p. 71.
2. *Strategic Digest*, 29 (4). April 1998. pp. 509-10.
3. Ibid., p. 514.
4. *The Military Balance. 2002-2003*, IISS. London. 2003. p. 244.
5. Gottfried. Paul, "The Multilaterist International". *Orbis*, 46(1). Winter 2002. p. 157.
6. *Jane's Defence Weekly*, 18 December 2002, quoted in Strategic Digest, 33(2), February 2003, pp. 189-90.
7. The *Military Balance. 2002-2003*, IISS, London. 2003, p. 232.
8. Hawkins. William R., "What Not To Learn From Afghanistan", *Parameters*, 32(2), Summer 2002, p. 27.
9. Watkins. Eric. "The Unfolding US Policy in the Middle East". *International Affairs*. 73(1). January 1997. p. 1.
10. Garfinkle. Adam, "Agenda 2000: The US Imperial Postulates in the Mideast". *Orbis*, 41(1). Winter 1997. p. 28.
11. Lewis. Samuel W., "The United States and Israel: Evolution of an Unwritten Alliance". *Middle East Journal*, 53(3). Summer 1999. pp.364-65.
12. Byman. Daniel, "Let Iraq Collapse'. The National Interest, Fall 1996, pp. 48-60, quoted in Garfinkle. Adam, *Orbis*, 41(1), Winter 1997. p. 26.
13. The Military Balance. 2002-2003, IISS, London. 2003, p. 96.

judging each issue on its merit, the basis of its policy of nonalignment, [illegible] the option to pursue a [illegible] national policy. As in the fifties once again Indian leaders are offered the choice of pursuing an independent foreign policy or joining the coalition led by USA. The choice is still open.

References

1. [illegible] p. 92.

2. [illegible]

3. [illegible]

4

US Paramount Reach with Iraq War

Rakesh Gupta

Prelude

The US intervention in Iraq was still an open question when the events in December 2002 unfolded. They were however a pointer to what was coming. Before we look into the reach of the American Imperium let us first have a look at the event the world over as a prelude to the war. We maintain that the military unipolarity that the US enjoyed since supremacy at the global level in the post–Iraq phase. This may well be the beginning of the new phase of American power as per Modelski's theory of historical cycles. Modelski is of the view that transition to Great power status (read unipolar) takes place practically after one hundred years and lasts for about fifty years. Others in neorealist paradigm refer to the status of the French power in the 17th century, the British position in the 18th and the 19th century, respectively, and, now of course to the US. Earlier in the 1980s, according to the Japanese scholars, who were applying Modelski's theory to its economic robustness Japan was the next candidate. Now US are considered to be in an unparalleled position in terms of technological predominance and military reach. At the same time world is witness to the new challenges that this imperium is springing and facing. These are from the popular upsurge against the meeting of the WTO at Seatle. Second, the demand of the Great powers like France and Germany supported by Russia, India and China to have the UN approval on intervention in Iraq. In contrast the US could manage only Britain and Spain. Of course all hues of Muslim countries are considered by it to be enemies and sources of national security threat apart from nuclear powered Third World countries. The current world politics is a fight for natural resources in which oil is the king and nuclear power is the sword. This is the face of the new Leviathan—a sea power transforming into a Centaur, i.e. sea and land power with no mercy in the name of credibility.

If someone asked the question to what is common between boobs and butts one answer is reproduction. The smoking cigar represents suck and push. If some one asked the question what is common between politics and war it is reproduction, which needs oil, natural gas, chemicals and petroleum and nuclear power. Both are related to ego, at another level. In the December, 2002 events on the globe, unconnected to the simple eye and removed from each other in their causes, contexts and frameworks had one thing in common. That is energy (oil and nuclear power). The power of oil is determining the politics of the world as of now. This it did and inaugurated the era of petro dollars in the 1970s. Who knows of this more than the US officials ? James Baker, Secretary of State then, said in 1991 'oil is our civilization, and will never permit any demon to sit on it'. Practically twenty years earlier Nixon and Kissinger had talked about the gunboat diplomacy in the context of the Arab world wanting to nationalise oil. Western democracies and the quest for oil are the reality. All other talk of enlightenment, enlightened self-interest and democracy vs terrorism is chaff. They can be friends and foes depending on the situation in which the dominant power is. Oil seems to demonise and humanize people no matter at which end of war and politics one is standing. Super powers get above law to use thrusts to suck oil by shedding blood. Weak are declared terrorists in case they do not comply with the suck and thrust argument. Or show a slight deviant behaviour. The crisis of the 1970s was met by the innovation of the petro dollar. Today there is a danger that there may be Euro petrol. If that case the power of the US military reach would bubble out. US will not let that happen. If Europe, Venezuela and Muslim world combine US will have it boy. Uncle Sam wills not any activity leading to this take place.

The events that have taken place since the Afghanistan 'operation enconda freedom' shows the power of oil has again reasserted itself. On the day the oil workers' Opposition against the leftist President Chavez of Venezuela was renewed. Asif Rizvi, the man linked with the death of the American journalist, Daniel Pearl. and, the bombings on the US counsulate in Germany, died in an accident? What is common to them? It is oil. One in Latin American and the other in South Asia has only shown that politics is related to oil either covertly or overtly. What is common between the US saying that there is an Iraqi 'breach' on weapons and the Russian troops suddenly landing in Kyrgistan? What is common between some US firms talking to Iraqi oppositon and some Russian firms taking over major shares of another firm of theirs? What is common between Angola Parliament's tax reduction and the British retail firms refusing to purchase a Venezuelan product? It is oil. What is common between the Indian discussions with Uzbekistan and Pakistani discussions with Iran? It is oil. What is common between the Russian and US interests in Iran? It is oil. What is common between Chinese and US interests in Iraq? It is oil. So King oil rules. It has the Midas touch. The Angolan price concessions were made to control the soaring gold prices as well. These had taken a new skyhigh that month.

Oil has close relationship with water. Around the sea and the defence of the sea lanes is the argument for vital interests and their protection by force. Central Asia is getting more attention from the US. It is because of the oil in the Caspian Sea. India is inching into Central Asia since it understands the need of the US to be therein to fight terror, ostensibly. It is now edged out of it since NATO has taken over Central Asia. As far as Central Asia is concerned US knows that the source of its extended accumulation is the region's oil wealth. India has energy, regional and political interests in the region. Central Asia is at the centre of three regional players, namely, Russia, Iran and

China. With all these India cooperates and competes. It has now also to consider the role that the US plays in the region. It has joined up with the Shanghai five to fight terror. Uzbekistan has joined this regional pact too. Uzbeskistan is though an unreliable friend of Russia and China since it wants the US. India has joined it as seventh member. There is feverish activity in this region which is vital to India. There is the stalled Chinese penetration in the region. The US has stalled the Chinese gains. It needs India to deter China and not give oil conracts to Indian firms in Central Asia. The US presence has put pressure on the Russians as well. The US forces have been operating from Kyrgistan in military terms. As a result the Russians landed their troops and military hardware in Kant airbase in Kyrgistan. This base is adjacent to the Mansa airbase from where the US military is operated during the Afghan campaign. The US is now offering money to the Russians to get out of Central Asia or parts thereof, especially from Tadjikistan. It is reported that there is a difference of opinion between Putin and his military General. The President thinks that the US does not have any malafide intention in coming to the region while the military brass disagrees. The Indian thinking may be closer to Putin's. India has also taken steps to engage in talks with Tadjikistan. Afghanistan and Turkemenistan have entered an agreement to lay the natural pipeline that will supply it to Pakistan and may extend it to India. A Japanese firm is interested in the project.

Since Iraq is the biggest producer of oil it has been in the forefront of news about of war. This scenario is very different from the one being faced by the Venezuelan President Chavez who was facing twenty--six day strike in December by the oil workers in his country. At the time of writing it is reported that he is preparing to stall opposition to fight the elections in 2004. The leftist President has come in for pressure for fresh elections and the British firms were refusing to lift oil from his tankers on the plea that the containers are contaminated. The Brazilian Government has shown support to Chavez. The British and the US firms are not losing out since the price of oil has not come down.[1]

The situation in Iraq is very different from the placid goings on elsewhere say in Venezuela. Placid it is in comparison to Iraq. There is a regular strategy of displacing the then and now fugitive President Saddam Hussein as part of the strategy of War. The former US President, Senior Bush wanted to finish him off. He did not. The present one is still pursuing him to bring to conclusion the unfinished task he could not do. Now the United Nations has been geared to it. This is evident by the statement of the Secretary General of the UN. The UN would have supported the US efforts as and when the inspections failed. The US and the British had taken the view that the document that Iraq had submitted had a 'breach'. The Chinese and the Russians who also have considerable oil interests in the region did not accept the breach argument. India's muted voice remained feeble but whatever its worth it was opposed to the breach thesis. This message had to be made clear since India under the Chairmanship of Rakesh Sood had to determine the disarmament agenda especially on outer space. The Iraqis, it seemed were going to be in for inevitable war by end January-beginning February since the US hospital ship ordered to be there was to take that much time to reach. Saad Qassem Harmmoudy, Secretary General of Arab Popular Forces, told an Egyptian daily that even if Saddam resigns, the US will conduct a war to *'colonise Iraq'* (italics ours). Obviously oil and geostrategy are the guiding principle. Iran was still to be dealt with; Libya was to be dealt with. Russia was to be deterred from any move in this direction and roll back its interests.

While India, Russia, China may be having coincidental positions on issues of Iraq and Outer Space they have not much in common on strategic and security issues. Their foreign policies were at variance on many issues, even if their orientation to achieve a multi–polar world existed. There is no single block to oppose the US in case it desired to go its own way on issues of war and peace. Another crisis was brewing in North Korea. This relates to nuclear weapons. Like in case of Iraq, so in case of North Korea. Some in the present US administration were involved in nuclearising it, e.g., Dick Cheney in this case, as reported in the US press. Iranians have recently said that their nuclear facility made by Russian support is for peaceful purposes. Post–Iraq they are put on notice to peaceful purposes. Common between Iraq and North Korea is that the leaderships of the US have hob–nobbed with their respective leaderships on the issue of weapons of mass destruction. A war on two fronts seems to be on the cards. Both because of energy production : oil and nuclear power. As for its impact the news was that the dollar as of December 26, 2002 had gone down to 1.0346 against the Euro it's lowest since January 2000. Turkey was gearing up its economy to face the fall out of the War on Iraq by requesting Russia to lower the price of its oil to Turkey and was afraid of refugees as well as of biological and chemical warfare on it. It is an ally of the US in the War as well as in it diplomacy to join the European Union in opposition to Cyprus. The European scene may be different on Iraq: atleast the German interests show that there is a German firm working inside Iraq. Does it mean that at some stage we may withness a new constellation of forces? Apparently oil is the king and nuclear power is the sword. This should put many political scientists out of the job with all their treatises on politics and war, state and civil society, democracy and dictatorship.

US Power

The pre-Iraq war noticed that the US was still within the post cold war structure of international relations. Waltz's neo-realist perspective called the new international structure pyramidicals. At the apex was the US military unipolarity. At the middle level it was nuclear bipolarity. At the base he thought that is was economically multipolarity. Most of the nations had visions of moving the structure to multi-polarity. The neo-liberal and the theorists of interdependence assumed that the world would move in the direction of complex interdependence if the NATO, UN, European Union, NAFTA and other macro regions expanded. The difference between the two was that neo-realists stipulated anarchy in the system to be a determinant. The other viewed that it could be managed by new institutionalism that interdepence implied.

The latter failed in this theorization since the UN, NATO, European Union or any other such body could not be involved in the war on Iraq. It was not involved in the settlement of the issues of Kosovo, Bosnia and Herzegovina. Even much earlier in case of the Nicaragua when a military campaign was launched against a popularly elected Government no such body was involved. Even before Iraq there was this issue of the implementation of the neo-liberal agenda the world over under globalisation. Did it mean that globalisation was offering a new paradigm on neo–realism and interdependence? New issues of common concern, new ways of constructing polities, new networks of telecommunication, common domestic and foreign policies offered a possibility that the traditional system of looking at international relations is on the decline. A new paradigm of globalisation was ascendant.[2] The issue at the heart of this academic exercise is whether unit level political and economic analysis is relevant or should there be a global economic and political level analysis. While the theorists have done this in the pre-Iraq phase the leader–statesman has concerned himself with the use of American power and their impact on these twin possibilities the world over. There is historical and contemporary dimension to the US hegemony in military terms.

Historical Dimension

After September 11, 2001 attack by Al Qaeda supporters on the US Twin Towers and symbols of political and military power the Bush administration theorized on the global structure differently. In a speech, Bush had called for looking at international relations in terms of post –Cold War. In this new phase he had redrawn the contours of security thinking of the US. In September 2002 Bush administration came out with another doctrine of national security in which it announced its intent to intervene unilaterally wherever its own interests were threatened. In a recent speech in Delhi one of the spokesman, Berges, from the US Air Force, said that when Bush came to power he came with a different vision from Clinton. Clinton was stuck with the post–Cold War vision. He wanted to move forward. Bush was inclined towards a more activist policy of intervention if dictated by national interests. As a result what we witness is that the Taliban, its own creation for purpose of fighting, was liquidated by making Pakistan a frontline state and saving it from economic ruin. After the ghastly attack on the Twin Towers and the Pentagon the Bush Administration that was planning to unilaterally set up National Missile Defense system in violation of the ABM treaty found that another of its own creation had become a monster: Osama Bin Laden. He was a business partner of the Bushes for poppy business in the region of borders of Pakistan and Afghanistan, a creation of CIA as a freedom fighter, and his Al Qaeda network, funded through the erstwhile BCCI[3], had become terrorist and needed a surgical operation. Terrorist, since he must have stopped listening to them. The two monsters were linked India, China, Russia and Central Asia knew the cost of terrorism that Taliban was and Pakistan remains (especially for India) till date. The Junior Bush also discovered another rogue-Saddam Hussein, to be terminated in national interest, though he had trained many Libyan agents on the US instructions, to destabilise Muammar Gaddafi. Senior Bush had nudged the same gentleman to launch an attack on a smaller neighbour, Iran. But his attack on Kuwait became the plea for the attack. He fell out of favour.

In 1902 former US President Mckinley had told the world that it is the will of God that the US take over the "rotten apple" Cuba and the Philippines. Macnamara and Kennedy use the logic of window of vulnerability vis-à-vis the rotten apple to launch the missile races with the then Soviet Union. Later it was discovered that there was no missile gap. In 2002 present US President said that Iraq must unilaterally be destroyed for no demon can be allowed to sit over oil in the words of James Baker in 1998. He was a demon for he hid weapons of mass destruction. Even this has proved incorrect. Blair is having problems in his country and Bush is unable to prove such weapons of mass destruction. In a matter of a little more than a year that elapsed between Operation enconda freedom and the war against Iraq US has regarded itself as one above law. This it has done since the end of the Second World War over various issues. Here are some examples.

US National Security documents 1/3 called for military operations in Italy, along with national mobilization in the United States, "in the event the communists obtain domination of the Italian government by legal means." Second, it egged on the Isrealis to attack Lebanon that had left tens of thousands dead and have repeatedly driven hundreds of thousands from their homes. There are massive killings and ethnic cleansing and other large scale atrocities conducted by Turkey, within NATO abetted by a huge arms flow of arms from the Clinton administration that escalated as atrocities peaked. Now Clinton backed Turkish terror. And it succeded. Another client state Coloumbia had the worst human rights records in Latin America in the 1990s. The process began with the Kennedy administration. In 1958 President Eisenhower supervised a major clandestine operation in an effort to break up Indonesia. That led to forty years of terror. Since the 1950s the US has tolerated, protected and promoted military dictators in Pakistan who have committed incalcuable harm to their own country as well as engaged in covert and overt aggression on India both declared and undeclared apart from sponsoring terrorism.

US Thinking

US rationale of a superpower needs to be comprehended to understand the second Iraq war. US must appear to be a credibile power. What better way to be credible than pose a nuclear threat? The logic of credible threat was advanced in Kosovo in early 1999.Chosmky details US credibility by referring to the post–Cold War deterrence study by the US Strategic Command (STRATCOM): Washington's "deterrence statement" must be "convincing" and immediately discernible by leaders of "rogue states" (meaning deviant small powers). The US should have available "the full range of responses, because "unlike chemical or biological weapons, the extreme destruction from a nuclear explosion is immediate, with few if any appliatives to reduce its effects."[4]

Noam Chomsky refers to the deployment of the expression of the rogue states and believes that the superpower that does not observe any international law, UN, International Court or any other body is the rogue state. In that context he finds the US to be one and only one along with Britain to be rogue states. The way US has deployed the term it means any State that hurts the national security interests as perceived by a particular administration of the US is to be described to be a rogue. This was related to Russia against whom Britain used chemical and biological weapons before the war. In the literature on post–First World War affairs any state that chose its way of development against the dominant US strategic or economic interests or any corporation thereof was considered rogue justifying unilateral action. Rolling back the frontiers of communism was one such justificatory doctrine to intervene. That explained why there was no voice against weapons of mass destruction being used against Soviet Union. After the second war it was containment. Italy, Greece, formation of NATO, destabilization in Indonesia, Egypt, nuclear proliferation in Israel, murder of Salvador Allende, intervention against Nicaragua, support to Pol Pot, action against India and Vietnam and opposition to liberation of Bangladesh and victory of Vietnam against the Chinese were all in the name of containment. Before the collapse of the Cold War and break up of the Soviet Union, Reagan highlighted national security threats in 1983. These were related to the Third World, especially from Horn of Africa, Cambodia, Afghanistan, Nicaragua and Southern Africa. This led to the pursuit of nuclear and strategic supremacy by not ratifying the SALT agreements and announcing militarisation of outer space through Strategic Defence Initiative.

With the collapse of the socialist system new sources of threat were pinned down. These emanated from the Third World States, especially those with the missile potential. Now ideology was given a go by. The much discussed theory of discriminate deterrence was then propounded for surgical strikes against the Third World targets. The theory was based on smart munitions and the agrument in favour of it was that these have least collateral damage and shall save property though not human lives. As the 1990s advanced the threat from Third World got linked with two issues. First was the propaganda about stolen nuclear weapons from the former USSR being in the hands of non-state organizations. Second the change in the Balkans and the problem of Serbian ethnic cleansing deemed the US unilateral intervention on humanitarian grounds to save the kosovars under Clinton administration without sanction from any one. The Clinton doctrine raised heckles and it is well known that Europe was uncomfortable with all this. Unipolarity had transformed itself into unilateral action and with the credible threat of the use of nuclear weapons.

Some sampling of the European perception shows the growing European unease with the US inclination to intervene as in Haiti and Kosovo. In a perceptive remark Glennon said about the failure of the UN "the problem was not the second Persian Gulf War, but rather an earlier shift in world power toward a configuration that was simply incompatible with the way the UN was meant to function. It was the rise in American unipolarity not the Iraq crisis that, along with cultural clashes and different attitudes towards the use of force, gradually eroded the council's credibility."[5]

Contemporary Dimension

This inclination to unilaterally deploy military powers–with or without weapons of mass destruction led to disquiet in Europe. In 1998 the former foreign minister of France said 'we cannot accept a politically unipolar world.' The French wanted a multipolar world. Germany joined later to contest US hegemony. Its foreign minister said in 2000 "the core concept of Europe after 1945 was and still is a rejection of the hegemonic ambitions of individual states." The Russians and the Chinese were committed to multipolarity. So is India. In contrast Bush announced in State of the Union message of 2003 "the course of this nation does not depend on the decision of others."

Parrallel to the US view of regarding the Third World States as threats to national security it moved in the direction of identifying a new threat, namely terrorism. Ian Lesser, Bruce Hoffman, John Arquilla David Rinfeld and Michael Zamin came out with the state department's thinking on terrorism.[6] This book is the State Department's reports. It narrated that in 1998 highest death number was in 1998 but the lowest was in 1971. It took the position that since the end of the Cold War while the number of terrorist related incidents are less the number of fatalities are more. Today's terrorist are different from their Cold War counterparts. Today's motivations are religion, milleniarianism, racism and financial gain. Religion is primary motive. The religionists have committed deadly attacks in the 1990s, including 1997 assault at the Luxor temple in Egypt which resulted in 62 fatalities.

Commenting on incidents in the US, including on embassies inTanzania and Kenya the State department's Patterns in global terrorism states over 40 per cent attacks last year show ad hoc terrorists who act largely on their own, but are sparked ideologically by religious, racist, or other types of edicts. These compartmental terrorists may receive financial support or direction from a larger benefactor, but they operate virtually independent of each other, making it difficult to counter terrorism authorities to stop them. Moreover these groups are difficult to respond against because clear linkages to higher sponsors may not exist or be evident."

The second book is based on the US Air Force data on international terror. It notes the growing lethality of terrorism and is the starting point from which postmodern terror is deduced. During 1980-92 it notes that there was a six fold increase in religious terrorists and increased throughout the mid 1990s. Terrorist organizations are more horizontal and fewer verticals and may use weapons of mass destruction.

Some points in these need to be made. First these documents in 1999 do not identify either a State or a criminal organization to be behind these groups of new terrorists. It mentions religion and racism but does not identify them. It did not refer to Al Qaeda. It does not note the Pakistani sponsored terrorism. These also do not refer to other States sponsoring terrorism despite the fact that there was already the history of the first Persian Gulf War. In preparation to the second Gulf War Iraq was alleged to have had Al Qaeeda links. Vague was the issue of source of terrorism. Who was the rogue it did not identify?

The US policy apart from legislating for meeting the threat domestically if followed the thrust of multilateral cooperation. Halifax summit in 1995, Sharm El-Sheikh summit in March, 1996, G-7 Declaration on terrorism at Lyon Summit, June 1996, Ministerial Meeting on Terrorism, Paris 30 July, 96, International Convention on Terrorist Bombings, 15 December 1997. Second track policy was to impose sanctions against States that were regarded as rogue. Continuation of exports restrictions against Cuba, Syria, North Korea, Iran, Iraq, Sudan, Libya, pursuant of the provision of the Export Administration Act. Then there was the Executive Order No. 12957 prohibiting trasnsations with respect to the Iranian petroleum resources. There was the Executive Order 12947 prohibiting transactions with terrorists, 24th January 1995. Executive order No. 12959 probibiting certain transactions with respect to Iran, 8th May 1995. Iran–Libya sanction act of 1996. Against Cuba there was the Liberty Solidarity Act, 1996. Two points need to be made here. First this was a hang over of the Cold War mind set springing from the Red Terrorist network though this could never empirically be proved. Second, Iran and Libya were more in the focus than Iraq.[7] Surprisingly it is reported that in 1986 Iraq was exported anthrax.[8] Walter Laquer, who usually represents the voice of the State department says that religion and terrorism are the newer facet as of the new menace. He mainly identifies it with the Arab world. These terrorists focus on the popular or sociaist terrorist regimes, like Algeria and Afghanistan, says Walter Laquer.[9]

September 11 changed everything US were in for a shock. Its placid orientation towards terrorism changed. All Muslims now overnight became terrorists. The earlier secular regimes were joined by the fundamentalists like Taliban in Afghanistan. Both Saudi Arabia and Pakistan came in for shock as well. The Pakistanis in no time agreed to overturn the regime that they were helped by the US to set up. The Saudis are under the shadow of the congressional report's classified portions on September 11. These deal with the Saudis. The Iraqis came in for focus attention first before Iran and Libya. The Palestininan cause of the homeland is now equated with the Muslim terror and the Muslim world everywhere is considered suspect. A fall out internally has been the security measures in public spaces like airports and new tighter immigration laws to suggest that the US is no longer the home to liberty. The Muslim population of India is also not beyond that shadow of terror network though Pakistan became the US Frontline State.

In this context one needs to take a look at US action on Saddam Hussein and Iraq. The preparation for intervention on Iraq was on the following grounds. First, Saddam must go. Second, there should be a democracy. Third, the oil interests need to be protected. Fourth Saddam has harboured the Al Qaeda terrorist and has links with them. So Iraq was faced with the double accusations of being a rogue state and one with terrorist links. Iraq replaced Libya, which was for a very long time considered to be a rogue state. So did it replace Iran? Why did this happen that first Osama Bin Laden and then Saddam became terrorists. The reasons are not far to seek. They were the good guys carrying on the US geostrategic games for decades. Even if it meant proliferation of deadly weapons of mass destruction (Saddam Hussein) or the missile systems like the Stinger missile (Osama Bin Laden). Both were asked to account for these. They refused. So the heat turned on them. Osama was chased since the CIA trained operatives were spread all over the place but only the CIA did not know and these operatives were with deadly weapons. Till 1998 this development must not have taken place since the State department documents quoted above called them faceless without any knowledge of who was behind them and where they were. Second, the Iraqis were given the ultimatum to account for the weapons and they refused. The Iraqis were held as deviant earlier since the Israelis bombed their Osiraq nuclear reactor given by the French. They were again held for their crimes since the senior Bush attacked them after being egged on to attack Kuwait. Now the third time was under junior Bush since the ten-year period, which had seen human casualties owing to sanctions, was not enough to kill the rogue.

We notice that the claims on all four counts are shallow. The grounds of removal of Saddam Hussein and introduction of democracy cannot be the reasons of intervention. Third, the oil interests could be secured by diplomacy and need not involve intervention. Fourth, CIA disputed the allegation of links with Al Qaeeda. The only grounds of intervention that could be left were the one on weapons of mass destruction. This was not conclusively proved either before or after the attack. The attack however could have following reasons: oil, eve of election year, domination of the region to prevent any other power to emerge as a threat to the US, to dominte the oil reserves not only of Iraq but also of the entire region from the Middle-East to Central Asia. The contracts have gone to the US, to begin with. For Central Asia, NATO has been brought to replace other forces and US. For Iraq the US is in trouble since it failed to carry its allies with it. Now it wanted to allow for removal of US troops to the peace stations. This is not happening. Instead, after the declaration of close of combat sixty-two US soldiers have died. The refusal by the other powers to join in has brought the US to the UN again. The other powers are saying that the proposed resolution is not clear about the role of the UN. So the UN troops cannot be sent. For Afghanistan Pakistan is allowed to do as it likes. India's Foreign Secretary Kapil Sibal and Russian Foreign Minister have noted the danger of the Taliban raising its head. The US imperium is not interested in reconstruction. That is the emerging pattern. The US has been viewed as an imperium in terms of economic aspect of globalisation for quite some time now. [10] US reach is commented upon by Zbigniew Brezezinski[11] thus "the unique position of the first and only truly global superpower" whose "vassals and tributaries' include the states of Western Europe." For the first time ever he wrote, "a non-Eurasian power has emerged not only as the key arbiter of Eurasian power relations but also as the world's paramount power."

It may be added that this is a superpower that will be found credible only with the intent to intervene with nuclear weapons.

Reference

1. Startfor. Com. December, 2002.
2. James H. Mittelman, 'Globalisation : An Ascendant paradigm?' *International Studies Perspectives* (2002) 3. pp.1-14.
3. Michael Ruppert. 'Osama Bin Laden's Bush Family Business connections' *bin laden html.*
4. Noam Chomsky, *The Rogue States. The Rule of Force in World Affairs,* Southend Press. Cambridge. M. A. 2000.
5. Michael J. Glennon. 'Why the Security Council failed' Foreign Affairs. May/June. 2003. p.18.
6. Ian Lesser. Bruce Hoffman. John Arquilla rin feld and Michael Zamin. *Countering the New Terrorism,* Washington D.C. Rand. 1999; Jessica Stern, *The Ulimate Terrorists,* Cambridge. M.A. Harvard University Press, 1999.
7. Thomas J. Bradley, 'US Anti–Terrorism Policy. The Clinton Administration, '*Contemporary Security Policy*, Vol.19. No.2. August 1998, A Frank Cass Journal, pp. 50-70.
8. Stephen R. Bowers and Kimberly R. Keys Technology and Terrorism Research Institute for the Study of Conflict and Terrorism.
9. Walter Laquer. *New Terrorism* OUP. 1999.
10. Leo Panitch. 'New Imperial State' *New Left Review*. March/April, 2000. pp. 5-21.
11. Z. Brzezinski. *The Grand Chess Board.* New York. 1997. p.40.

5
Geo-Strategic Significance of US-UK Action in Iraq

Maj. Gen. (Retd.) Afsir Karim

The Bush doctrine was evolved in response to the growing threat of weapons of mass destruction and international terrorism. The policy was evolved in view of the increasing possibility of WMD falling into the hands of stateless terrorists, who could not be deterred from using them. The United States according to this doctrine reserved the right to take preemptive action or wage war, even use nuclear weapons against non-nuclear states, to safeguard its national interests. This policy was considered necessary to prevent proliferation of Weapons of Mass Destruction (WMD), after the breakdown of the policy of nuclear deterrence at the end of the Cold War. The Bush doctrine stated that "given the goals of rogue states and terrorists, the United States can no longer solely rely on a reactive posture as we have in the past... traditional concepts of deterrence will not work against a terrorist enemy whose avowed tactics are wanton destruction and targeting the innocents; whose so-called soldiers seek martyrdom in death and whose most potent protection is statelessness".

The National Security Strategy of the United States of America deals in great detail with methods and means of waging war against international terrorism. The policy also lays down methods to deter enemies from threatening the US and its allies with WMD. The attack on Iraq demonstrates the determination with which this policy is being pursued by the US administration.

Preemptive action against Iraq, however set a dangerous precedence and unfolded an entirely new strategic scenario. Whether Iraq was a legitimate target under the new US doctrine will remain a debatable point because weapons of mass destruction were neither found anywhere in Iraq, nor used by Iraq during the war. There is still no evidence to show that Iraq had any links with Al-Qaeda or any other international terrorist organization. The impression that is gaining ground is the main aim of the US administration was to control the oil wealth of Iraq that was not possible without ousting Saddam Hussein and occupying Iraq.

War in Iraq created great international turbulence as it was evident that it was not only a war against Iraq but the beginning of a much larger campaign to bring far reaching political changes in the entire Arab World. It was apparent that the US chose Iraq as much for its oil as for strategic location in the Middle East. Iraq is ideally located to be used affectively as a strategic pivot to overawe all those regimes in the Middle East that seem unwilling to further US interests, or were suspected of providing bases or sanctuaries to the global terrorist groups like Al-Qaeda. Taming the Arab world could prove a long and difficult process as use of excessive force against civilian targets in Iraq by the US forces has created bitterness against the US on an unprecedented scale in the entire Arab World and winning of the war may not result in the intended impact on intransigent Arab states. The expectation that the removal of Saddam Hussein will hold a lesson to defiant nations to toe the line or drive out terrorists from the Middle East did not come true.

The US is presently feared and hated in most Arab countries; even friendly nations and allies are not comfortable with the belligerent US posturing and its large military presence in the Middle East. From a geopolitical angle the US, however, is now in a position to intimidate and coerce more countries of the region to support its policies, but countries such as Iran and Turkey may not comply and others may sulk.

There can be little doubt that the US-led occupation of Iraq will give several long-term politico–strategic advantages to US but gradually opposition to hegemonic US policies may gain momentum in Russia, China and India and some other countries like France and Germany, who may resist the US capability of dominating both Europe and the oil–rich Middle East.

The US would not like to share the economic and strategic advantages for which it waged the war on Iraq and is therefore unlikely to accept a primary role for the United Nations in Iraq. It is more likely that US will opt for preemptive strikes or show force to dominate the region rather than fritter away the strategic gains it has sought by the change of regime and occupation of Iraq. Some reports indicate that the US defence officials and civilian advisers close to the Pentagon are working on widening the scope of war in the Middle East:

The armed resistance in Iraq has not ceased even after the disappearance of Saddam Hussein with his entourage, and the US authorities in Iraq still have to cross many political and military mine fields. In most parts of Iraq chaos prevails as the US planners failed to visualize the consequences of a political vacuum and the likely resistance of the Iraqi people. There is a growing sense of anger and desperation among the people because of the indiscriminate US bombardment of the civilian areas during the war resulting in stunning disbelief of the US callousness. It is still not clear whether this strong psychological blow will lead to continued turmoil but if the persistent attacks on US troops are any indication resistance is likely to increase in intensity and geographic spread. Will all Iraqis pull in one direction and cause further casualties on occupation forces or will the radical anti-Americanism decrease over a period of time will depend on handling of the situation by the US forces.

The United States forces so far come out of the war as mindless victors and not as benevolent liberators as they had declared. It is still unclear weather Washington will be able to win over the people or will use force and strategic coercion to achieve its ends. The US leadership by its utterances and actions seem inclined to depend more on lethal force rather than presenting a benign face. The apprehensions of the entire Arab countries have greatly increased because of the belligerent attitude of the US administration towards the Arab World. US has already accused Iran and Syria of undermining peace in the Middle East by harboring and encouraging and allowing terrorist groups to operate from their soils. It has also put Saudis on notice in many subtle ways.

The United States cannot afford a rift with all countries of the region because of its geopolitical compulsions. Turkey will remain important for the US in relation to southern Europe and Iran. The US will have to limit Kurdish ambitions of an independent state that claim some areas of Turkey to avoid a showdown. Northern Iraq can prove a powder keg if the situation is mismanaged there by the US.

The conditions in Iraq are not likely to settle down soon as sporadic attacks against the coalition forces indicate. Shiite population of southern Iraq can wage guerrilla war against the United States if they are not given their due in a democratic set up; similarly Kurds may raise the ante if their claims for a separate state are ignored. Although the US has proved to the world that it was not dependent on or responsible to anyone for its actions, this may not hold good if the United States decides or is forced to enlarge the theatre of war in the Middle East. Enlargement of areas of armed conflict may lead to such geopolitical turbulence that the US policy-makers may not be able to handle, if the present volatile situation in the Middle East is any indication. The claims of 'democratic imperialism' to safeguard US mainland and its allies may find few takers in the future; this policy on the other hand may create widespread resentment against US and increase its international isolation to an intolerable degree.

It seems the general agreement has been that post-war Iraq must be democratic but Saddam Hussein's ghost still haunts the Americans.

The United States has yet to prove that it means to fulfill its declaration that the war's aim was not to colonise but to free the people of Iraq. Presently very few people in the world are likely to take US pledges seriously. The war ended with a total military victory for the Americans, Baghdad was captured without difficulty but Saddam and his entourage became elusive. The chaotic conditions prevailing in various parts of Iraq give little hope for formation of a representative government in Iraq. The entire country has dissolved into chaos as basic services such as medical, water and electric supply have collapsed and Americans seem to watch helplessly as looting and lawlessness continue unabated. Surprisingly, Washington failed to foresee or cater for the consequences of destruction caused by their own troops. Whatever situation may emerge ultimately creating a new order under the overall control of the military does not seem feasible. It is evident that turbulence and chaos will continue in Iraq for quite some time under the present dispensation. So far the most apparent consequence of the war is the immense destruction caused by American bombings and ground action. Thousands of Iraqis are dead or are maimed and in these conditions the resentment of the people is bound to reach a boiling point soon. The task of rebuilding Iraq is urgent but extremely difficult as lawlessness and political infighting show. Sunni minority that ruled Iraq so far is highly restive and the ultimate goal of establishing a democratic and representative government seem to be receding. Rashid Khalidi, a historian of the Middle East at the University of Chicago has said, "there are some very dangerous cleavages there. If exploited by outside forces they could cause problems" seems to be proving correct.

It is clear that neither the political order of Iraq nor the Middle East can be changed by the Americans in a hurry. In the aftermath of the war much will depend on Washington's handling of the situation in the next few years and the reactions of the diverse segments of the Iraqi population. A freely chosen democratic government may not be easy to establish because of various challenges from the diverse factions and external forces. Most Arab governments will be uncomfortable with a democratic government in Iraq. Therefore they work against such an arrangement.

The military and political objectives of the US in the Middle East have not been achieved so far, doubts about US motives will continue to generate fear and bitterness against the Americans on a scale never witnessed before. Reports of indiscriminate firing by American troops, killing a large number of unarmed civilians is hardly helping the peace process. If such incidents are not controlled immediately, bringing back normalcy may prove elusive. It has been clearly demonstrated that winning a war is not sufficient to achieve ultimate geopolitical objectives. It is evident that American unilateralism and its scant regard for the security concerns of other countries in the wake of the Iraq war have created a new uncertain security environment around the globe. This could lead to an arms race in certain regions of Asia and a showdown between countries where deep rooted unresolved conflicts are simmering. One such region is South Asia where India and Pakistan seem poised for a dangerous confrontation over Kashmir.

The global war on terrorism seems to have reached a plateau, but the American worldview has not changed. The US policy has gone beyond the tactical requirement of combating terrorism and is now based on *strategic* domination of all those powers that do not accept its dictates. The strategic aim of the US now extends to gain political and economic control of all oil rich states in the Middle East. This strategic stance, however, appeared to be a diversion from the war against terrorism that was launched after the events of 9/11.

The US administration now seems to be seeking alliances with India and certain Central Asian republics to combat terrorism and may depend less and less on its traditional allies such as Saudi Arabia and Pakistan. Although Al-Qaeda and the Taliban have been driven out of their strongholds in Afghanistan, it seems they have found a safe haven in certain regions of Pakistan. After the emergence of Muttahida Majlis-e-Amal (MMA) as a political force in Pakistan it is much easier for these elements to find safe houses and bases in Pakistan. In these circumstances the US forces have to provide protection both to Karzai and Musharraf to maintain their present positions. The USA will have to maintain a strong military presence in the Afghanistan-Pakistan belt till the situation stabilizes in the region and this may take a long time.

It appears that Al-Qaeda has suffered irreparable damage after 9/11 and Osama bin Laden (dead or alive) or his followers may not be able to revive the global Jehadi movement against America, although they are still capable of mounting terrorist attacks in most parts of the globe including the American mainland.

No one can guarantee the emergence of a pliable regime in Iraq as events after the war indicate. As after the Israeli invasion of Lebanon in 1982, Hizbullah, a dreaded terrorist group came into being and the Palestinians eventually launched a new form of war that combined guerrilla warfare, terrorism and *Intifida.* The US problems in Iraq continue unabated despite massive use of military force. It was easier for the US to win the war than to ensure peace after the destruction wrought by its flawed policy.

It seems the initial framework for targeting only those countries responsible for terrorist attacks on US targets has gradually changed to 'regime change' by force of arms. It appears the so-called 'Neocons' (neo-conservatives) on the Capitol Hill have succeeded in unduly influencing many others to support change-by-force policies.

6
Iraq: War to Reorder the World

Prakash Karat

The war on Iraq was waged not to pre-empt any threat to the United States, nor, to eliminate weapons of mass destruction in the hands of a dictator. In the name of "regime change" it was nothing but an audacious step in the thrust for total American domination of the world. The 21st century is seeing the proclamation of an US imperium. The goal being to maintain and consolidate global hegemony, secure the interests of US multinational capital and the use of military power to prevent any challenge to its imperial interests.

Imperialism, at the beginning of the 21st century is marked by the overwhelming dominance and exercise of American power. With the advent of the Bush presidency, this has become overt and brazen, but the processes were set in motion in the last decade of the 20th century. Iraq stands as an emblem for this new aggressive imperialism.

The war on Iraq marked a turning point. The US has occupied an independent Arab state and aims to convert it into a protectorate, a la Afghanistan. The US, after the Second World War, stationed troops and maintained bases in the Arab world - in Saudi Arabia, Lebanon and the Gulf states. It intervened a number of times in West Asia to topple regimes or prop up client ones. For this, it had a reliable ally and base in Israel. Yet this is the first time, the United States is an occupying power in an Arab country, despite the puppet regime that it will eventually set up. There can be no more dramatic manifestation of the new American imperial order than the setting up of its new outpost in Iraq in the oil-rich region.

The war on Iraq was foreordained. It was bound to happen, even had the attacks on September 11, 2001 not taken place. September 11 provided a convenient pretext. It is the Bush doctrine of pre-emptive war in action. The war on Afghanistan was only the prelude. The "axis of evil" speech, targeting Iraq, Iran and North Korea was made soon after. The "global war against terrorism" and the concept of an unending war was propounded. The ease with which a global coalition against terrorism was rallied, emboldened the "new imperialists" in the Bush administration.

Why Iraq?

Iraq was the subject of an unending war since 1991. The 12-year sanctions regime was a continuation of war by other means. It was maintained by the United Nations mainly due to the insistence of the US. Iraq was the target of not only the present Bush administration, but of the Clinton presidency which succeeded the Bush Sr. administration. Both the 1993 air strikes and the 1998 "Desert Fox" operation when Iraq was subjected to seventy-two hours of bombardment were conducted in the Clinton years. These attacks were apart from the constant aerial bombardment in the no-fly zones carved out of Iraqi airspace. The reality is that Iraq has been a prime target of American imperialism without any let-up.

What motivates this unremitting hostility? Iraq was the only major country (apart from Iran and Syria) which was outside the grip of the US in the region. The Saddam Hussein regime's intransigence must be seen in the context of the strategic importance of Iraq. With the world's second largest oil reserves and a modern state based on the Baathist party's authoritarian rule, Iraq posed a threat to the hegemonic position of the US in the region and more immediately to the Israeli state's role as the latter's chief agent. The occupation of Kuwait in 1990 by Iraq confirmed the American fears that Iraq under Saddam Hussein would prove intractable and more dangerous than Iran. During the 1980-88 Iran-Iraq war, the US had supplied arms to both countries in a cynical move to divide and weaken both powers at one stroke.

The manner in which the Bush administration ratcheted up its case for war and embarked on its military aggression, itself revealed the new calculus of an unbridled imperialism bent upon world domination.

The rightwing think tank the "Project for the New American Century" had prepared a document "Rebuilding America's Defences: Strategy Forces and Resources for a New Century", in September 2000[1]. It had stated: "While the unresolved conflict with Iraq provides the immediate justification, the need for a substantial American presence in the Gulf transcends the issue of the regime of Saddam Hussein". The PNAC had people associated with the earlier Reagan and Bush Sr. administrations.

Earlier, in a 1998 letter to President Clinton, they said: "We should establish and maintain a strong US military presence in the region, and be prepared to use that force to protect our vital interests in the Gulf - and, if necessary, to help remove Saddam from power." The letter was signed by Donald Rumsfeld, Paul Wolfowitz, John Bolton, Richard Armitage and others who are key figures in the Bush administration.

It is these men who prepared the National Security Strategy of the United States of America presented by Bush to the US Congress in September 2002. The document sets out clearly the strategic goals of US imperialism today. Firstly, it strives for maintaining total world domination. Secondly, it proclaims the willingness to strike pre-emptively at perceived or potential threats to the interests of the US. Thirdly, it states explicitly that the US will act to prevent any other power from equaling or challenging US power. The document concludes with the warning: "Our forces will be strong enough to dissuade potential adversaries from pursuing a military build up in the hopes of surpassing, or equaling, the power of the United States."

The use of military power for aggression, conquest or destabilizing regimes, are manifestations of processes within the world capitalist system in the era of imperialism. Conflicts between nation-states and between imperialist states themselves are a result of competition and exploitation engendered by the imperialist system. Both geopolitical and economic interests are interwoven in military conflicts.

How does one see the unprecedented superiority of US military power and the way it uses it? There is no doubt that the military power of the US gives it a pre–eminent position in the imperialist system. The US alone spends 40 per cent of the world's total expenditure on defence. The US spends more on its defence budget than the next 25 major countries put together. But this military strength is not mirrored in comparable economic power and dominance. Here the competition with Western Europe and Japan is less unequal. While Germany and Japan, after the Second World War, had always accepted US leadership on the political/global plane, on the economic front, there has always been competition and conflicts. In the last decade of the twentieth century, the US conscious of this rivalry has sought to exploit every opportunity to build and consolidate its economic strength.

A Marxist analysis of this unbridled use of military power by the imperialist superpower would necessarily look at its economic underpinnings. The US ruling circles are anxious to maintain its hegemony over the international economic order. A system which benefits America the most, among all the advanced capitalist countries. Free capital mobility, free trade (except where it affects one's domestic interests) and having the dollar as the main reserve currency. Such a system enables the US to finance an unlimited trade deficit and to keep the flow of capital from abroad coming. Coincidentally, the Iraq invasion occurred at a time when the US economy was stalling after the weak recovery from the 2001 downturn. Though the Federal Reserve was lowered short-term interest rates 12 times in three years and there is a $300 billion deficit this year, as compared to a $237 billion surplus in 2000, the combination of increased government spending and low interest rates has not worked.

The decline in the US economic growth in the recent period is pushing the US military circles to increase military expenditure and stimulate the economy with war expenditure. While the burden of military expenditure is increasing the deficit, "Nevertheless, military expenditure is unquestionably providing the Administration's most direct stimulus to the economy, as registered in the fact that, in the year following 9/11, the equities of the nation's largest defence contracts performed 30 per cent better than those of S&P 500." [2]

It is in this background that we must see the Iraq war and the occupation. There are both geo-political and economic motives behind the drive to establish unchallenged suzerainty over the Gulf region. Oil is no doubt a key issue. By 2020, the US will be importing 60 per cent of its daily oil requirements. Control over the oil resources of Iraq will immeasurably strengthen its preeminent position in the imperialist bloc - to the disadvantage of the European powers and Japan and eventually helps the US confront the real potential threat, China.

But it is not oil alone, which drives the current war on Iraq. The global hegemonic strategy of the US requires it to put down all recalcitrant states, especially those with the potential to be regional powers who can defy the US will. After the Cold War, the US strategists have in their quest for total domination posited the threat from "rogue states", listed countries as sponsors of terrorism and finally under Bush the "axis of evil". The US has been consistent in its hostility to Arab nationalist movements and Arab states who assert their independence. These stem from a two-fold reason, firstly it requires client states for the control of oil and secondly for protecting its gendarme, the Israeli state.

Significance of Sept. 11

The September 11 terrorist attacks in New York and Washington were a watershed. It provided the pretext and became the catalyst for the brazen attempt to reorder the world[3]. The "global war against terrorism" as defined by Bush should have logically targeted Saudi Arabia next, because that country proved to be the biggest reservoir of recruits for the Al Qaeda. Fourteen of the nineteen hijackers on September 11 were of Saudi origin. The Saudi royal regime has been the biggest source of support for fundamentalist projects all over Asia and Africa. Egypt which is another client state of the United States has reared many Islamic extremists given the repressive nature of the regime. But the attention of the Bush administration was directed towards Iraq where the fundamentalists did not have any worthwhile influence.

Iraq came on the horizon immediately. The day after September 11, at a National Security Council meeting, Rumsfeld, the Secretary for Defense, raised the issue of going after Iraq not just the Al Qaeda. Next day at Camp David, both Rumsfeld and his deputy Paul Wolfowitz raised the matter again[4]. The inescapable conclusion is that the "global war against terrorism" is an extension of US imperialist interests. Much before September 11, the United States was in search of a new strategy after the Cold War which could justify its imperial ambitions.

The Spoils of War

There are immediate and substantial profits to be made from the occupation of Iraq. The UN authorized the revival of the oil-for-food programme under the 'defacto authority' in Iraq. $10 billion accruing from oil sales will be made available for essential supplies and humanitarian relief. The US will, as the occupying authority, have at its disposal. the funds generated from the sale of Iraqi oil. So America, after inflicting the devastation on the lives of the Iraqi people, will be providing relief to them at their own expense. Not only that, the "reconstruction of Iraq" will be a lucrative affair.

Apart from the oil revenues being used by US companies to "rebuild Iraq" the whole reconstruction programme will be directed by the US occupying authority. The USAID has already put out tenders for the building of roads, power and infrastructure. In the $75 billion requested by the President from the Congress for the war, $ 3.5 billion is set aside for reconstruction in Iraq. American companies will get most of the lucrative contracts. The Bechtel Corp. was awarded the first contract for reconstruction which is expected to go up to a total of $ 680 million in the next eighteen months. Halliburton, which was formally headed by Dick Cheney, the US Vice President, is being favoured with most of the prime contracts in the oil industry. The neo-conservative advisors of Bush are pressing for the privatisation of the Iraqi oil industry. Such a privatisation would be the model for privatisation by other OPEC members to weaken its domination of the oil market.

In the old days when British colonialism ruled the roost, there was the Iraq Petroleum Company which was owned by the Anglo-American and Dutch companies. What is happening is a reversion to the old style colonialism which existed between the two world wars.

Iraq and the Imperial Order

The global war against terrorism proclaimed after September 11 led to the US entering Central Asia in a big way and establishing its military bases in Kyrgyztan, Uzbekistan and Tajikistan. The Caspian basin oil-rich region has been opened up to American oil companies. After the Gulf, the Caspian basin has the biggest oil reserves. The US has gone back into the Philippines and is steadily increasing its military presence in South Asia with Afghanistan and Pakistan having permanent military bases and military collaboration agreements with India, Bangladesh, Nepal and Sri Lanka.

The conversion of Iraq into an American protectorate will mean a significant expansion of the military-imperial network in the Middle East. Turkey, the only country in this region to be part of NATO, is a longstanding ally, despite the recent rupture over allowing American troops access to Northern Iraq through Turkey. Between Afghanistan and Turkey only Iran and Syria remain who are not allied to the US.

Saudi Arabia, Yemen, Egypt, Jordan and the Gulf states are all within its orbit with their governments cooperating with the US.

The condemnatory remarks of Donald Rumsfeld and Secretary of State, Colin Powell, during the invasion of Iraq regarding the help Syria gave the Iraqi government and of Iran's promotion of terrorism, portend America's next round of attrition against these two states.

The concept of imperialism was something unmentionable and unacceptable to the ruling class ideologues of the West after the Second World War. It was only the Marxists who persisted in analyzing the world in terms of imperialism and its dynamics. After the collapse of the Soviet Union, even sections of the Left abandoned the use of the term. The term has come back into usage after September 11. Ironically, it is the rightwing ideologues who have embraced the term and unashamedly advocate the virtues of an American empire. Michael Ignatieff who teaches at Harvard University has written about such an American empire. According to him the new US empire "is not like the empires of times past, built on colonies, conquest and the white man's burden. We are no longer in the era of the United Fruit Company, when American corporations needed the marines to secure the investments overseas. The 21st century imperium is a new hegemony whose grace notes are free markets, human rights and democracy, enforced by the most awesome military power the world has ever known."[5]

As for the conquest of Iraq, he claims that "Iraq is an imperial operation that would commit a reluctant republic to become the guarantor of peace, stability, democratization and oil supplies in a combustible region of Islamic peoples."

One of the editors of *Wall Street Journal,* Max Boot, called for the military occupation of Afghanistan and Iraq citing the role played by the British during the 19th century in the region. He wrote: "The September 11 attack was the result of insufficient American involvement and ambition; the solution is to be more expansive in our goals and more assertive in their implementation." Another journalist, Robert Kaplan wrote a book, *Warrior Politics* which demanded that the US leadership "bring prosperity to distant parts of the world under America' s soft imperial influence". Kaplan stated "There is a positive side to empire. It is in some ways the most benign sign of order".

American rightwing propagandists, supporting the Bush administration do not shy away from terming the role of the United States as an imperialist one. Their British counterparts are not far behind. One of Blair's senior policy advisers Robert Cooper called for a new liberal imperialism. In an article published in the leading British paper *The Observer,* Cooper stated "What is needed then is a new kind of imperialism, one acceptable to a world of human rights and cosmopolitan values. We can already discern this outline: an imperialism which, like all imperialism, aims to bring order and organization but which rests today on the voluntary principle." He then goes on to spell out what he calls the "voluntary imperialism of the global economy". He lauds the role of international financial institutions such as the IMF and the World Bank. This coming out of the closet by the neo-imperialists indicates the arrogance and confidence with which they see America as the sole hegemon and superpower in the world. The war against Iraq with the sole purpose of the removal of President Saddam Hussein and occupying the country, indicates what is in store for all the nation states who do not adjust themselves to the new imperial order.

India's Imperialist Supporters

America's grab for Iraq has brought out in sharp relief the pro-imperialist trends which are inherent in the BJP-RSS outlook. From the outset, the Vajpayee government refused to oppose the war moves of the United States and to mobilise other countries to take a common stand. After a period of silence, faced with increasing criticism, all that the BJP–led government was prepared to state was that any action to be taken against Iraq must have the endorsement of the United Nations. This was followed by the refusal of the government for a resolution by Parliament condemning the war. The plea given was that the government's hand should not be tied before the non-aligned meeting at Kuala Lumpur where flexibility was required to arrive at a common position. At the NAM summit, India was among those countries which played a role in diluting the draft prepared by Malaysia on the threat of war against Iraq. Finally, the talk of a "middle path" was a signal to the United States: India would while stating that it did not want a war, be happy to go along with the United States once the aims of the war were accomplished. It is this double-faced stand which satisfied the United States and led its Ambassador, Robert Blackwill, to assert that there was no difference between India's stand and that of the US on how to deal with Iraq.

Despite the pro-American stance of the BJP, among the people there were strong sentiments against the war and sympathy for Iraq. It is this public opinion which compelled the BJP to eventually "deplore" the war and term it as unjustified. This was followed by the unanimous resolution of Parliament criticising the war and calling for the withdrawal of US and British troops.

The BJP-led government was inclined to accept the American request for sending troops to Iraq to stabilise its occupation. If India had sent a division of Indian army amounting to 17,000 troops, this would have been the second largest contingent after the Americans. The decision to send troops was stopped in its tracks only by widespread public opinion and the united stand of the entire opposition. The very fact that the Vajpayee government was initially in favour of sending troops itself indicates the big shift that has come in India's foreign policy.

Sending troops to Iraq would have been an eerie repetition of history. During the First World War, the British acquired Iraq when it fought the Ottoman empire. The occupation of Basra, Baghdad and Mosul provinces were accomplished by ninety thousand soldiers of the British Indian army. For the BJP-led government, the sending of troops for the recolonisation of Iraq was a matter of *realpolitik*, but for most of the Indian people, it would have been a shameful repetition of colonial history.

The pronounced rightwing trend is also evident in sections of the intelligentsia and the media. All through the build-up for the war, a number of editors, strategic affairs experts and former diplomats argued for India openly supporting the American war. In two successive articles, Shekar Gupta, the Editor-in-Chief of *The Indian Express* set out reasons for supporting America's war.[6] According to him, the US takeover of Iraq will be the prelude to democracy in the Middle East and the elimination of Islamic fundamentalism. "The war will lead to a prolonged American occupation of Iraq and they will first shift the centre of gravity to the Islamic world from Riyadh to Baghdad and then do what it takes to defang, if not de-Islamise, the politics of the Muslim (particularly the Arab) world..Not all analysts agree with what Bush is doing, but they all say his team has concluded that band-aid solutions won't work in the Muslim world, that it needs reconstructive surgery and some minor amputations, like Saddam. Does that work to our benefit or detriment? Given a chance - and the power - wouldn't we have liked to do just that? This war will not be about oil, but about militant Islam and everybody's future." It is not naivety which leads Gupta to put out such arguments. Borrowing ideas from the US rightwing think-tanks and newspapers like the *Wall Street Journal* has become a habit for much of the big business run media in India. The United States is the biggest patron and protector of the Saudi Arabian regime which has been the chief centre to spread fundamentalism around the world. A little reading of history would show how America brought in Pakistan, Iran and Saudi Arabia into this strategic chain in the Middle East to control the Gulf region in the fifties. The Baghdad Pact, mentioned earlier, was one of the first such moves.

By smashing the Baathist regime in Iraq, America has struck against one of the few major secular states in the Arab world. This will not "defang" or "de-Islamise" the politics of the region but provide a fillip to fundamentalism and religious extremism. Nor can anyone subscribe to the make-believe world of democracy flourishing under a Pax Americana in the Arabian deserts. Leave alone the medieval system of the Saudi royal family, the US-backed "democracies" of Egypt, Jordan and Morocco are different versions of authoritarianism which exist all over the region. The alacrity with which *The Indian Express* editor advocates the cause for an American imperium mirrors his eagerness to get the Indian print media tied up with the media barons of the West.

Resistance of People's and Countries

The occupation of Iraq was an inevitable outcome of the US war of aggression. But this latest exhibition of unbridled power has not been without resistance. The opposition to the war on Iraq has been unprecedented in many ways. Firstly, the United States faced opposition from some of its major allies in Europe like France and Germany. In the Security Council three permanent members, France, Russia and China refused to accept that resolution 1441 provided an automatic endorsement for US military action on Iraq. The fiasco of the attempt to get a second resolution passed is significant because for the first time in recent history, the United States could not pressurise or coerce the United Nations to fall in line by endorsing its war. The fact that the United States could not muster the nine votes required for passing the resolution by the Security Council was in itself indicative of the widespread opposition to the US move. There was no doubt, that the US would go ahead with its war even if the UN did not sanction it. However, the refusal by the Security Council to legitimize the US war shows that the resistance to American unilateralism is growing.

Underlying the failure of the United States to gain UN authorization was the sharpening of inter-imperialist contradictions, a phenomenon not in evidence for more than two decades. France and Germany, the two biggest countries in the European Union, were apprehensive of the prospects of the US capturing Iraq and consolidating its dominance over the Gulf region. Both in terms of Europe's dependence on the oil supplies from the region and the brazen efforts to assert American dominance, made the war of Iraq an issue on which both the major European powers had to voice their opposition. Underlying this divergence was also the conflict about the preeminence of the dollar and the challenge posed by the Euro. Russia, another major country in Europe now in the capitalist orbit, lined up with France and Germany.

The struggle in the Security Council and the diplomatic skirmishes during the build up towards the war took place in the background of the biggest anti-war mobilisation ever seen particularly the February 15 protest marches. The spectacular protests definitely show a growing mass consciousness about the dangers of the reckless and adventurist course embarked upon by US imperialism. It is significant that the biggest mass protests took place in those very countries whose governments are supporting the US war effort–Britain, Australia, Italy and Spain. In the West, the mass anti-war movement was preceded by three years of anti-globalisation protest movements. Increasingly, the link between imperialist driven globalisation and war became established for millions of people.

The anti-war protests during the Vietnam war did radicalize a section of the people particularly the young who were drawn into the movement. The historic mobilisations which preceded the Iraq war saw another noteworthy feature. In Britain and Australia and to some extent in the United States school students organised and came out into the streets to protest the war. Such large-scale participation of school students in the anti-war movement has never happened before. The radicalization which will come about among sections of these youth, augurs well for the Left in these countries.

The relentless American drive for total domination in the past one decade, the military pummeling of small states, the threats of intervention to change governments and systems not to its liking, its unilateral acts bypassing international norms and forums, have led to a sense of despondency in some progressive circles. The unrelenting onslaughts, the patently unjust economic order imposed on the poorer countries and the use of blockades, sanctions and open military intervention, create the grounds for pessimism and anxiety.

But it would be a mistake to see only this side of the picture. As with all "empires" there are limits to the powers of the sole hegemon. These limitations express themselves in the political, economic and military spheres. Firstly, the imperialist driven globalisation and the imposition of neo-liberal policies around the world have their own dynamics. The operations of predatory finance capital and the imposition of neo-liberal policies in country after country have led to growing inequalities, loss of livelihood and widening poverty which are now finding expression through gathering discontent. Both the gulf between the rich and the poor countries and the sharp division between the rich and the poor within nations are setting off reactions over which the US imperial order have no control. This is starkly seen in South America. In country after country, the neo-liberal policies stand discredited and it is becoming difficult for the ruling classes to impose that model.

The spectacle of the use of American military power with its vast technological superiority is a deliberate and conscious demonstration. The Bush administration is increasingly flaunting military power and to use it as a lever to reorder the world. Such brutal and destructive power is a serious threat to the lives and security of people all around the world. However, the brute use of military power cannot be the basis for the enduring success of US imperial aims. The limits of such military power was evident in Afghanistan. The use of missiles, precision guided bombs and other high-tech weaponry helped minimize US casualties and to subdue the weaker adversary but it has not led to political and social structures which America wants to put in place. In Afghanistan, this is exemplified by the fact that the handpicked ruler of Afghanistan, Hamid Karzai, has to be constantly guarded by US special forces and his writ does not run in many parts of the country. Even the much vaunted aim of eliminating the Taliban leadership and the Al Qaeda could not be fully accomplished.

In Iraq, a much more developed society with a deep nationalist tradition, it will be all the more difficult for American military occupation to provide any political and social legitimacy to a pliant regime. Iraqi resistance and a protracted struggle against the colonial occupation is bound to develop. Not only will the conflict in Iraq not end, the entire region will be thrown into turmoil. Israel will seize the opportunity to crush the Palestinian movement and the pro-American regimes in the region will come under severe strain. Hence, Iraq, unlike Afghanistan, will prove to be a turning point. The rhetoric of American imperialism with its hypocritical cant of ensuring a world free of terror safe for democracy and human rights is violently different from the experience of American power for people around the world. They see the imperial power as greedy for super profits, bent upon cornering natural resources like oil and willing to trample upon national sovereignties and resort to brute military force to maintain its hegemony. Notwithstanding the compromises and patch-up arrived at between US-Britain and France, Germany and Russia, the challenge to a unipolar US dominated world has begun.

By any reckoning the struggle against this new bestial form of imperialism and American power will be a protracted and difficult one. It is important to draw the proper lessons from the latest imperialist adventure in Iraq. While outrage against the beast on the rampage is natural, there is no scope for despair and pessimism. After a long time, since the danger of fascism moved millions of people, the spectacle of a US empire founded on brute military might moved tens of millions of people around the world to protest and oppose the war. The "global coalition against terrorism" was reduced to a pathetic "coalition of the willing". At no time since the Second World War, when US supremacy in the imperialist bloc got established, had America been so isolated from the rest of the world.

What the United States and the Britain are seeking to accomplish is the recolonisation of Iraq which had slipped out of their grip in 1958. The occupation of Iraq has not ended the resolve of the Iraqi people for independence. The struggle, which has now erupted against the occupation, will be a protracted one. The United States will find itself faced with another round of popular anti-imperialist struggles sparked of by its imperial occupation of Iraq. The challenge in the coming days will be: how to carry forward the rising feelings against brute imperialism by shunning sectarian-fundamentalist responses. This requires a world-wide secular and militant mobilisation against the imperialist driven globalisation.

Reference

1. See Vijay Prashad: The Arrogance of Empire, an assessment of the Bush Doctine, The Maxist, July-December 2002.

2. Towards thePrecipice: Robert Brenner, London Review of Books, February 2003.

3. See Prakash Karat: Global War Against Terrorism, Extension of American Hegemony. The Marxist. July-December, 2001.

4. Bob Woodward: Bush at War, Simon & Schuster, 2002.

5. Quoted from Fred Goldstein: Bush can't sell war for empire, Worker World, Junuary 17, 2003.

6. The Indian Express, 1 February and & 8 February 2003.

7

Genesis of US-UK Military Operations in Iraq and its International Significance

V.D. Chopra

Any objective analysis of the U.S.-U.K. military operations in Iraq, which have destroyed its entire Baathist led political, social and economic structures, must take into account its geo-strategic and geo-economic reasons. Though, Middle East is not a well defined area, it includes Egypt, Israel and Arab states of southwest Asia. Some historians include Morocco and Afghanistan in this concept. Prior to World War II, the Middle East Command of the British Royal Air Force even included Kenya within its sphere of operation. Quite apart from this within the Islamic world, a division has resulted in the creation of Shia and Sunni sects. Despite this, there are strong social and cultural bonds among them. It is significant to mention here that Islam as a religion is based on well defined tenets and principles. Islamic religion is the main driving force. Thus, the Arab world forms part of the larger Islamic world. Moreover, the common consciousness and experience has created the concept of Arab nation, despite diversities of the various states in culture, stage of economic development and different political power structures. It is relevant to mention here that Arabic language is spoken by overwhelming majority of people in a large number of the countries in Africa and Asia. There is no doubt that Islam is the religion of the majority of the Arab people. However, there are religious minorities who are not Muslims but belong to the Arab nations such as Christian. There are also other ethnic minorities such as Kurds and Berbers of northwest Africa, who have their own language and culture.

It is pertinent to mention here that this region before the World War II was under British influence except for Syria and Lebanon. The British were responsible for the mandated territories of Palestine, Transjordan, and Iraq, while in the Crown Colonies of Cyprus and Aden, British rule was direct. In the Persian Gulf, the British position was sustained by treaties with local Sheikhs that gave Britain responsibility for defence and the right to establish military bases. The Egypt, despite the opposition of the Egyptian government and despite nominal Egyptian independence, British troops were stationed in the Suez Canal Zone. After the World War II the processes of decolonisation took place and one country after another became independent and sovereign. Nevertheless, Balkanization of the region and creation of boundaries arbitrarily have thrown up a large number of conflicts among the newly created states, which continue to create conflicts and tensions.[1] In the post World War II period, the countries of Middle East have been following different internal and external policies. They have been asserting their national independence. Some of them came under the influence of the United States and Western model of socio-economic development and others were influenced by the egalitarian policies of the erstwhile Soviet Union. This was in reality manifestation of different historical experiences. It may be mentioned that Turkey under Mustafa Kemal, Iran under Reza Shah and Egypt under Nasser followed different courses of nation building. Iraq chalked out its own nation state structure. However, to influence the course of development in this region, the Western Powers, the United States in particular set up Baghdad pact, later known as the Central Treaty Organisation (CENTO). This shows how in the post World War II period the political vacuum created by the British rulers began to be filled by the United States. This is how some of the nation states of this region became pro-United States and others were suspicious about the American policies. In this sense historically speaking the Arab people by and large have gone through an experience which makes them critical about the policies of the United States. This sentiment has continued to have expression in the state policies of some of the countries. This aspect has been further compounded and intensified by the oil factor, which assumed a new dimension after the nationalisation of oil industry in the various states of the region. Recent developments in Iraq should be analysed in this historical background.

Geo-Economic Factor-Oil

The Middle East is the world's largest oil-producing region. Iran, Saudi Arabia, Iraq and Kuwait have the richest proven oil resources and perhaps are among the top six oil-producing countries in the world. As early as in the 60s, the countries in this region are estimated to have produced 496 million tons of crude oil according to one estimate. In one decade this oil production increased to nearly 700 million tons. Thus, three decades ago this region in the world economy came to occupy a strategic position. Above all, this region is estimated to have 60 to 65 per cent of proven oil wealth of the world. This estimate, according to some experts underestimates the proven oil wealth of the region. Recent discoveries for instance have been made in Iran, the United Arab Republic, and Syria. Again by the end of last century, Iran surpassed Venezuela. It is one of the biggest oil producing countries after the United States. It should be mentioned here that Russia is one of the top oil producing countries of the world and according to one estimate it has 27 per cent of the proven oil wealth of the world.

This leads to the conclusion that oil wealth of this region plays a key role in the regeneration of the economy of these countries and is one of the most important factors in the international economy. Seen in this context the United States has strategic economic interests in oil wealth of this region because according to one estimate the United States alone consumes 30 per cent of the energy produced in the world. The economy of the United States and the standard of living of the people in this country in this sense are dependent on their control over the oil wealth of the world, of this region in particular. That after having demolished political and economic structures of Iraq, the political elite of the U.S.A. is threatening Iran and Syria conceals more than what it reveals. The establishment of the Organisation of the Petroleum Exporting Countries (OPEC) in 1960 was a major development. Even at the time of its creation, the five members (Iran, Iraq, Kuwait, Saudi Arabia, Venezuela of OPEC produced over 90 per) cent of all crude oil crossing international boundaries. These oil producing countries have been receiving higher and higher percentages of the revenues as the once 50-50 division between country and company had shifted to 75-25 and even 80-20. As a result of an agreement signed in February, 1971 for instance, by six Persian Gulf oil-producing nations Iran, Iraq, Saudi Arabia, Kuwait, Abu Zaby, and Qatar and twenty-three international oil companies mostly American and a few British and Dutch firms-oil company payments to the six nations rose by more than £ 4,000 million.

High production and huge revenues, however, do not necessarily indicate development and modernization. Such resources can be used to prop up decadent and unpopular political regimes as well as to reinforce crumbling traditional institutions. There is no doubt that petroleum is an important catalyst of change. The oil industry stimulates development in the sense that it (1) helps to raise the Gross National Product and contributes to foreign-exchange receipts; (2) stimulates the growth of other industry, especially in related areas such as petrochemicals and natural gas; (3) provides opportunities for local employment and technical training; (4) generates revenues that can be used for national development programmes; (5) introduces new personnel and business relationships into the culture; and (6) heightens aspiration, and expectations among the citizens.[2]

This brings us to the conclusion that oil factor in the internal politics of the various countries in this region plays a very important role, the chief being rising national consciousness and national aspirations. All the countries of this region have been undergoing a process of political transformation, though the level of its development is uneven. However, the crux of the problem is neither military might nor installation of puppet regimes can reverse this process. Any attempts to control the natural resources of these countries : from outside will be resisted by various formations political and religious. The revolution in Iran, the growing oppositions to monarchies are illustrative of this social change. However, it is unpredictable how these currents and cross-currents will mould the political and social structures of the societies of this region. The moral is that the Middle East is passing through a process of change. However, the Western Powers, the United States in particular instead of adjusting themselves to the new realities have not given up their game. Their ambition to control oil wealth of this region for their narrow national interests is un– satiable. Let us examine this aspect.

American Ambitions

Recently a Kyrgyzstan daily, *Times of Central Asia*, quoted an Israeli internet site as reporting that the US forces in Uzbekistan planned to deploy tactical nuclear weapons in Central Asia. If this is true, it indicates a new strategic geo-political war game. Oil strategies of Russia and China in this region do not support such a possibility, though. But the recent overtures of certain Central Asian States looking to the West for dollars do not rule out such a scenario.

According to a Kazakhstan political scientist, Anderi Chebortrarev, in this case, 'the zone of vital interests' and terminology used by the U.S. Administration was to provide a legal cover for their military bases in other countries located far away for deploying their specially created direct action corps.

They affirm that, till August 2001, the Bush Administration saw the Taliban regime as a "source of stability" in Central Asia that would enable the construction of an oil pipeline across Central Asia from the rich oilfields in Turkmenistan, Kazakhstan and Uzbekistan, through Afghanistan, Pakistan and the Indian Ocean's warm ports. [3]

In the context of this new development, Russia's geo-strategic and geo-economic interests should not be ignored. It seems that Moscow has evolved its own alternative strategy. It has for instance struck a big deal with Turkmenistan to build a South-North pipeline to carry much of the Turkmen gas to Russia. This development has taken place after both Turkmenistan and Unocal were trying to lay a pipeline from Turkmenistan to Turkey.

It may be mentioned here that even after a decade of promises, western companies have not laid any pipeline from Kazakhstan. On the other hand, Russia has built a pipeline from Tengiz oil field (holding 10 billion barrels of oil) all the way through Russia to Novorossiysk on the coast of the Black Sea and then to Blue Stream Gas pipeline to Europe - a 1,850-km-long pipeline, with deep undersea laying of pipes in The Black Sea.

Above all, China has secured a $ 1 billion oil exploration contract in Kazakhstan. There seems to be a tacit understanding between China and Russia to resist expansion of US oil interests in the Central Asian region.[4]

There are clear indications that American oil policy in general and its Middle East oil policy in particular is undergoing certain changes. In view of the political and economic changes taking place in the oil producing countries including in Saudi Arabia, the American policy makers have worked out a new policy. It is important to mention here that at present one-third of the oil requirements of the United States are met from the oil producing Middle East countries. It has been estimated for instance that 10 per cent cut in supply of Saudi oil to the US could hike the price of a barrel of oil to $ 64. The new contour of the American oil policy is directed towards Afghanistan, Central Asia and now Iraq. The American policy makers therefore have evolved a military strategy with this objective in mind. If they are tightening grip over Afghanistan penetrating into Central Asian Republics, now Iraq has become their target. Let us not make any bones about it. The logic of this development is that American and Russian interests, American and French interests are coming into conflict at the present stage of development in this region. This is the economic content of the so-called theory of "liberation of Iraq".

This brings us to another aspect, who will exploit the oil wealth of Iraq, which is the seventh largest oil producing country in the world and second in the Middle East after Saudi Arabia, after occupation of Iraq and installation of a new power structure. The international community, the countries which are sending peacekeeping forces to Iraq, the United Nations in particular cannot afford to ignore this development in the post -Saddam era. In this connection far reaching importance is the fate of the oil contracts which Saddam Hussein regime entered into with others countries. The relevance of this question has to be seen in the background of the fact that occupation of Iraq by foreign troops is going to be a long affair. In view of the growing resistance of the Iraqi people, particularly the followers of Saddam Hussein.

If that is the case, will the US then represent Iraq in OPEC during this period? There can be no greater irony than the largest oil-importing nation sitting in a producer's cartel discussing production quotas to fine-tune prices.

The US President, George W. Bush, has already sought $ 75 billion from the US Congress to past fund for the war effort. Michael O' Hanlon of the Brookings Institution puts the post-war cost of military occupation at $50 billion to $100 billion a year. William D. Nordhaus of Yale University estimates the reconstruction to be anywhere between $ 75 billion and $ 500 billion.

The new sovereign, by virtue of its sovereignty, can do what it pleases with the country's resources, even abrogate existing contracts, but under international law that would be considered as expropriation requiring compensation by the repudiating party.

The validity and extent of the title of the various contenders for the Iraqi oil fields will depend on the nature and terms of the contracts themselves, about which there is little information in the public domain. But the US need not even fuss over the finer legal details. It could install in Iraq a regime favourable to its interests and get it to annul existing contracts on the plea that they were awarded on political considerations. Along with Russia and France, which have the biggest stakes in Iraqi oil, a whole host of countries are closely watching the US moves, wondering which excuse would be used to jettison their hard-won oil concessions in Iraq. [5]

Weapons of Mass Destruction

The worst happened on March 20, 2003 after the World War II when America launched a full-scale war with cruise missiles on Iraq, an independent sovereign state with the declared objective of dislodging "Saddam Hussein and his clique" from power, dismantling its stockpile of weapons of mass destruction and rebuilding a new Iraq. This is the "boldest" roll of the dice any American President has done in the 30 years and "dangerous too", as American Senator Joseph Biden has put it. Whatever may be the pious declaration of the US about the objectives of this war, it marks the beginning of a new era in international relations and has far reaching implications than what appears on the surface. But there is something more to it. It exposes the double talk about weapons of mass destruction practised by the US administration in the 80s and today that too in relation to the Gulf regions especially Iraq.

Before we examine this specific question, it will be pertinent to recapitulate that during the entire period of war and in the post–war period against Iraq no concrete evidence has been put out to bring out that Iraq did not destroy all its weapons of mass destruction.

U.S. Defence Secretary, Donald Rumsfeld for instance refused on April 8, 2003 at a Pentagon news briefing to get into the specifics of reports that the United States forces in Central Iraq had found weapons and chemicals that could be called to be in the realms of mass destruction. Rumsfeld was asked to comment on a report coming out of the 101st Airborne Division that investigations of the 14 barrels at a training camp in Central Iraq on 6 April revealed deadly nerve gas agents such as sarin and tabun. Defence Secretary confined himself to the comment "we don't speculate".

A second report had come from the National Public Radio, which had attributed this to a top official of the First Marine Division. According to this report, missiles of BM-21 variety were equipped with sarin and mustard gas and were ready to fire.

These and other reports were never substantiated with concrete evidence.

This raises the question of Iraq's stockpile of weapons of mass destruction, which was supposed to be the driving force behind this military operation. The coalition forces did not stumble on any weapons type chemical munitions or factories that were producing them.

U.S. and British soldiers in the desert of Iraq and Kuwait had put on their gas masks countless times only for practise to be ready for an attack with chemical and biological weapons.

Reporters accompanying the troops were often seen in dramatic live broadcasts wearing their gasmasks. But while troops and reporters were seen prepared for a chemical warfare, the U.S. has not come forward with evidence that Iraq had still stocks of chemical or biological weapons.

Significantly, the U.S. and British government were repeatedly emphasising that they had no doubt that Iraq had biological and chemical weapons to justify the war. Iraq on the other hand denied this allegation. Above all the United Nations weapons inspectors had not found such weapons during inspections in the country during the entire operation.

Famous lawyer Rajeev Dhavan has brought into focus that "America's justifications for the war on Iraq fall into no recognisable justifications for a just war. It cannot claim that it is implementing Resolution 1441 of the UN Security Council has not authorised the war. It is not a form of anticipatory self defence. As for nuclear and chemical arsenals, the biggest repository of these weapons is America, which did not hesitate to drop atomic bombs on Japan or use chemical weapons in Vietnam."[6]

However, the postures of the US and Great Britain policy makers stand as a complete contrast to their policies in the 80s and today. Peoples' memory is proverbially short but it is not so short as the ruling elites of these two countries believe. There is a telling evidence to prove that in transforming Iraq into a state possessing weapons of mass destruction (WMD) and enhancing its nuclear bomb capability both these countries made available to Iraq massive financial and technical support.

According to the information from the site www.iraq.watch.org., before the Gulf War of 1991 the major part of double purpose equipment suitable for creation of biological and chemical weapons of mass destruction worth more than 1.5 billion dollars had been supplied to Iraq by American companies with approval of the US Commerce Department.

A large number of the financial institutions of the United States and Great Britain, such as Bank of New York (USA), Irving Trust Bank (USA), Midland (GB), Lloyds Bank (GB), Barclays Bank (GB) and some others, took part in rendering financial assistance to Iraq for increasing its capabilities of weapons of mass destruction (WMD) and nuclear bombs. This cold fact speaks for itself. But there is something more revealing than this fact.

It will be embarrassing for Washington to recollect how it helped the Iraqi former President Saddam Hussein, build his arsenal of chemical and biological weapons during the eighties with a view to cut to size Iran. It will be awkward for the US Defence Secretary, Donald Rumsfeld, when he is reminded of the role he played as a special envoy of President Ronald Reagan to West Asia.

The documents published by *Washington Post* in the end of the 2002 show that Mr. Rumsfeld met Mr. Hussein in Baghdad on December 20, 1983 and conveyed to him the US Government's willingness to help him in his war with Iran and to restore diplomatic relations with his regime.

This followed a National Security Directive signed by President Reagan that the US administration was willing to do "whatever was necessary and legal" to prevent Iraq losing the war. This directive was issued despite intelligence reports available to the then Secretary of State, George Shultz, suggesting, "almost daily use of CW (chemical weapons)" by Iraq against Iranian troops. Above all *The Times* said describing the disclosures as "timely reminder" of the US involvement in the creation of Mr. Hussein's arsenal of WMD. These disclosures are based on testimonies of former US officials, including supply of cluster bombs and biological agents, including anthrax according to this report.

It is relevant to mention here that American Intelligence Services knew that Iraq was believed to have been manufacturing mustard gas at a production facility in Samarra since the early 1980s. Moreover, by the start of the Gulf War, Iraqi forces had developed chemical delivery capabilities and possibly landmines and cruise missiles.

On July 30, 1991 Ambassador Rolf Ekenus, director of the United Nations Special Commission on Iraq (UNSCOM) charged with overseeing the elimination of Iraq's chemical and nuclear arsenals, told the Security Council that UN inspectors had found chemical warheads armed with nerve gas.

This shows that how in early 90s the US did not exhibit any anxiety about Iraq's alleged capability of WMD because they were directed against Iran. On the contrary it was financially and technically supporting Iraq in its drive to build its stockpile of WMD. This is confirmed by the fact that as late as on 10 February, 1994 the American media reported that during the 1980s "the US government approved shipment of biological agents to Iraq that could be the cause of the debilitating illness plaguing Persian Gulf War veterans". "The viruses and bacteria, commonly used to develop biological weapons, were shipped to Iraqi government agencies by American Type Culture Collection, a non profit group in Rockville that collects and distributes biological specimens worldwide".

"Richard Roblin, associate science director for American Type Culture Collection, said his group had sent two types of dangerous specimens to Iraq after receiving a request from Iraqi government representatives. One was Bacillus anthracis, the organism that causes anthrax, an often fatal ailment. The other was Clostridium botulinum, the organism producing botulinum toxin that can cause vomiting, constipation, weakness and headaches, but this tragic narration of facts does not end here. "We don't make decision about which cultures are shipped there" said Roblin, whose firm is one of the nation's largest biological specimen banks and acts as a clearing house for scientists. We rely on the Department of Commerce. It's their job". Iraq requested specimens were routinely approved by Commerce's Bureau of Export Administration during the Reagan administration. This shows how US administration was directly responsible for export of such deadly material to Iraq.

No further evidence and documentation are needed to prove that it was primarily the American Administration, which provided strategic material to Iraq to manufacture chemical and biological weapons of mass destruction. In this sordid drama Great Britain too made its contribution. The anthrax strain had a British military pedigree for instance. Significantly, after Iraq imported these strains from the United

States and Great Britain it embarked on the path of their multiplication on a large scale with the active support of British trained scientists.

In March 1991, Molly Moore reported from Jubaly, Saudi Arabia that Marine Commanders found no indications of chemical weapons stockpiles on the battlefields of Kuwait. According to a *Washington Post* report that day (March 7,1991) U.S. intelligence analysts claimed that these weapons never got distributed down to the battlefield from storage sites north of the Euphrates River.

These exported biological materials were not diluted or weakened. They were capable of reproducing. Thus by the time of the invasion of Kuwait, Iraq had developed biological weapons. Its advanced and aggressive biological warfare programme was the most advanced in the Arab World. The programme probably began late in the 1970s and concentrated on the development of two agents, botulinum toxin and Anthrax bacteria. Large-scale production of these agents began in 1989 at four facilities near Baghdad. Delivery means for biological agents ranged from simple aerial bombs and artillery rockets to surface-to-surface missiles. We will come to this question in more details on the basis of media reports. It may be mentioned that included in the approved sales are those biological materials, which have been considered by various nations for use in war.

Let us at this stage examine what type of material was exported to Iraq before Iran–Iraq war.

1. Bacillus anthracis—Anthrax is a disease-producing bacteria. This material was allegedly used in the Persian Gulf War. Anthrax is an often fatal infection caused by indigestion. It begins with high fever, difficulty in breathing and chest pain. The indigestion eventually results in septicemia (blood poisoning) and the mortality is high. Once septicemia is advanced, antibiotic therapy may prove useless, probably because the exotoxins remain despite the death of the bacteria.

2. Clostridium Botulinum—A bacterial source of botulinum toxin, which causes vomiting, constipation, thirst, general weakness, headache, fever, dizziness, double vision, dilation of the pupils and paralysis of the muscles involving swallowing. It is often fatal.

3.Histoplasama Capsulatum—Causes a disease superficially resembling tuberculosis that may cause pneumonia, enlargement of the liver and spleen, anemia, an influenza like illness and an acute inflammatory skin disease marked by tender red nodules, usually on the shins. Reactivated infection usually involves the lungs, the brain, spinal membrances. Heart peritoneum and the adrenals.

4. Brucella melitensis—A bacteria which can cause chronic fatigue, loss of appetite, profuse sweating when at rest, pain in joints and muscles, insomnia, nausea and damage to major organs.

5. Clostridium perfringens—A highly toxic bacteria which cause gangrene. The bacteria produce toxins that move along muscle bundles in the body killing cells and producing necrotic tissue that is then favourable for further growth of the bacteria itself. Eventually, these toxins and bacteria enter the bloodstream and cause a systemic illness.

In addition several shipments of Escherichia coli and genetic materials as well as human and bacterial DNA were shipped directly to Iraq Atomic Energy Commission.

These exports of strategic materials to Iraq for manufacturing chemical and biological weapons clearly establish who enabled Baghdad to develop these weapons of mass destruction. But this alone doesn't tell the whole story, for almost five years from mid 1985 different types of strategic materials were exported from the United States to Iraq, if one fully examines the various sources. At least 50 consignments of such materials were sent to Iraq. These facts have been reported in the American media. These facts speak for themselves and prove how when Iraq was engaged in war with Iran, it was liberally helped to develop weapons of mass destruction.

This brings us to the question why Iraq was encouraged to manufacture and develop chemical and biological weapons. This needs to be investigated. One obvious reason was that this strategy was evolved to drive a wedge between Iran and Iraq. Both these countries are rich in oil wealth. They have built an industrial base. Above all, they have a well trained army. In the Middle East these two countries hold a key position. That being the position, both geopolitical and geoeconomic interests of the United States demand that these two countries should be weakened militarily, economically and politically. Without this the US administration cannot consolidate its hold over the oil rich Gulf region.

Moreover, Iraq and Iran give a moral support to the Palestinian demand for vacation of Israeli occupied Palestinian areas and creation of an independent state of Palestine. The weaker Iraq and Iran are the more difficult it will be for Palestinians to achieve their objective. Therefore, in the mid-80s Iraq was helped to possess and develop chemical and biological weapons to be used against Iran. But when this policy of 'divide and rule' did not work, the fire has been now directed against Iraq and both Iran and Syria have been administered warnings. The irony of the situation is that those who encouraged and helped Iraq to manufacture weapons of mass destruction had undertaken a military action against it on the pretext that they want to destroy its weapons of mass destruction and democratise it. This brings us to the conclusion that the United States has two phases, one manifested itself in the 80s and the other has unfolded itself now. However, this double talk has evoked worldwide opposition including among the people of Great Britain and the United States.

There is yet another dimension of the U.S. led military action against Iraq. Does it not reflect that in the beginning of the 21st century the biggest military–cum–economic power of the world has begun to establish its hegemony over the world? Moreover, "America not only recovered the $40 billion spent on the 1991 Gulf war but also gave itself and its arms and oil conglomerates a further benefit of about $70 billion. The net benefit of Iraqi war will be much greater and will also place the U.S. in charge of one of the largest oil reserves in the world."

This brings us to another aspect which relates to the fact that the pretext that Iraq possessed weapons of mass destruction has proved to be a very thin cover now the emphasis has shifted to 'liberating' Iraq and ending its 'dictatorial' regime and that too without the sanction of the United Nations. There are many other states with a political system which does not fit into the Western concept of democracy. Does this not imply that uni-polarism has not begun to 'liberate' and democratise other countries to suit its narrow geo-political and economic interests.

There is telling evidence, which shows that the theory of destruction of weapons of mass destruction in Iraq was invented both by the United States and Great Britain to cover their real intension of world domination step by step. It will be not out of place to mention some factual evidence to this affect.

U.K. prime minister Tony Blair on July 17, 2003 night made a significant admission in the US Congress when he declared that "history would forgive him even if no weapons of mass destruction are found in Iraq". This speaks for itself and needs no comment. But there is something more to it, which in itself is a chilling disclosure.

"BBC has a tape of David Kelly expressing serious concern about how Downing Street made the case for war". Susan Watts, science editor of Newsnight recorded her conversations with the weapons expert, who killed himself on Thursday (24 July 2003). In her report she quoted a source - now known to be Kelly - suggesting No 10 was "desperate" for information and had exaggerated "out of all proportion" the claim that Iraq could launch weapons of mass destruction within 45 minutes.[9]

After this disclosure no further evidence is needed to prove how facts were fabricated by the power that be both in the United Kingdom and USA to prove their theory of weapons of mass destruction to justify their war in Iraq.

US Congress, Republicans included, questioned the Bush Administration's use of the intelligence material for launching the war, with one view being that the White House manipulated intelligence assessment to mirror its perception. However, Senior administration officials, including top Cabinet members, dismiss this contention. [10]

This shows how theory of launching military action in Iraq to destroy its weapons of mass destruction was entirely subjective and did not reflect the objective reality.

This brings us to another question: how the Bush administration's Iraq policy has evoked world wide opposition and in this sense the hegemonistic ambitions of the United States are now being resisted in the various parts of the world including in the United States and Great Britain.

Resistance to U.S. Hegemony

Never before since the end of the Cold War, and disintegration of the Soviet Union, has resistance to US hegemony unfolded itself on such a wide scale as it has during the recent months. This graphically is reflected on American's policy on Iraq and North Korea. It shows that a wind of change has begun to blow over our planet on unipolarity and forces of multipolarity have begun to gain momentum, both on the popular level and in the ruling elites of a large number of countries. Its undercurrent is the human urge to solve problems through political dialogue and not through military confrontation. This is a new trend in the international politics. It underlines that the American policy of building a world order in its own national interests has come under heavy stress. This is a refreshing development, though it will be naive to exaggerate it.

It is in this background that the recent aggressive and bellicose postures of President George W. Bush should be examined on his stand on war in Iraq. The American objective has not merely been disarmament of Iraq but something more than that. They want to bring about a basic change in the political landscape of the Gulf region. Let us examine the other side of the political situation the mood of the people through out the world.

Firstly, popular demonstration transcending party barriers in the various cities of the United States, London, Berlin, Paris and other European capitals against war are clear manifestations of the new temper of the people in Europe. The hostility of the people of the entire Arab world and of the Muslim population towards the American policy needs no recapitulation. Even in countries like Russia, which has a Muslim population of about 20 million, a section of the Muslim population had offered to volunteer itself to fight on the side of Iraq.

Secondly, four leading member of the Security Council, i.e., Germany, France, Russia and China had made their positions clear on the military attack by America on Iraq. In Great Britain, a section of the Labour Party has serious reservations on the Anglo–American policy on Iraq. Several MPs and a few ministers had threatened to resign.

Thirdly, Arab League and NAM summits had declared that there was an urgent need for a peaceful solution of the Iraq crisis under the UN's auspices.

Fourthly, NATO is facing a crisis of credibility; France, Belgium and Germany had vetoed a US request for the alliance to begin military planning against Iraq.

Finally, the top United Nations weapons inspector Hans Blix informed Security Council on March 7, 2003 that the destruction of the Al Samoud missiles constituted a "substantial measure of disarmament" and argued that Baghdad's cooperation could be "seen as active or even proactive". Significantly, the Head of the International Atomic Energy Agency, Mohammed ElBaradei, also took issue with the United States intelligence agencies by maintaining that the suspect aluminum tubes were not destined for any equipment that could be used to refine uranium for nuclear weapons use. These facts are revealing and clearly bring out that Iraq had implemented U.N. directives. Despite this United States and Great Britain launched an unprecedented military offensive against Iraq and destroyed its military defence.

The worldwide movement against American brinkmanship and the fact that no evidence has been produced about Iraq's stockpile of weapons of mass destruction even after dislodging of Saddam Hussein regime show that reasons for this military action were different than what was proclaimed.

According to both, the International Energy Agency (IEA) and the U.S. Department of Energy's Information Administration (EIA) proven oil reserves are around one trillion barrels, enough to meet demand well beyond 2020. That being the position the American policy makers are looking beyond the next two decades. The reason is obvious. The United States is the biggest oil consumer in the world today.

The American Gulf policy has another dimension. There is no doubt that the majority of the world's future supplies will be sourced in the Gulf region, which holds 66 per cent of the world's oil reserves. Next to Saudi Arabia, Iraq has the richest oil reserve, as already mentioned.

There is another significant factor. Apart from depletion in the oil wealth of Saudi Arabia and Kuwait, the American policy makers cannot ignore widespread Anti–American feeling in the entire Arab world including in Saudi Arabia. This will have its own political impact on the ruling elites of these countries. Above all, the American policy makers seem to have planned to create a new belt of their area of influence, consisting of Iraq, Central Asia and Afghanistan. There are clear indicators to confirm this. This will have its own chain reaction on geo-politics of Arab and Asian countries.

Therefore, American Gulf policy is directed to create 'client' states in the Gulf region. Washington wants to install in Iraq a regime which is friendly to it.

It is relevant to mention here that Saudi Arabia is one of the major oil producing countries in the Gulf region and also a major oil exporting state. For the U.S., Saudi Arabia, under the helm of the al-Saud family, holds up one of the two main pillars of U.S. strategy in West Asia at present. As a result, the British and the US Governments have helped to repress and suppress any challenge to the Saudi regime. More and more Saudis are openly questioning the credibility of the present Saudi regime. In such a situation a powerful and oil rich Iraq can pose a challenge. This leads to the conclusion that in the Gulf region, all sources of threat or irritants to the American interests should be removed. This was the driving force behind Bush administration's Iraq policy.

Another important component of the American drive to consolidate its position in the Asia-Pacific region relates to its policy towards North Korea.

The present situation around North Korea is caused mainly by the policy of the United States. It has violated the framework of 1994 agreement with North Korea. This has upset energy supplies to the North Korea, though Pyongyang had completely fulfilled its obligations. The fact is that Americans have never approved light water nuclear reactors' construction by North Korea in accordance with this agreement.

On the other hand Washington is baselessly accusing North Korea of research and development of nuclear weapons. These accusations are unfounded because it is generally known that for production of weapon-grade plutonium one must have a special technology, which North Korea doesn't possess.

Washington's double standard policy may prompt other countries to withdraw from the NPT and initiate a large-scale arms race in the Asian-Pacific Region. Japan and Taiwan have already exhibited recently their nuclear ambitions. It is a well known fact that Japan has become plutonium 'giant' and can manufacture nuclear bombs at a moment's notice.

Nuclear programme of North Korea has an exclusively peaceful character. It is not directed towards creation of nuclear weapons. North Korean problem should be solved by diplomatic ways with active mediatory participation of countries of the region.

The US is following a tough policy towards North Korea to isolate it from the international community. The American policy of creating tension in Korean Peninsula is not in the interests of the Asian people. Therefore, any resolution by the United Nations Security Council as suggested by US which condemns North Korea will worsen the situation.

This analysis brings us to conclusion that for the first time after the disintegration of the Soviet Union and emergence of the United States as a uni-polar world power, certain new tendencies in international relations have crystalised the main content of these tendencies is that unipolarism has begun to demonstrate and assert that it is the real world leader and all the other nations, particularly developing nations must accept this reality. The tragedy of the present situation is that there is Afro-Asian unity and movement to block this development. This is the biggest weakness of the present situation.

Conclusion

Now let us examine the American policy in the post Saddam era. At a time when there is international pressure on the United States to have the United Nations play a more meaningful role in the reconstruction and stabilisation of Iraq, the top American civilian official in Iraq, Paul Bremer, has said that at the present time he did not see any indication that Washington was looking for a UN force.

But Mr. Bremer has made the distinction between a United Nations force and a request from the UN to other countries to send peacekeeping units.[11]

There is growing apprehension in the various countries that the United States now will embark on the path of asserting itself in its own national interests in the post Saddam era. This shows that the international community's fears of a superpower on the rampage untrammeled by collective control may be coming true. If this happens, this will lead to erosion in the role of the United Nations and its policy making body, the Security Council. No major world powers including Russia and China so far have gone beyond deploring the American policy in Iraq. India, the leader founder of the Non Aligned Movement also falls into this category. However, the Russian President, Vladimir Putin, has stressed that the pivotal role in defusing crises in the world must belong to the UN Security Council. France and Germany have expressed their opposition, with Jacques Chirac warning of the serious consequences of the flouting of international norms. The embarrassment of India's muted, ambivalent response during the runup to the crisis has been somewhat minimized by the parliament resolution describing that war was "deplorable". India has now taken the stand that it will be willing to consider the proposal to send peacekeeping force if the United Nations gives a mandate. However, the question as to who will head this peacekeeping force has been still kept vague.

As against this, peace loving forces throughout the world, in the Arab world in particular, have accused US and UK of carrying out an illegal invasion amounting to a war of aggression. The militants in the Arab world have charged that the US acted as a terrorist state by attempting to assassinate Iraqi leadership.

A war waged without a clear mandate from the UN Security Council according to the Geneva-based International Commission of Jurists, constitutes a flagrant violation of the prohibition of the use of force, a rule enshrined in the UN Charter precisely with the aim of preventing states from using force as a plea.

This brings us to the conclusion that US–UK war in Iraq and subsequent developments bring in to sharp focus a new trend in international relations when militarily and economically powerful states have begun to dictate and interfere into the internal affairs of the other countries openly. There are some scholars who have begun to describe this new phase of international relations as "rise of 21st century model of neo-colonialism".

This also shows that the American forces cannot restore peaceful conditions on their own in Iraq and this in turn makes it difficult to reconstruct it, create democratic political system, ensure social security for the common people, combat criminality in post–conflict Iraq and above all stop conflict in Iraq.

It also has to be admitted that there have been more and more incidents of protests and armed resistance of local population.

Political circles and societies of the United States and Great Britain have expressed concern over the increasing number of soldiers killed in the post–war period. It is in this context that President George W. Bush and Prime Minister Tony Blair want to hand over the difficult task of stabilisation to military contingents of other countries including India and Bangladesh. The objective is to minimise the American and British losses at the cost of other nations.

The Americans are in a hurry in using foreign contingents in this process before the UN Security Council gives a mandate for sending peacekeeping forces to Iraq under its command. Moreover, an internationalisation of the situation in Iraq in this manner will give a trump card to Washington during the discussions in the United Nations, first of all at the United Nations Security Council.

India's military participation in Iraq without the UN mandate will amount to its identification with anti-Iraqi coalition. This will tarnish India's image as a peace loving country and leader founder of the Non Aligned Movement in the entire Arab and Afro-Asian world. If this happens, this will be a departure from India's traditional foreign policy and create mis–giving about its intention to all the other developing nations including those in its neighbourhood. Above all, its chain reaction on the entire Arab and Muslim world would be devastating.

In this background it will be relevant to recall that United Nations Secretary General Kofi Annan called publicly on July 30, 2003 for a rethinking of the international institutions that were "largely sidelined" during the Iraq war.

"Many of us sense that we are living through a crisis of the international system," he said. The war and other crises "force us to ask ourselves whether the institutions and methods we are accustomed to are really adequate to deal with all the stresses" of the present.

He was of the opinion that UN General Assembly should address itself this basic question. This reflects a new mood in the international community after the Iraq war.[12]

References

1. *The Middle East*, edited by Alice Taylor, pp. 3-6.
2. *The Middle East*, edited by Alice Taylor, pp. 12-14.
3. *National Herald* dated February 3,2002.
4. *Ibid.*
5. *The Hindu* dated April 4, 2003.
6. *The Hindu* dated April 4, 2003.
7. *Ibid.*
8. *Hindustan Times* dated July 19, 2003
9. *Hindustan Timed* dated July 24, 2003.
10. *The Hindu* dated July 11 ,2003.
11. *The Hindu* dated July 25, 2003.
12. *Hindustan Times* dated August 1, 2003.

8

American Aggression against Iraq–Who is Terrorist ?

Asghar Ali Engineer

(I)

The aggression against Iraq by President Bush of America and Prime Minister Blair of the U.K. has attracted worldwide condemnation and rightly so. The forces of these two countries are ruthlessly bombarding Iraq. Even market places and civilian buildings have not been spared - probably deliberately targeted. Hundreds of civilians have been killed in last two weeks. More they (USA and UK) get frustrated more ruthlessly they bomb particularly Baghdad. And ironically now it is Bush and Blaire who are villains and President Saddam Hussein is a hero.

This raises one question - who is greater terrorist - Osama bin Laden or Bush and Blaire? When the New York twin towers were attacked on 9/11th world media raised hell and condemned not only bin Laden (which would have been justified) but Islam itself and equated Islam with terrorism. There were host of articles in leading newspapers and magazines round the world condemning Islam as responsible for terrorism and that Islam is a violent religion which urges upon its followers to wage jihad.

Now that President Bush is committing all these crimes against humanity in the name of 'liberating Iraq' who shall we blame for it?

Osama bid Laden was of course an individual, a head of Al-Qaeda, an organisation floated by Osama himself, and not elected by any people or Muslims of the world or any country, for that matter. Even then American media wrote as if all Muslims were responsible for the crime committed by Osama.

Can the crimes against humanity being committed by Bush - an elected representative of USA - on the people of Iraq be blamed on Christianity since he invokes Christianity, like Osama who invoked Islam for the crime he committed against three thousand or so people working in those towers. Bush is also invoking Christianity but organising Christian prayers in White House or conducting the Bible study circles and invoking God time and again?

No, clear no. Christianity or Christians are in no way responsible for what Bush is doing. Like Osama, Bush himself alone is responsible for his crimes. His greed for oil makes him shed pints of human blood. And, let us make no mistake, it is not oil alone. He is being backed in his crimes by scores of American multi-nationals, apart from Israel, are also backing this aggression against the innocent people of Iraq. The military-industrial complex is well known for its greed for money and this formidable combination in the USA keeps war machinery going in one part of the third world or the other so that it can make tons of money. The Zionists of Israel also are powerful block urging American ruling establishment to destroy the Arab countries around them so that it can fulfill its expansionist dreams.

It is well known that whenever vested interests want to grab power or someone else's wealth or property they invoke God on their side and create religious sanctions to legitimise their misdeeds. Laden and Bush-Blaire are no different in this respect. If one examines the terminology being used by Bush-Blaire it makes things abundantly clear.

Bush makes it out as if he is doing all this to 'liberate' Iraq from a dictator. Mr. Blaire also recently said when confronted by some for killing innocent civilians, that one had to pay this price for ridding this world of dictators. If such wars are not fought, the world, according to Bush and Blaire will be full of dictators. What an excuse for war. As if America has not supported dictators in Asia, Africa and Latin America all these years.

These dictators have committed worst crimes against their people with full support of American ruling establishment for years during Cold War. Mr. Blaire is also fully aware of all this. And yet today America wants to project itself as champion of Iraq's liberation by getting it rid of Saddam Hussein.

America has been demanding for years now that Iraq be disarmed and weapons of mass destruction (WMD) be destroyed. Now this war of aggression has clearly shown who possesses weapons of mass destruction— Iraq or America? America is the only nation in possession of huge piles of WMD, no one else. It can destroy the world several times over. It has used these weapons in several countries in killing innocent people. In Vietnam it killed unarmed peasants working in their fields. For what? To destroy communism.

What kind of liberty it wants–liberty for people or liberty for American ruling establishment to loot and exploit poorer nations? However, though American ruling establishments have been using rhetoric of freedom only to establish their hegemony all over the world. To retain this hegemony it can destroy all those who come in its way. As far as America is concerned the words like freedom, liberty, human rights and so on are nothing but empty rhetoric. Any person of common sense knows this.

As for WMD America has been insisting on this for last 13 years. Who does not know that America had supplied technology to Iraq to manufacture poisonous gases so that these weapons could be used against Iran to destroy Khomeini's revolution. It was American ruling establishment, which wanted to use Iraq to destroy Islamic revolution in Iran. It is for this reason that Bush is so sure that Iraq posseses WMD. USA itself had supplied this technology for its own selfish ends.

Iraq did try to develop nuclear capability for manufacturing weapons. But much before it could do so Israel destroyed Iraq's nuclear plant through air raid. It was also an act of great aggression but USA allowed it and it allowed it with impunity. Unfortunately no other country condemned it, not even the Arab countries.

In the Arab countries all monarchs and Sheikhs who suppress democracy in these countries have been friends of American rulers as they serve American interests in a most servile way. America has launched its war of aggression from Kuwait and without support from Kuwait and without use of Kuwait territory it could not have launched this aggression against Iraq. Who is ruling over Iraq? Is the Sheikh of Kuwait not a dictator? Why is then America so keen no support the ruling Sheikh in Kuwait? It is greatly handicapped since Turkey's Parliament did not allow USA to land its army in Turkey and launch invasion against Iraq from Turkey. Now Powell is on the visit to Turkey to persuade its rulers to allow American army to invade Northern Iraq.

Thus most of the Islamic countries do not have democracy today thanks to US support for dictators in Islamic countries. And in Iraq they want to establish 'democracy' and want to 'liberate' people of Iraq. US did not have time to study the social and political history of Iraq. People of Iraq may or may not like Saddam but they do love their country, their nation. They will not allow outside aggressors to 'liberate' them.

It is heartening to note that unlike the Cold War era people cannot be easily deceived now by deceptive rhetoric. The US and UK ruling establishments can no longer deceive people of their own countries by this deceptive rhetoric of 'democratic values' and 'liberating' people of 'corrupted and ruthless dictatorship'. People today can easily understand the real intent of aggressors and their naked interests.

In fact the American aggression against Iraq is any time worse than 19th century colonial invasions of European countries.

Earlier the Christian church used to remain silent as USA often used anti–Communist rhetoric to invade other countries. This time in the absence of any communist power USA cannot deceive Christian Church to justify its aggression against Iraq. The Churches, both Catholic and Protestant, did not buy American position and have protested, in most cases, vehemently, against war against Iraq. The Pope appealed to his followers throughout world to fast on a particular day to protest aggression against Iraq. The World Council of Churches has also issued a strongly worded statement against the USA for its war against Iraq. Many Catholics in Latin America are also strongly condemning the US for launching aggression against Iraq. Some activists of these churches even tried to appeal for forming human shield in Iraq against American bombing.

Such an act of solidarity by the Christian Churches is a matter of great significance and must be enthusiastically welcome by all concerned. Bush's Christian rhetoric thus cannot deceive anyone. God is being invoked by Bush (the American soldiers have been asked to pray every day and even send their prayers to White House as if they are fighting a 'just' war and God is on their side. God cannot be on the side of those who kill innocent civilians who have nothing to do with either Bush's vested interests or Saddam's political designs. These innocent people want to live in peace.

Christ is considered the prince of peace and he cannot be on the side of aggressors who kill innocent people ruthlessly even though they may take his name a thousand times. Christ always talked of peace and was always on the side of the oppressed. According to the Bible the meek shall inherit the earth. The Qur'an also says the same thing in 28:5. Thus the Church is on the side of the poor and weak and so is the Qur'an. It is only the vested interests and the powerful are on the side of Bush and Blaire, none else.

We also have to reflect deeply about the way our democracies are functioning. Democracy tends to become pocket borough of the rich and the powerful. They can manoeuver it quite successfully. The people of America, at least a large number of them, are against the war in Iraq. There have been huge demonstrations against war in New York, Washington and Los Angeles and so many other cities of America. Similarly there were massive protests against war in London and other cities of UK and yet the rulers in USA and UK went ahead with war dismissing these protests with contempt. Not only this these powerful individuals manipulate media and propagate lies and half-truths to legitimise their aggression against another country.

It is ironical that these very people criticize those countries, which lack democracy. America has declared war ostensibly to eliminate the dictator Saddam and gift people of Iraq 'democracy' so that they can enjoy 'freedom'. And Bush is even prepared to kill hundreds of innocent citizens of Iraq so that the people of Iraq can enjoy 'freedom and democracy'. It is also a matter to be reflected upon that due to such aggressive invasion against other countries the quality of democracy in USA is being eroded.

Dissent is no more tolerated by the Bush administration. While Bush is keen to gift freedom to the people of Iraq, he is unhesitatingly suppressing freedom at home. The police is pouncing upon the demonstrators against war and those journalists who do not agree with the analysis of war situation in Iraq are losing their employment. The case of Mr. Peter Arnett, a veteran war reporter with the NBC T.V. has received enough attention worldwide. Since Mr. Arnett appeared on Baghdad T.V. and gave opinion that the war is not going as planned by the USA and its allies, lost his job.

It clearly indicates that democratic freedoms are under attack in USA. It has never happened before. After the terrorist attack on twin towers in New York democratic values have come under serious challenge. Of course it is for the people of America to struggle against such violations of democracy in their own country. They should not, under any circumstances allow McCarthian era to return.

It is difficult to predict the outcome of war in Iraq at this stage. America had terrible superiority of arms over Iraq. Iraq has been virtually disarmed over last one decade. A few weeks before war it was compelled to destroy its Samoud missiles having more than 150 kms range. It is virtually fighting against most powerful allies armed to teeth without arms. It now possesses only some outdated small arms.

It is irony of the situation that the country which possesses most dreadful arms of mass destruction is considered 'champion of world freedom' and Iraq which hardly possessed any arms was being pressurised by the whole world to disarm and disclose all its weapons of mass destruction. In the region if any country possesses WMD it is Israel. Israel possesses all sorts of weapons including nuclear weapons. But since it is faithful ally of USA and guards its interests in the region, it is no threat to world security. According to American rule, those who threaten American interests are 'threat' to world security.

Everyone knows the world has totally skewed structure and everyone bows before power and minds his interests. Principles and values are only to be invoked by the weak. The powerful has to dismiss such a discourse. America also uses human rights rhetoric when it comes to third world countries. But there too, if the regime is US friendly the discourse can be dispensed with.

(II)

We would now like to turn our attention to the role of Islamic countries in this whole affair. There too Islamic rhetoric is used by vested interests to protect themselves. This Islamic rhetoric is, of course, meant for Muslim masses. The most obvious rhetoric used is of 'ummah'. Muslim ummah is supposed to be united like rock and stand up to all crises. However, such unity of ummah is never to be seen from earliest part of Islamic history. Muslim ummah split into various interest or sectarian groups within few years of Holy Prophet's death.

Such unity is nowhere to be seen since that early period. Today the ummah is as much divided with no signs of ever taking a united stand on any issue. On aggression against Iraq too Muslim countries are deeply divided. Unfortunately Kuwaiti rulers are more than eager to provide all facilities to the US and its allies to launch aggression from its territory. The Allied troops were first a massed in Kuwait and all the provisions for the troops are also being supplied from there. Thus Kuwait is the lifeline for the Allied Forces for their war against Iraq.

Saudi Arabia, Jordan and Egypt also are amongst the supporters of the USA in the region. Though they are not actively helping the US they are all silent spectators. They are not even protesting, as it will harm their interests. Pakistan has also been cowed down and its military rulers are cooperating with the US. They are afraid of earning wrath of US masters. Syria is of course protesting and will invite wrath of America.

Of course the Muslim masses in these countries are seething with rage and are eager to help Iraq. In some countries like Pakistan Muslims are staging massive demonstrations under the leadership of Ulema. However, it is possible to demonstrate in Pakistan but people in other countries are not that lucky. In Saudi Arabia, for example, though there is no less anger against America but they cannot even demonstrate and vent their spleen. The accumulated anger can have disastrous consequences.

It is also important to note that such acts of imperialist aggression lead to terrorism in the Muslim world. There are two things, which are mainly responsible for promoting terrorism: acts of aggression against Muslim countries and suppression of democratic freedoms with the help of authoritarian rulers ready to align with the US.

Unfortunately Osama bin Laden's acts of terrorism thus find justification in the eyes of Muslims due to such acts of aggression on the part of US. Many people including Hasni Mubarak, President of Egypt are now suggesting that there will be many more Osamas now in the Islamic world. This will in turn be blamed on Islam and 'clash of civilisation' theory will find even more acceptability in the western world.

The technological progress has enabled nations like the USA, which want to dominate the world, to develop weapons of mass destruction and kill hundreds of thousands of people across the world. There is nothing to be proud of in 21st century. Even Chengez Khans of the medieval world could not have killed as many people as countries like USA are killing in wars today. In the two world wars in 20th century millions of people were killed because of this killer technology. We should feel ashamed that despite so much progress of science we have not been able to suppress our desire to rule or dominate over others at any cost. Succeeded in refining our aggressive instinct.

It is here that we need value based approach to our problems. Science without human values can be an unmitigated desire. From Hitler's Germany to Hiroshima to Vietnam to Iraq it has been long history of this unmitigated disaster. Unfortunately most of these people were killed in the name of saving democracy and freedom.

All religions of the world can be great boon for humanity if their leaders do not ally with vested interest as they have done in the past and stand by spiritual values like compassion and mitigating suffering. Like Buddhism and Christianity, Islam too, lays great emphasis on compassion and justice. The religious leaders across the world should come together to fight against mass killings by powerful nations of the world by invoking hollow words like freedom and democracy.

It is highly gratifying that religious leaders have given a call to protest against American designs in Iraq. Some of them even proposed human shield against ruthless American bombing. Unfortunately many Muslim religious leaders - though not all - are not showing enough courage to give a call to resist American aggression in Iraq. Islam is a great religion, which inspires people to fight against injustice, though not necessarily violently. We must use the concept of non-violent struggle to fight against injustices all over the world. It is the only way to fight terrorism too.

If Muslim religious leaders take initiative to promote non-violent resistance against such acts of aggression by USA and its allies, it will be a great service to humanity. It will save hundreds of innocent lives in future. If there is no such non-violent resistance which needs tremendous courage, likes of Osama will again be causing tremendous suffering to the people. We must impress on Muslims that taking innocent lives is an unIslamic act (5:32). Also, a Muslim has to act with wisdom (Allah is Hakim) and has to suppress his/her anger (3:134). Suppressing anger, however, does not mean compromising with injustice but to elevate it to higher form and combining it with wisdom and using non-violent means so as to save human lives and minimise human suffering while fighting against injustices.

Let us hope our religious leaders would not issue *fatwas* resulting even in more human suffering and would give creative lead to struggle against injustices being inflicted on Muslim world by America in its arrogance of power. In the Qur'anic language America is resorting to *istikbar* and Allah brings downfall of all *mustakbirin* (arrogant rulers drunk with power) and this downfall can be hastened by human agents acting with wisdom.

9

USA, Iraq and the World

Manohar Singh Batra

Iraq had invaded Kuwait on August 2, 1990. It was considered guilty to have committed aggression against a UN member state. In the scenario of a collapsing Soviet Union, the US in an anxiety to establish its political and diplomatic supremacy asked the UN to step in or be labelled irrelevant. Many UN members joined the US initiative. When Iraq refused to pull out of Kuwait, the Security Council imposed economic sanctions. But when the sanctions did not produce the desired result, the UN Security Council passed Resolution 678 authorising countries to use all necessary means to achieve the purposes of its previous resolutions. The aerial phase of the Gulf War started on January 16, 1991 and the ground operations began on February 24. On March 28, the US and the UK introduced "the mother of all resolutions", which after some amendments was adopted on April 3 as Resolution 687, and a de jure cessation of hostilities was established. A war between Iraq and a group of states acting under the UN's authority was thus ended.

Iraq had to pay a very heavy price for attacking Kuwait. It was admitted by the US Secretary of State, Madeleine Albright in a television interview in 1996 that 50,000 Iraqi children had died of economic sanctions. It was "a very hard choice", she said, but, according to her "we think the price is worth it." During the war, coalition forces dropped more than 85,000 tons of bombs on Iraq in a six-week period. In addition to military installations, life-support systems like production and distribution of clean, potable water were destroyed. Owing to the collapse of the economy due to the embargo, a high rate of unemployment was generated along with acute scarcity of essential articles and medicines. After imposing a blanket ban on all imports and exports, the Security Council decided to allow only the import of 'supplies intended strictly for medical purposes and, in humanitarian circumstances, foodstuffs.' It was left to the discretion of the sanctions committee, created under Resolution 661, to determine what constituted humanitarian circumstances. By March 1991, the United States and its allies had driven Iraqi forces out of Kuwait by military force, in the process destroying or disabling most of Iraq's civilian infrastructure, including factories, electric power stations, and water treatment and sewage plants.

After the September 11 terrorist attacks in New York and Washington D.C., President Saddam Hussein again became an anethema for the US. In a major address to the United Nations, President George W. Bush "set stiff and immediate conditions for Saddam Hussein to meet to avoid being overthrown at the hands of US-led forces." The Secretary of State, Colin Powell said: "We still believe strongly in regime change in Iraq." The Vice President, Dick Cheney added. "There is no doubt that Saddam Hussein now has weapons of mass destruction. There is no doubt that he is amassing them to use against our friends, against our allies, and against us." William Safire of the *New York Times* noted in his column that Saddam Hussein is "gaining the power to threaten our cities with annihilation." We must therefore "liberate Iraq."

The US and the UK kept on unilaterally bombing Iraq. By the end of 1999 they had flown more than 6,000 sorties, dropped more than 1,800 bombs and hit more than 450 targets. The Pentagon alone spent more than $ 1 billion in 1999 to maintain its force of 200 aeroplanes, nineteen warships and 22,000 troops which were part of the operation. In 2000, even more sorties were flown than in 1999. The war on Iraq became the longest sustained US air operation since the Vietnam War. The Pentagon continued to enforce "no-fly" zones over northern and southern Iraq and these "kept our skills high on knowledge of the area and kept our competency high in flying over the area."

Iraq has the world's second-largest proven oil reserves, after Saudi Arabia, containing some 11 per cent of the world's oil. As early as 1945, the US State Department had noted that oil "has historically played a larger part in the external relations of the United States than any other commodity." Since World War II, West Asia has been of very great importance to the US and UK planners. In late 2002 Bush launched a diplomatic initiative sending special envoys to major powers to seek support for his plans to launch a military campaign against Iraq. British Prime Minister, Tony Blair orchestrated Bush's efforts. Both of them initiated a new resolution in the Security Council stipulating stricter and more punitive provisions for international inspection and elimination of weapons of mass destruction reportedly manufactured by Iraq. The arguments advanced were that Iraq still possessed vast amounts of chemical and biological weapons and it still had residual capacity of developing and deploying nuclear weapons. Iraq had not opened its weapons facilities to UN inspectors, nor had it fulfilled its promises of eliminating weapons of mass destruction in its arsenals. The US therefore wanted to take punitive action against Iraq to destroy its weapons of mass destruction capacities and to bring about a change of regime to ensure security and stability in West Asia and the world at large.

The US Defence Secretary Donald Rumsfeld was more specific when he said that Saddam Hussein had the choice of facing a military operation or he could go into exile. Bush gave notice to UN that he expected the Security Council to support his policy decision and even otherwise US would go ahead even if he were denied the UN support. All major powers excepting Britain showed clear reservations about the US decision. Germany, France, Russia, China and India opposed a new military campaign against Iraq. Arab countries also indicated their opposition with Saudi Arabia asserting that it would not allow its territory to be used for launching operations. India's Prime Minister,

Atal Behari Vajpayee said in the middle of November 2002 that other nations should not impose their will on the Iraqi people. This amounted to a direct snub to the Bush Administration. But the Foreign Office clarified that Vajpayee wanted Iraq to fully comply with the UN resolutions and abandon its weapons of mass destruction. When the international community was satisfied that Iraq was in full compliance, the sanctions should be lifted.

In his State of the Union address, President Bush warned that the gravest danger facing the US and the world was from outlaw regimes that sought and possessed nuclear, chemical and biological weapons. He talked of Saddam having terrorized, oppressed and murdered his own people. He insinuated about open channels and ties between Iraq and terrorist organizations, including Al Qaeda. Secretary of State Colin Powell claimed that Iraq had responded to Resolution 1441 with empty claims, empty declarations and empty gestures. The resolution declared Iraq to be in "material breach" of disarmament obligations and called for immediate and full cooperative compliance. Failing this, Iraq was warned of "serious consequences." Para 4 of the resolution said that a false declaration by Iraq or failure to "cooperate fully in the implementation of this resolution shall constitute a material breach of Iraq's obligations and will be reported to the council for assessment in accordance with paragraphs 11 and 12. Para 11 directed the inspectors to report immediately any breach by Iraq. Para 12 required the Council "to convene immediately upon receipt of a report in accordance with paragraphs 4 or 11....... in order to consider the situation and the need for full compliance with all the relevant council resolutions." A joint statement by France, Russia and China stated: "Failure by Iraq to comply with its obligations.......will be reported to the Security Council. It will be then for the council to take a position on the basis of that report." But the US Administration made it clear that while the council would meet, the US would be free to act as it pleased. President Bush said that "the US has agreed to discuss any material breach with Security Council, but without jeopardizing our freedom of action." Immediately after the vote, the US told the council : "If the Security Council fails to act decisively in the event of a further Iraqi violation, this resolution does not constrain any member State from acting." US National Security Adviser Condoleeza Rice said that a delay of only two hours in a requested entry would constitute a violation. "It would be time at that moment for the Security Council to act."

The UN Secretary General Perez de Cuellar had said on April 16, 1991 that the first Gulf War was "not a UN war." On the New Year Day, 2003 Kofi Annan voiced his sentiment by observing that he did not see an argument for military action against Iraq. This should take us to two documents for a keener insight into the US thinking. One is "rebuilding America's Defenses : Strategy, Forces and Resources for a New Century" published in September 2000 by the Project for the New American Century (PNAC) and the second is entitled "The National Security Strategy of the United States of America" published in September 2002 by the US administration. It sets out the "grand strategy" of the US. The PNAC decument sets the strategic goal as Pax Americana, feels military missions are needed to achieve the expansion of democratic peace, to defend key regions and holds the view that this unipolar moment in history should be grabbed. On the Gulf, the document recommends "retaining forward-based forces in the region given the long standing American interests in the region." The NSS document asserts that......."The United States has long maintained the option of preemptive actions to counter a sufficient threat to our national security. To forestall or prevent hostile acts, the US will, if necessary act preemptively.........." The mention of the UN in conflict resolution is missing.

In pursuance of the UN resolution requiring Iraq to disarm, the Iraqi government submitted an 11,800 page document detailing all its chemical, biological, industrial and research and development activities. This way, Iraq lobbed the ball into the court of the UN inspection team. But President Bush reacted by saying: "We will judge the declaration's honesty and completeness only after we have thoroughly examined it and that will take sometime." The President's scepticism went up to saying in his weekly broadcast that the declaration must be credible and complete, or the Iraqi dictator would have demonstrated to the world that once again he had chosen not to change his behaviour. In the meantime US continued to mount attacks on Iraq in protest against which the latter complained to the UN Secretary General. "These daily violations........facilitated by the government of Kuwait, and the barbaric bombing of Iraq's cities and villages, have reached the level of an undeclared war," Iraqi Foreign Minister, Naji Sabri wrote to Kofi Annan in December, 2002. But such complaints did not deter Bush from his unwavering aim of building a case against Saddam Hussein. In his New Year statement he expressed an apprehension that the Iraqi President posed an immediate danger as an attack by him "would cripple our economy." Condoleezza Rice told a state-run Cairo daily on Februray 1, 2003 that the US expects to administer Iraq for a "certain period of time" after its "liberation from the regime of Saddam Hussein." Hardly a week later, the Chief of UN weapons inspectors, Hans Blix talking to Tony Blair, distanced himself from the US claims that Iraq clearly possessed weapons of mass destruction. The same day, the UK Foreign Secretary, Jack Straw said that Saddam and terror groups such as Al Qaeda were "part of the same picture" and warned that both posed a similar threat to national security and world peace. He dubbed Iraq and North Korea as "rogue" states and the "most likely sources" of technology and know–how for terrorist organizations. President Saddam Hussein accused UN inspectors of engaging in "intelligence work" instead of searching for nuclear, chemical and biological weapons Iraq had denied it was hiding.

In the meantime the US and the UK combine started playing the war drums aimed at overthrowing the regime in Iraq and setting the tone for a long-term political transformation of the entire West Asian region. The planners in Washington were hoping that the people of Iraq would welcome the invading forces for ending the tyranny of

Saddam Hussein. Cynically they were using the fig–leaf of Resolution 1441 of the Security Council, according to which Iraq was in material breach of existing UN resolutions; that Iraq's non-compliance with the Council resolutions posed a threat to international peace and security; that Iraq had "a final opportunity to comply with its disarmament obligations under relevant resolutions of the Council"; that Iraq would face "serious consequences as a result of its continued violations of its obligations" and that the Security Council was "determined to secure full compliance with its decisions". Five months after the resolution was passed and three months after the Iraq regime had submitted an almost 12,000 page document detailing all its facilities, the U.S. administration reached the conclusion that Saddam was still hiding WMD and his decree to dismantle Al-Samoud missiles was just a subterfuge.

The assault on Iraq led by the U.S. coalition marked a turning point in history. A worldwide popular revulsion to this war came to be witnessed. The U.S. administration had threatened possible nuclear retaliation against Iraq if its forces or allies were attacked with weapons of mass destruction, which, it was proved later, never existed. The coalition forces had made elaborate preparations for a lethal strike. The warships had been moved into the Mediterranean, which was in response to a delay by Turkey to permit the US forces to station and transit through its territory to open another front against Iraq. By positioning warships in the Red Sea, the U.S. could fire missiles without intruding into the Turkish air space.

On the 13th day of the conflict, President George W. Bush told the Iraqis on April 1, 2003 that he would pursue "until your country is free". "We are coming with a mighty force to end the rule of your oppressors", declared Bush. But the harrowing footage of civilian casualties broadcast by Arab satellite channels fuelled opposition to the war and sparked angry protests in the Muslim world and beyond. Saudi Arabia's Foreign Minister urged Saddam Hussein to make a "sacrifice for his country" and step down to spare Iraq more pain.

"This war can only lead to strife, to bloodshed and to increased hatred," Prince Saud–al Faisal said. Even the 100,000 or more US and British troops could not find any weapons of mass destruction in Iraq. Nevertheless, a Central Command official said the military was ready for heavy casualties to oust Mr. Hussein. "We are prepared to pay a very high price because we are not going to do anything other than ensure that this regime goes away," the official proclaimed. "If that means there will be a lot of casualties, then there will be a lot of casualties."

Eight days before the attack, India's Prime Minister Vajpayee made a statement in both Houses of Parliament on March 12 in which he said that India consistently stood for a peaceful resolution of the Iraq issue. The peace and prosperity of the Gulf was of vital interest to India given our long standing political, cultural and economic ties with the countries of the region. There were 3.5 million Indians working in the Gulf, whose welfare was of great concern to us. Over 60 per cent of India's crude oil imports were sourced from this region. India recognized the validity of the unanimous decision of the UN Security Council in its Resolution 1441, which provided for the disarmament of Iraq and also reaffirmed the sovereignty and territorial integrity of Iraq, Kuwait and the neighbouring States. India had voiced its concern on various occasions about the difficult humanitarian situation in Iraq. The Iraqi people had suffered severe shortages and hardships for over a decade. While we sincerely hoped, in the interest of all humanity, that the matter could be resolved peacefully through the United Nations, the Indian government had made contingency plans to deal with any eventuality. India announced a $ 20 million immediate humanitarian assitance to the people of Iraq in response to an emergency appeal made by the United Nations. This aid included 50,000 tonnes of wheat to be made available to the World Food Programme.

The easy conquest of Baghdad by the US-UK-led forces brought relief and elation to the perpetrators of this unequal war. The militarily and economically strongest nation of the world brought down a tiny and weak West Asian country for the rescue of which no other significant state took any step or made any tangible contribution. The toppling of Saddam Hussein's statue in the heart of the Iraqi capital by the US soldiers became a matter of great celebration for the coalition governments. But soon the world was faced with certain discrepancies and loopholes in the original premise on which an attack on Iraq was tried to be justified. The National Intelligence Estimate on Iraq which represented the consensus of the US intelligence community, contained cautionary language about Iraq's connections with Al Qaeda and the reliability of conflicting reports by Iraqi defectors and captured Al Qaeda members. Moreover, in his State of the Union address in January 2003, George W. Bush had stated that according to the British, Iraq was attempting to buy uranium in Africa and on this the President made an assertion that Iraq had embarked on a nuclear weapon programme. Questions about the reliability of the intelligence that Bush cited were raised shortly afterwards. The Chief UN weapons inspector, Hans Blix had stated on March 7 that there was no evidence of underground weapons in Iraq and that UNMOVIC was receiving full cooperation from Saddam Hussein's regime. Bush had termed Iraq's disarming a charade. All the excuses and rationales put forward by the US to support its war have fallen flat. And in the bargain the sole superpower has rendered the UN a non-entity, though it would have no qualms to try to resurrect its dignity, if it thought it was necessary. It also sidelined all the other four veto-wielding members of the Security Council, besides other major players like Germany and India. It has proved that it is determined to have its way in world affairs irrespective of the popular opinion and the future of the UN. This situation has the potentiality of causing widespread fear, paranoia and anxiety. Moreover, the conquest of Iraq does not mean the end of terrorism. Instead of vanishing it might become more damaging and threatening. Hatred is likely to translate into vengeance.

The present Secretary of State, Colin Powell had said in 1991 (when he was chief of the US armed forces), "Think hard about it, I am running out of demons. I am running out of villains." The New Yorker reported in April 2002 that the National Security Adviser Condoleezza Rice said "that she had called together the senior staff people of the National Security Council and asked them to think seriously about how do you capitalize on these opportunities to fundamentally change American doctrine, and the shape of the world, in the wake of September 11th." But what will happen, one is tempted to ask, to the US economy, which is under the heaviest debt in the world. The value of the dollar has been going down vis-à-vis the euro, which has been challenging the dollar's position as the only currency exchange accepted worldwide. But, perhaps, control over oil would bring enormous economic benefits to the USA and also to British oil interests. Thus, to the present day policy makers in USA, the conquest of Iraq is an important step to long–term worldwide dominance.

In this context, the "Act of the Liberation of Iraq" adopted by the US Congress is quite relevant. It was based on the necessity to topple the political system of Iraq by the US government and to instal a puppet government there by using all means including terrorism. For that purpose the Congress had allocated 97 million dollars, from which the US governments have been paying to the mercenaries.

Speculation has been rife in the world as to which country would be the next target of USA–whether it would be Syria or Iran. US accused Syria of harbouring Iraqi fugitives and concealing the weapons of mass destruction given to her by Saddam for safekeeping. The young Syrian President assured the US authorities that his country had done nothing of the sort and its hands were clean. Iran was accused of harbouring the Al Qaeda terrorists and of running a nuclear weapons programme. Iran provides a good market and Washington is reluctant to let Russia or Europe to monopolise it. US pressurized the European Union not to sign a programme of trade and economic cooperation with Iran. The strategic importance of Iran too cannot be lost upon anyone. In early June a top official of the Bush administration admitted: "We are already in a life and death struggle with Iraq over the future of Iraq." Though Iran adopted a silent posture during the Iraq war, it cannot be expected to stay aloof from the post-war settlement any more. After some suicide terrorist bombings in Riyadh in May, Al Qaeda terrorists based in Iran were suspected of having committed the outrage. The Pentagon busied itself with the task of engendering "public and private actions" that could lead to the toppling of the Iranian government through popular uprising. Though Iran has denied complicity in the terror acts, US officials have talked of "very troubling intercepts" about the involvement of Iran-based Al Qaeda men in the Riyadh incident in which 34 persons were killed. US Secretary of Defence, Donald Rumsfeld has publicly castigated Iran for harbouring Al Qaeda extremists.

Considerable attention is focused on the nuclear reactor cooperation programme between Russia and Iran. Iran's nuclear programme has been accorded IAEA approval, as it is of purely non-military nature. Nonetheless USA is keen on pressurizing IAEA to declare Iran being in material breach of its nuclear obligations. Washington has been trying to portray Iran's declared plan to establish facilities to have a complete nuclear fuel cycle as a clear violation of its IAEA obligations. Russia, however, is determined to continue its nuclear cooperation with Iran as an indication of its desire to safeguard its economic interests as well as to show its concern about USA's aggressive foreign policy. In the event of Iran falling a prey like Iraq, Russia would feel endangered, as that would mean its encirclement by pro-US states. American forces are already stationed in Pakistan, Afghanistan, Uzbekistan and Kyrghyzstan. Russia is scheduled to supply enriched uranium to fuel the Bushehr reactor after a few months, while US is opposed to this. Any harm to Iran would inevitably affect India, as it has close economic and trade ties with that country.

Though US and UK have won the war in Iraq, they have not gained legitimacy. If they together or USA alone tries to trigger a global war, that would be disastrous and catastrophic. At present, however, out of fatigue and fear of casualties and to prevent mass uprising in the conquered territory, they are persuading, cajoling and pressurizing countries like India to deploy their contingents to stabilize Iraq. The complexities of the situation have prevented the Indian goverement from promising compliance of the request. Donald Rumsfeld took up the issue with the Deputy Prime Minister of India, L.K. Advani at Washington June 9, 2003 but the latter wanted to gain time. Though there is a record of India having sent out about sixty thousand troops on various UN peacekeeping missions and 2735 troops were deployed in UN peace keeping missions during 2002, this country did not want to fall foul of various Arab countries and also needed clarifications on significant issues relating to its prestige and financial implications. Feelings were running high among Arab states over the high–handedness of the US-led coalition in their attacks on Iraq, in which an estimated 7,000 civilians were killed, besides tens of thousand of military casualities. After the fall of Baghdad, the American patrols were being attacked by trained and motivated fighters in an organized manner. In his two released speeches, Saddam Hussein had called upon Iraqis to treat all foreign forces in their country as occupiers and invaders.

The Pentagon sent a team led by the US Assistant Secretary for Defence, Peter Rodman to Delhi to persuade the Vajpayee government to send a Division of the Army to act as stabilization forces in Iraq. The opinion in India wanted a UN mandate and also raised the question of control and command. The Pentagon team drew New Delhi's attention to the Security Council Resolution 1483, which appealed to the member states "to assist the people of Iraq in their efforts to reform their institutions, rebuild their country and to contribute to conditions of stability and security in Iraq." The Indian government sought clarifications on a range of issues like the interim political administration in Iraq, the kind of roadmap for its political condition as well as the humanitarian situation prevailing there. The Indian government finally decided not to send its troops, the fact which was greatly lamented by the US officials but, they still hoped that India would at some stage contribute its forces to reduce the pressure on the US soldiers.

Saddam Hussein's two high profile sons, Uday and Qusay were killed on July 23 in the northern town of Mossul in a gunfight. The former Iraqi President described them as martyrs. The armed resistance put up by the Iraqi nationals has been explained as "a classical guerrilla–type campaign", by the American generals. But addressing the Iraqi armed forces in an audio tape dated July 20 and broadcast by a Dubai-based mass media unit, Saddam Hussein called upon them not to surrender and not to be defeated as the war was not yet over. On the other hand, President Bush personally hailing the deaths of Saddam's sons, expressed satisfaction that the "former regime is gone and will not be coming back." Bush reminded the people that Uday and Qusay were responsible for torture, maiming and murder of countless Iraqis. Bush emphasized what he considered as a positive development that 19 nations were providing 13,000 troops for the stabilization of Iraq and "more than two dozen nations have pledged funds that will go directly towards relief and reconstruction efforts." President Bush's exultation over the killings of Saddam's sons was matched only by the avowal of Iraqi insurgents to "raise hell" against the United States and Britain and their threat to bring their fight to the countries of the coalition partners. Amid the spurt of killings of American soldiers by the Iraqi guerillas, the US Deputy Secretary of Defence, Paul Wolfowitz said on July 27, "it is a sacrifice that is going to make our children and our grandchildren safer because the battle to win the peace in Iraq now is the central battle in the war on terrorism."

Alongwith the sniper attacks on the US soldiers in various parts of Iraq, another dimension of a complete breakdown in the US intelligence that helped steer that country into war emerged. The CIA Director's briefing to the Senate left no doubt in anybody's mind that the episode of the Nigerian uranium was just a scandal, the implications of which were quite damaging to the White House. George Tenet, the Director of CIA officially took the responsibility for the claim in

January that Iraq had been trying to buy uranium, but he also said that his agency had been pressured to justify a war the administration had already decided on. Dick Cheney had been demanding a more 'forward-leaning" interpretation of the Iraqi threat.

Out of a sense of remorse, the UK Prime Minister, Tony Blair speaking to the US Congress in mid July hoped that history would "forgive" him even if no weapons of mass destruction were found in Iraq. Singnificantly softening his stance on Iraq's weapons, Blair admitted that eventually he might be wrong on the weapons issue.

The US introduced a resolution in the UN Security Council on August 13 that would welcome the establishment of the 25–member Governing Council set up by the US and UK in Iraq. But George Bush abandoned the idea of giving the United Nations more of a role in the occupation of Iraq as demanded by countries like India and France as a condition for their participation in peacekeeping there. The US officials said that their country would widen its effort to enlist other countries to assist the occupation forces in Iraq, which are dominated by the US troops there. Defence Secretary Donald Rumsfeld vehemently opposed any dilution of military authority over Iraq by involving the UN either through UN peacekeeping forces or indirectly in any UN authorization of forces from other countries. Such paranoia on the part of the US officials and also the way the intelligence reports and assessments were handled brought a drop in the rating of the President, George Bush.

In spite of the brave talk by the White House and the Pentagon, the Bush administration came face to face with the prospect of approaching the Congress with an appropriations request for \$ 50 billions for Iraqi reconstruction next year, as against a total estimate of \$ 100 billions for a three years period, though the private estimates run into \$ 600 billions over a period of the years. Lawmakers were reportedly found in a quandary how could such requests be made by the administration in the face of a huge Federal deficit running close to \$ 500 billions.

A massive truck bomb ripped through the UN headquarters in Baghdad on August 19, killing at least 24 people and wounding scores of others. Sergio Vieira de Mello, the UN Secretary General's special representative to Iraq was among those killed. It was a big blow to the UN. It was suspected that the suicide attack was engineered in collusion with some Iraqi employees and guards who worked at the UN headquarters. It was also suspected to be an effort to discredit Bush's promises to bring stability and prosperity to the war-shattered Iraq. Some people were under the impression that US is losing control over the Iraqi situation and that some more attacks on the US installations and UN facilities could be expected. Incidentally on the day of the attack, Taha Yassin Ramadan, former Vice President of Iraq under Saddam Hussein was captured by Kurdish allies in northern Iraq.

On August 22 the Bush administration gave an indication that the US wanted to eat the cake and have it too. While the US wanted the world body to broaden its role and functioning, the security aspect of this new role would certainly have to be under American command. They overlooked the Indian view that unless substantial and meaningful changes were made to the mandate of the UN, it would not like to send its troops for the socalled stabilization of Iraq. Simultaneously with this US stance, Collin Powell launched a drive to get more nations to send soldiers to help US forces in Iraq. In an immediate reaction France expressed doubt over whether more troops should be sent by foreign countries to help US forces there. Foreign Minister, Dominique de Villepin impressed upon the coalition powers to change the logic of occupation to that of sovereignty in Iraq. Kofi Annan ruled out the prospect of the UN "blue helmets" taking over from the coalition forces and running Iraq.

It has become increasingly clear that the US presence in Iraq has been attracting terrorists and Islamists to oppose its forces. West Asia is in a flux. There are ripples in Iran and Syria. Everything is not right with Saudi Arabia. Israel and Palestine have been in a long combat. The Iraq imbroglio cannot be entirely separated from the Palestinian-Israeli stand off. Alternate terrorist attacks by both on each other are too frequent and ferocious to be swept under the carpet. The US involvement both in Iraq and Israel-Palestine conflict may not allow the situation to explode immediately, but heightened hostility in the region and restiveness among the Iraqis can lead matters to a stage not to the liking of the world.

References

1. Iraq Under Siege— *The Deadly Impact of Sanctions and War* edited by Anthony Arnove.
2. US has a plan to Occupy Iraq— David E. Sanger, *New York Times*, October 11, 2002.
3. *Iraq War 2003*— K. Santhanam and the IDSA Insight Team, 2003.
4. Anatomy of US Miscalculations in Iraq— Vladimir Kuzar and Sergei Sumbayev, *Mainstreams*, May 3, 2003.
5. US Foreign Policy Under Bush— Spotlight on Iraq; *World Focus* April-May, 2003.
6. The Way We Live Now— Tony Judt; *The New York Review*— March 27, 2003.
7. Death in Baghdad— Tim Judah; *The New York Review*— May 1, 2003.
8. On the Front Lines— Tim Judah; *The New York Review*— April 10, 2003
9. The Fall of Baghdad— Tim Judah; The New York Review— May 15, 2003.
10. US Motive on Arms Inspectors suspect, says Iraq— Atul Aneja, *The Hindu*, 31. 7. 2002
11. The Uitimate Hegemon — Muchkund Dubey,*The Hindu*, September 19, 2002.
12. Why We Not Worry?— J. N. Dixit, *The Hindustan Times*, October 9, 2002.

13. US, Iraq and the UN— Chinmaya R. Gharekhan, *The Hindu,* October 11, 2002.

14. India, US and the Gulf War— C. Raja Mohan, *The Hindu*, November 25, 2002.

15. Bush the Bully— Prem Shankar Jha, *The Hidustan Times,* December 7, 2002

16. India and the Gulf War— C. Raja Mohan, *The Hindu,* December 5, 2002.

17. Iraq submits Arms declaration— *The Tribune*, December 9, 2002

18. India's moment of Truth on Iraq— Subramanian Swamy, December 11, 2002.

19. Bush warns Saddam of Nuclear Attack— *The Hindustan Times*, December 12, 2002.

20. US warns Iraq of Stern Measures— *The Hindu*, December 21, 2002.

21. Final Peace offensive to disarm Iraq?— Atual Aneja, *The Hindu*, January 3, 2003.

22. Special Forces in Iraq for months— *The Indians Express*, January 6, 2003.

23. Iraq in a No-win situation— Chinmaya R. Gharekhan— *The Hindu*, January 6, 2003.

24. Bush's Reckless Militarism— United Nations Dares to Differ— Sunanda K. Datta-Ray, *The Tribune*, January 11, 2003.

25. Consequences of War in Traq— V. P. Malik, *The Tribune*, January 15, 2003.

26. Baghdad Has Not Done enough to avert War— US, *The Hindu*, January 28, 2003.

27. Preparing for Regime change in Iraq— C.Raja Mohan, *The Hindu*, January 30, 2003.

28. Saddam Hussein is Terror's Exhibit A— Colin L. Powell, *The Indian Express*, February 4, 2003.

29. No Proof yet: Blix— Hasan Suroor— *The Hindu*, February 7, 2003.

30. Oil as Weapon— editorial, *The Hindu*— February 8, 2003.

31. Arms and the Man— J. N. Dixit— February 13, 2003.

32. We have Not Found weapons of Mass destruction: Blix— Sridhar Krishnaswami, *The Hindu*, February 15, 2003.

33. Obscured by War clouds— Prem Shankar Jha; *The Hindustan Times*— February 17, 2003.

34. The Idea of Regime Change— Sunanda K. Datta-Ray, *The Tribune*, February 18, 2003.

35. It's Baghdad's Call— Robert D. Blackwill; *The Hindustan Times*— March 6, 2003.

36. Battles for Baghdad— V. R. Raghavan; *The Hindu*, March 12, 2003.

37. A grave decision— Kofi A. Annan; *The Hindu*, March 12, 2003.

38. US Campaign a prelude to War— Atul Aneja, March 16, 2003.

39. India's Stand on Iraq— K. K. Katyal; *The Hindu*, April 7, 2003.

40. The World Order after the Iraq War— Muchkund Dubey, April 9, 2003.

41. Filling the Vacuum— editorial, *The Hindustan Times*, April 12, 2003.

42. Stand up for your Rights— Arjun Sengupta; *The Hindustan Times*, April 17, 2003.

43. Should Chaos be the New order— Mohamed El Baradei, *The Indian Express*, April 25, 2003.

44. The UN and Post-war Iraq— V. S. Mani; *The Hindu*— April 30, 2003.

45. Blind Spot in Iraq— Bhaskar Ghose; *The Hindustan Times*— May 2, 2003.

46. True Lies in Iraq— Amulya Ganguli; *The Hindustan Times*— May 12, 2003.

47. Pentagon seeks action against Iran— S. Rajagopalan; *The Hindustan Times*, May 26, 2003.

48. Liar, liar— Prem Shankar Jha; *The Hindustan Times*, June 6, 2003

49. Sending Indian Troops to Iraq— V. P. Malik; *The Tribune*, June 6, 2003.

50. Advani buys time on Iraq— Chidanand Rajghatta; *The Times of India*, June 10, 2003.

51. Iraq: Why we must stay away— Taufiq Subhan; *The Indian Express*, June 12, 2003.

52. Get us UN nod, we'll be there: India— Jyoti Malhotra; *The Indian Express*— June 17, 2003.

53. Troops to Iraq— Chinmays R. Gharekhan; *The Hindu*— June 18, 2003.

54. Demand for Indian troops— Vijay Oberoi; *The Tribune*— June 20, 2003.

55. Bush speech overstated Iraq report— Walter Pincus; *The Indian Express*— June 23, 2003.

56. Grey Areas in UN resolution on Iraq; Sibal— Sridhar Krishnaswami; *The Hindu*— July 4, 2003.

57. No troops for Iraq, home truths loom— *The Hindustan Times*— July 15, 2003.

58. Baghdad Blues— editorial; *The Times of India*— July 15, 2003

59. Iraq— a continuing headache for US— M. Ahmad Kazmi; *The Tribune*— July 16, 2003.

60. Spy Agency that wanted war— *The Hindustan Times*—July 18, 2003.

61. Blair: Iraq may not have WMDs— *The Hindustan Times*— July 19, 2003.

62. America's war before the war— Michael R. Gordon; *The Hindu*— July 21, 2003.

63. Iraqi insurgents vow revenge— *The Hindu*, July 24, 2003.

64. US changes tack on Iraq— Sridhar Krishnaswami; *The Hindu*— July 29, 2003.

65. Hitting the US, through UN— Michael Georgy & Luke Baker; *The Indian Express*— August 20, 2003.

66. Bush ratings indicate changing perception?—Sridhar Krishnaswami, *The Hindu*— August 12, 2003.

67. Iraqi reconstruction, a headache for Bush— Sridhar Krishnaswami; *The Hindu*— August 13, 2003.

68. 16 die in bomb blast at UN's Iraq HQ— *The Times of India*— August 20, 2003.

69. US zeroes in on Saddam secret service— Dexter Filkins; *The Indian Express*— August 23, 2003.

70. Annan rules out takeover by UN 'blue helmet's— Sridhar Krishnaswami; The Hindu— August 23, 2003.

71. Fighting the Big One— Thomas Friedman; *The Indian Express* August 25, 2003.

10
India should not Send its Troop to Iraq

Rajindar Sachar

US, it is reeling under the response of Iraqi nationalism. The Iraqis have realized that getting rid of Saddam Hussein was not the only item on Washington's agenda. The real agenda was what was spelt out by the US Secretary of State to I.K. Gujral who, as India's Foreign Minister, met him in 1990 (during Gulf War) to discuss the evacuation of Indians from Iraq. His response was direct and acerbic: "Oil is our civilization, we will not let that demon (meaning Saddam Hussein) sit on it."

The Iraq venture is not going to be a picnic for the US. There are no welcome hugs or arches. In a recent Senate Foreign Relations Committee meeting, the US Army Chief made it clear that Washington needed a large peacekeeping force and that conditions in Iraq were more serious than in Bosnia. The US forces have, after all, been in Bosnia for over eight years and there is still no end in sight. Are our politicians ready to do the dirty work of the neo–conservative group controlling George W. Bush?

One was surprised at the attitude of the Congress and the BJP (Vajpayee–Sonia meeting) on the issue–working for a consensus on whether to send our troops to Iraq and holding consultations with Iran. Did they seriously believe that Iran would want Indian troops to be sent to the region when it is being accused by the US of forming part of the "axis of evil" and is mischievously being targeted for a regime change? The Congress spokesperson and the Foreign Minister made the same noise about developing a consensus. This when millions of people in the US and Europe had already demonstrated against a war, which, as has been well established, was fought by the US and Britain on the basis of lies, deception and forgery.

Fortunately public pressure at that time forced Central Govt. to decline to send troops. But now again pressure by USA is mounting. BJP may not be sensitive to the compulsion and the sacrificial spirit of nationalism. Surely, the Congress should be sensitive and appreciative of the hostility to foreign troops. The presence of British forces in our country during the World War II period generated tremendous anger and resentment.

Must our young solders, besides falling victim to Iraqi bullets, also be demeaned and disgraced by being treated as an occupation army? There is another angle to the U.S. request for Indian troops. Apparently, it has been suggested that the troops will be posted in the Kurd-dominated area where there is massive resentment against Saddam Hussein. The Kurds are fighting for separation from Iraq.

Neighbours Turkey and Iran, which have sizeable Kurdish populations, would not want any trouble. But Kurds are waiting for an opportunity and will not sit quiet. In such a situation the Indian troops may have to fight them and would not Pakistan exploit the situation, though illogically, as an excuse to foment terrorism in Jammu and Kashmir? Recent incidents are adding to the fuel of terrorism. The implications of sending Indian troops to Iraq are thus horrendous and unimaginable. The chapter must be closed at once.

It was always clear and the recent blast and killings in Iraq though to be deeply regretted from humanitarian point of view must in all fairness be considered in the background of Iraqi nationalism as a protest at being treated as a vassal of US Neo Conservative imperialism. Now efforts are being made to give it a veneer of UN fig leaf coverage. In spite of all that has happened US even in the draft resolution brought before the Security Council is willing to go only to the extent of saying that UN must be involved in the stabilization.

in Iraq. But it was not willing that the overall command and control of day to day working should be given to the Iraqi people. Their objective of UN cover is extremely limited so as to obtain troops from countries like India. The US position is very clear it will not give up its control of Iraqi oil or to decide how the economy of Iraq is to be determined in future.

It was always an open secret that the main purpose of Iraq invasion was not to flush out any WMD, which it was well known did not exist but only to capture the oil fuel and give this as a boon to the American companies. These apprehensions have now been confirmed by the Executive Order 13303 by President Bush in May 2003 directing the development fund for Iraq and certain other properties in which Iraq has an interest. This order provides that US oil companies operating in Iraq will have immunity for their working and also specifically provided that their assets will be free from any decree or execution or other judicial process and any such order shall be deemed null and void until December 31, 2007 at the minimum. All this benefit obviously will go to the multi-national companies and with high officials close to Bush administration.

As more and more information comes out it is becoming clear that this whole venture of US invasion on Iraq was of the same prototype as old Pirates on the sea looting of ordinary ships in the middle of 16th Century. It is now an open secret that one of the companies that have bagged immediate extractive contracts has close connections to members of the Bush Administration, in particular, on oil industry related contracts have been awarded to the subsidiary of Halliburton, one of the biggest oil service companies in the world. United States Vice-President Richard B. Cheney was the Chief Executive Officer (CEO) of Halliburton from 1995 to 2000. This favoritism shown by awarding of contract, without inviting competitive bids of contracts worth 300 million US$ to K.B.R. a subsidiary of Halliburton, has invited loud criticism in US Senate and rival competitors. Thus an open loot and carry by powers within Bush administration are the direct beneficiaries of this war. No wonder US forces are on twenty four hour alert and taut - they have killed Palestinian photographer journalist in cold blood leading to mass resentment, in response a fairly effective guerrilla war by Iraqis is being fought without being arrested by US troops with all the resources at the command of the USA Government.

Thus even the immoral temptation to send troops in the hope of booking some crumbs of reconstruction money thrown from the table of US Multinationals is apart from showing low conscience not even reasonable prospect.

Our heritage is noble. Our young generation deserves better. Or has neo–liberalisation, backed both by the BJP and the Congress, made us so impervious that self-respect and honour have ceased to be the condition precedent in Indo–US relations? How unnatural and out of reality is the strategy of USA is shown by the fact that pivotal role in the formulation of the war plans was played by Ahmad Chalabi, a refugee from the Iraqi revolution of 1958 who has been resident of the US for much of the time since. Nominated by the US to serve as one of nine members who will hold the presidency of Iraq's governing council in rotation, Chalabi's extradition is now being sought by parliamentarians of Jordan, who are keen to see him serve out a 22–year sentence for corruption and embezzlement awarded in 1992.

Again a final attempt is being made by USA to persuade the government to agree to send the troops. Even in our country some people are falling into the trap apparently overwhelmed by the recent bomb blast of Bombay and J&K. The argument is that sending troops will help India and USA would put pressure on Pakistan to stop terrorism. This is a perception which has been exposed already. USA will only give public statement apparently to confuse Indian leaders into agreeing to send troops to Iraq. USA officials are visiting India to interact with the foreign office and put pressure. I would hope that the public opinion, political opposition would firmly impress upon the government that once and for all India must decline to send troops to Iraq. Frankly, I am against sending troop to Iraq even if Security Council was to pass a resolution to give some kind of voice to the UN. This is for the reason that the troops are being asked by USA because unfortunately there are too many deaths and destruction of USA forces in Iraq. For Bush to face this tragedy of body bags with presidential election coming next year is a nightmare. USA went to make war on Iraq on its own in spite of main opposition and overwhelming countries of the world.

We in India at least have no right or obligation to draw chestnuts out of fire for USA to ease its internal problem. I would have thought that single fact alone that Iraq was invaded is a sufficient and principled reason for India to resolve that under no circumstances would it send its troops to that country to help an occupying USA invading powers. A free country with its thousands of years old cultural contact with Iraq can never contemplate to send its troops to fire at Iraqi people. That would be sacrilege and not all the waters of Ganges would be able to wash off our sin at shedding the blood of ordinary Iraqi who is fighting for his freedom from USA enslavement.

We are a free nation and we have no reason to send our forces to Iraq to help the invading army. Indian lives are not cheap. Gandhi's India cannot be a party to the ruination of a country with which we have had cultural and civiliational contacts and links for centuries.

11
India's Options in Iraq

Shri Prakash

No country decides its options in foreign policy matters without reference both to the long term principles it might have set out for itself in relation to the International system as well as the specific situation and the nation-state which is involved. In India's case the maintenance of peace, the use of non-conflictual strategies to resolve disputes, the fostering of democracy, independence and development were all integral elements of the doctrine of *Panchsheel* or peaceful and cooperative coexistence first adopted by the *Bandunq* Conference in 1955.

In the case of the crisis situation confronting Iraq today, India has not only to consider short term gains for itself, but the wider questions of international law and political morality which have been thrown up by the unilateral decision of USA and UK assisted by a few other countries to involve and occupy Iraq militarily. The reasons given by the occupying forces have been mainly concerned with the allegations at different times (1) of Iraq possessing and manufacturing Weapons of Mass Destruction - Nuclear Weapons, Chemical and Biological Weapons; (2) of the Saddam Hussein Regime under his personal instructions of killing political opponents and terrorizing them to the extent that they fled the country; (3) of the violation of the human rights of those who dared to disagree with Saddam Hussein through torture and inhuman treatment by agencies under the control of his sons; (4) of the monopoly of power by the minority Sunni

Muslim elite especially those coming from Saddam Hussein's hometown of Tikrit; (5) of the non-inclusion of Kurds and Shias in the running of the government and (6) of mismanagement of national revenues for personal gains by Saddam Hussein and other leaders of the Baathist Party.

After occupying Iraq the US-UK coalition forces despite facing armed resistance and non–cooperation from many quarters have proceeded to set up (i) a nominated Governing Council; (ii) a Cabinet appointed by the Governing Council; (iii) the rudiments of a new police force; (iv) resumption of some exports of oil; (v) handing out of contracts for reconstruction of Iraq to American Companies.

India has to take into account not only the fact that it had enjoyed a close and multi-dimensional relationship when Iraq was being run by the Baathist Party. It has to recognize that USA-UK military intervention in Iraq had no UN sanction. The Indian Parliament has already passed an unanimous resolution asking for the withdrawal of the occupation forces. The Union Cabinet issued a 'Statement on the current situation in Iraq' , in New Delhi on 18 March 2003 in which it clearly said that in the UN Security Council on the issue of Iraq, India had consistently counselled against War and in favour of Peace. "We have stated that any move for change in regime in Iraq should come from within and not be imposed from outside. We have also been drawing attention to the precarious humanitarian situation of the Iraqi people which war would only aggravate."[1]

In order to clarify India's actual options in Iraq today and in the forseeable future three sets of questions need to be answered first. What was the nature of the support actually given by the Iraqi people to the Baathist regime which had enabled Saddam Hussein to be elected and appointed as the President of Iraq? How did the various wars Iraq got involved in - against Iran to confront the religious fundamentalism of the Ayatollah's regime; against Kuwait to try and recover territory which the Iraqi Parliament claimed historically to belong to Iraq and finally the sanctions regime imposed by the United

Nations affect the economy and society in Iraq? Included in this very question is that of how far the occupation forces and the administration nominated by them has even enabled a process of recovery to start? How widespread is the process of armed resistance to the occupation forces and who is organizing it considering the fact that most of the leading functionaries of the Saddam Hussein Regime whom the US authorities wanted to arrest are already in their custody? Finally, as far as India is concerned how does its present relationship with a US controlled Iraq compare with the times when the Baathist Party used to govern the country? In making its choices relating to Iraq today should India bow down to the power of international realpolitik or stand up for the right of every nation-state to exercise their national sovereignty through democratic means so that the New World Order would be based on peace and voluntary consensus rather than the principle of might is right?

Before taking up these questions it would help to clarify our understanding of the issues mentioned by USA and UK mainly as the actual reasons for their military intervention in Iraq. Time and again the White House and Pentagon Officials have not only alleged that the Saddam Hussein regime was manufacturing Biological, Chemical and Nuclear Weapons of Mass Destruction, and (WMDs) that the time in which it could actually deploy and use these weapons was getting shorter and shorter.(2) In any case, the manufacture of these weapons constituted a violation of the many International Treaties Iraq had signed under the leadership of Saddam Hussein. As of now neither the United Nations nor the US Occupation Forces have been able to find any Weapons of Mass Destruction. In his October 1996 Report the Chief of the UN Inspection team Ekeus noted that during its five and a half year existence, UNSCOM had dispatched 373 inspection teams involving 3574 experts to Iraq without finding any WMDs. The UNSCOM had by then spent US Dollars 120 million, most of it taken from Iraq's assets frozen abroad.[3] Later UN Reports also affirmed their inability to find any WMDs right down to the many statements made by Hans Blix the last of the UN Chief inspectors.[4]

A Report in the *Asian Age* of 4 July 2003 said very clearly that in Iraq "US lacks WMD proof." In addition to not being able to produce any real proof so far, that Iraq had made WMDs, nor has USA been able to show any links between terrorists and the Saddam Hussein regime. After a thorough investigation the US intelligence agencies concluded that Iraq was not involved in the September 11 terrorist attacks on the World Trade Centre. This conclusion was confirmed in March in London by a report by John Scarlett, Chairman of Britain's Joint Intelligence Committee, which stated that there was no evidence to link Baghdad with the 9/11 attacks or to the Al Qaeda network. [5] It is indeed noticeable that in his most recent speech at the UN General Assembly on 22nd September 2003 President George Bush of USA (according to a Report in the *Hindustan Times)* "made no reference to the post war situation in Iraq - other than pinning the blame on "terrorists" which is forcing Washington to come back to the Security Council. Neither did Mr. Bush dwell on Saddam Hussein's Weapons of Mass Destruction, his Chief rationale for going to War this March.[6]

The oft repeated US criticism that the Saddam Hussein Regime was a one man show of a tyrant and dictator has to be assessed objectively. Saddam Hussein's system may have countered conspiracies against his government or insurgencies led by some Kurds or Shia clerics with military counter offensives which could include excessive violence. The purpose given was to maintain national and party unity and a secular system or to fight off the onslaught from Iranian religious fundamentalism being articulated by the government led by Ayatollah Khomeini. In any case, Saddam Hussein even as President of Iraq has to be viewed as a part of the Baathist Socialist Party, which had grown in Iraq from a tiny membership of 200 in 1954 to 5000 active members by 1967.[7]

The basis of Baathist Social support came not only from an increase in the numbers of its active members but some of its new policies. Popular support existed for the land redistribution carried out by the Baathist governments even before Saddam Hussein became the President of Iraq in 1978-79. In 1953, 1.7 per cent of landowners owned 63 per cent of the land. About two–thirds of the population owned 5 per cent of the land and over three - fourths of the rural population was made up of landless labourers. By the early 1970s this scenario had radically altered after the Baathists took over power in 1968, albeit through a coup. Big estates were broken up and redistributed without any compensation being paid to the original owners. A more propertied peasantry came into existence, which did not suffer from the inequalities of yesteryears.[8]

Another major cause for there being support amongst the people for the Baathist movement was the nationalization of the Iraq Petroleum Company in which the major shareholders since 1931, when it was set up were the British, the French, the Dutch Companies and two US Corporations. The Company was nationalized in June 1972. This meant that when oil prices were increased between 1973 and 1974, the Iraqi government had a five fold increase in revenue from petroleum exports. On an average during the period 1973-1985 Iraq's oil output was 3.5 million barrels per day (bpd) and exports 3.3 million bpd providing an income of between US Dollars 21.3 billion and 26.3 billion per annum respectively to the public treasury unlike in the Gulf monarchies or Iran with a class of small landowners. Oil revenues tended to filter down because the government having to fight elections wanted to win the support of the people. Investment in all economic sectors trebled, the government raised the salary of its civil servants and military personnel dramatically. A strong Public Sector came into existence and free medical and educational services were provided with special emphasis on the education and employment of women thus providing a new layer of support for the Baathist Party.[9]

There were two major consequences of the increased revenues and expenditures received and promoted by Saddam Hussein's government. The first result of the developmental orientation of Baathist strategy was that they were easily able to win in the general elections.

That these were broadly fair, contrary to some American critics' claims may be seen from the fact that quite a number of seats were won by opposition candidates. In the General Elections of 1980 and 1984 the Baath Party won 183 and 188 seats respectively out of 250. In the 1989 vote, the Baath's share fell to 138, which shows that the deteriorating economic and employment situation after the end of the Iraq - Iran war did affect the number of seats Baath Party used to win.[10]

The second consequence of increased oil incomes was the building of a large army and a modern military infrastructure especially during the eight year of Iran-Iraq War. Iraq's military expenditures in constant 1991 US Dollars (USD) increased from USD 343 million in 1970 to USD 10121 million in 1981 (about 30 times) and then attained a wartime peak of USD 21360 million in 1984. The strength of the army reached 24 regular divisions or 360,000 backed up by an equal number of reservists and atleast one million *jehadis* or para military forces who could fight an urban guerilla war. This should be compared with the 200,000 US coalition troops now in Iraq. Saddam Hussein is also reported to have set up an extensive network of secret accounts in banks virtually all over the World so that in case he is deposed or Iraq occupied he could still continue to wage a clandestine war and pay for it.[11] This is one aspect of the current situation India has to keep in mind while deciding on its options about Iraq.

Even the scanty reporting on Iraq available in Indian newspapers shows a steady armed resistance against the US occupation forces even when the leading figures of the Saddam Hussein regime are in US custody. According to the BBC atleast 12 armed attacks take place on the occupation forces daily. This is confirmed by newspaper reports. According to one report in the *Asian Age* of 12 June 2003, "since the American command quadrupled its military presence here last week, not a day has gone by without troops weathering an ambush, a rocket propelled grenade attack, an assault with automatic weapons or a mine blast". According to a specialist reporter on guerilla campaigns "it is a mini war".[12] Another Report stated that "In Iraq a US soldier dies every day." The same report said "The BBC reported recently that resistance is growing and has spread from the pro- Saddam Hussein areas like Tikrit to cover almost entire Iraq. The occupying forces were facing resistance almost everywhere they went.[13]

Hopes of restoring normal oil export to pay even for the 3.9 billion US Dollars, the Bush government is spending daily on its armed intervention in Iraq have remained hopes.[14] The main pipeline which carries Iraq's oil exports via Syria has been blasted twice.[15] The United Nations mission supposed to supervise the implementation of human rights in Iraq has been attacked twice killing the head of the mission. One of the members of the US nominated Governing Council has been killed in broad daylight. Saddam Hussein has now been arrested. His two sons have been killed but to date no tribunal has been started to try alleged human rights abuses by ex-officials of Saddam Hussein's regime.

The economic and social situation remains as bad, if not worse than during the 12 years of the UN imposed sanctions after Iraq's abortive attempt to annex Kuwait. Then the Iraqi currency had depreciated several thousand times, child mortality rates had tripled, school drop out rates and unemployment increased by a large margin. Recent reports show little change in the situation. "No food, No water, No ruler", says one headline. Looting, lawlessness and chaos make people long for Saddam's rule. "Ofcourse we miss Saddam Hussein now", says Kazemal-Fartisti, 52, who owns electronics and clothing stores in the al-Arabi area. "Under him this would never have happened.[16] The *International Herald Tribune* reported that only "one to three hours of electricity was available in Abu Ghrain, a town close to Baghdad. Drinking water was being taken from polluted semi–dry canals". According to a western educated English speaking councillor Sheik Dari Hamis at–Dari "Conditions have never been worse. He could do nothing for the man who lacking electricity stayed up all night fanning a sick child left legless by unexploded ordnance, a sight that caused him to weep. He could do nothing for the multitudes complaining of cars, weapons or relatives taken by the US forces, other than give their names to the Americans. He could do nothing for those lacking drinking water or waiting for food rations.[17]

What has been the US response to the real situation in Iraq. The US government is asking other major Powers including India to send a multinational force to Iraq. There has been only a negative response from the major countries inside and outside the United Nations Security Council. There have been promises about starting the reconstruction of Iraq. To this end contracts worth one billion USD have been given to US Companies only. "Not a single other country has been accommodated".[18] However, the security situation being dismal no work has started on these contracts. Iraq continues to be burdened by hundreds if not thousands of billions of USD debt and compensation claims.

According to one recent Report "Everywhere he turns from the United Nations and Congress to allied capitals and to Baghdad and Tikrit - US President George Bush is finding major obstacles to his effort to secure and rebuild Iraq. Administration officials are acknowledging that there is an embarrassing lack of foreign donations to rebuild Iraq. European diplomats said that the United States would be lucky to get USD 1 bn in pledges at the donor's conference it is organizing in Madrid in October 2003, about 10 per cent of what the US wanted.[19] According to the decision taken at the Madrid conference the 60 countries present pledged 33 billion dollars in loans mainly for the reconstruction of Iraq.

This situation compares very unfavourably with the times when there was the elected Baathist government of Saddam Hussein ruling Iraq.

If one were to compare the overall hostility and the many disputes which have characterized India's relations with several of its neighbours over trade, territory, and people's migration - this includes India's ties with Pakistan, Bangladesh, Sri Lanka and on occasions with Nepal -

the relations between India and Iraq provide a much more positive example of friendly, cooperative and productive relations between two Third World Countries or nations of the South, both members of the Non-Aligned Movement.

At the time of gaining its independence from the British and for a few years after 1947, India was represented in the Middle East or West Asia only by its embassies at Cairo, Teheran, Kabul and Ankara. It was in September 1949 that the Indian legation was started in Baghdad and in 1952 that the governments of Iraq and India agreed to raise the level of their representation to that of Embassies.

A trade agreement was signed between India and Iraq in May 1953 and renewed on 1 January 1955 for another year. An Air agreement was also signed, and a cultural agreement in July 1954. The cultural agreement provided for the exchange of university and college teachers and members of scientific and cultural institutions; scholarships were instituted as well as cultural centres set up in both countries. Sports competitions between the two countries were to be encouraged. These agreements showed the secular nature of the bilateral relations which were developing between independent India and Iraq. The emphasis on economic aspects was demonstrated by the fact that one of the first Indian delegations to visit several West Asian countries including Iraq, Iran, Baharein, Kuwait, Syria, Lebanon, Turkey, Egypt and Sudan was led by Shri M.P. Birla, the industrialist. [20] By 1968 the value of Indo-Iraqi trade had increased to a level of 5.4 million pound sterling. On September 17, 1968 it was agreed in New Delhi to increase the volume of their bilateral trade to 6-7 million pound sterling. With the Baathist movement gaining in influence in Iraq, the two countries wanting to create a good precedent of South–South cooperation also agreed to enlarge purchases by government organisations and exchange more trade and business delegations.[21]

The widening ambit of India-Iraq cooperation resulted in 1973 in a new Economic and Technical Cooperation Agreement which included a provision for setting up the Indo-Iraqi Joint Commission which was constituted in 1974. At its meeting in 1976 an expanded programme for cooperation in education, science and culture was signed envisaging further cooperation in education, science, technology, art, culture, sports, medicine, health and Press, Radio, Television and Films.[22]

The coming to power of Saddam Hussein's government only speeded up the pace of Indo-Iraqi cooperation. The start of the Iraq-Iran war in September 1980 with India trying its best to mediate in order to bring about Peace still did nothing to prevent the expansion of India-Iraq cooperation. The sixth session of the Indo-Iraq Joint Commission which met in New Delhi in April 1981 identified new areas of cooperation in various fields including irrigation, agriculture, oil and petrochemicals. The Protocol signed at the end of the meeting stated inter-alia that India and Iraq should set "an example of cooperation in the economic field leading to national and collective self–reliance which should serve as an example to the rest of the developing world.[23] These years also saw a significant increase in the number and value of projects awarded by Iraq to Indian Companies. There were a number of major contracts both in the private and the public sectors. The total value of Indian projects rose from Rupees 400 crores 1979 to Rs.1800 crores by the end of 1980.[24] By December 1981 their value had increased to Rs. 2500 crores. [25] By 1982-83 there were 97 Indian Companies in Iraq executing projects worth over Rs. 5000 crores. India participated in the Baghdad International Trade Fair and this was greatly appreciated by the Iraqi government. [26]

The scope and range of India's constructive involvement were truly extensive and its project exports to Iraq "probably the single largest to any country in the World".[27] India was extensively involved in various construction activities in Iraq ranging from office buildings to putting up housing colonies building and management contracts for railways were awarded to RITES, India Ltd. in May 1988. The Associated Cement Company was awarded an Organisation and Maintenance contract for the Kubasia Cement Plant. They have run the plant at over 110 per cent capacity. The Oberois are presently running Hotel Babylon Oberoi in Baghdad and Hotel Nineveh Oberoi in Musul. Engineers India Ltd. (EIL) had signed agreements for the supply of skilled manpower to various Iraqi clients. India has a joint venture to build a phospate based fertilizer industry in Iraq.

It is also not true that due to shortage of oil revenues and its diversion for prosecuting the War against Shiite fundamentalism in Iran payments were not made to Indian Companies. In view of the friendly relations with Iraq, India agreed to defer payments against projects executed by the Indian Companies. By 1985 Iraq owed India approximately 1 billion US Dollars against deferred payments. During 1986, Iraq agreed to pay 50 per cent of the amounts due that year in oil. Similar arrangements were followed during 1987 and 1988. As per the deferred payment agreement for the outstanding dues for 1989-90, an amount of 290 million was to be repaid by way of adjustment against oil imports and the remaining amount is to be deferred to a later period. *Not only does this option remain open for the future in case of investments by Private Companies a system of payment for each phase of the project completed can be suggested to prevent the contractors from becominq over indebted.*

India which imports 65 per cent of its petroleum from the Gulf region has continued to rely on Iraq even during the period of the UN sanctions after Iraq's abortive bid to annex Kuwait in 1990. India has almost always run a current account deficit in its trade with Iraq, importing more petroleum in value terms than its commodity exports. For example, in 1988-89, India's exports of products to Iraq amounted only to Rs. 52.08 crores whereas India's imports from Iraq during the same period were worth Rs. 192.6 crores. India's exports included both traditional items like Tea, Spices etc. as well as nontraditional items like autospare parts, clothing, pumps, small engineering goods etc. *Once the UN (sanctions are lifted) and the Iraqi economy begins to function normally after rebuildinq its war ravaged and sanctions constricted oil industry the potential for Indo–Iraqi trade is tremendous.* However, this has still to happen in the absence of a legitimately constituted interim government which the US-UK occupying forces have so far failed to put together. The Governing Council nominated by the Chief of the US forces in Iraq and the subsequent Cabinet appointed by it might be administrative bodies running the country. They are, however, not an interim government recognized by the existing Iraqi Parliament or the Army which have neither been dissolved through duly constituted constitutional procedure. There is no sign that the people of Iraq recognize the American nominated committees as a legitimate successor to the earlier Baathist government.

The potential for Indo-Iraqi trade can be seen from the fact that even when the UN sanctions regime was in place and Iraq was being allowed to sell a limited and specified amount of oil, India was both one of its important customers and sources of imports. Between April 2000 and March 2001 India imported 27,037,000 Kilograms of Petroleum from Iraq valued at Rupees 315,267,958.[28] After Saudi Arabia, Kuwait, Baharain, Malaysia and Iran, Iraq was number sixth in the quantity and value of petroleum exports to India. In turn, India was exporting 22 major commodities which are listed below: Black Tea, Meat, Wheat, Soyabean, Tobacco, Salts, Medicines, Books, Jute, Rubber footwear, Glassware, Galvanised Pipes, Copper Tubes, Chemical Plants, AC Motors, Electric Sound Amplifiers, Power Cables, Printed Circuit Boards, Motorcycles, Electric Meters, Sports Goods and Artware. [29] *Quite for petroleum products in the future. India can look for a growinq market in Iraq for its exports in the future.*

It should also be emphasized that India has managed to maintain good diplomatic and political relations with Iraq through good times and difficult days. During the Iran-Iraq war which lasted for 8 years India sent and received many special envoys, put forward solutions and peace plans, organized meetings of NAM countries in a bid to defuse the situation. Right towards the end in 1987 (the Iran–Iraq War ended in 1988) the Principal Adviser to both the Iraqi and Iranian governments visited India for consultations.

Due to the goodwill retained by India with Iraq and the latter's secular approach the government of Saddam Hussein wanted to pursue in foreign policy matters, the latter firmly refused to include the Kashmir question in the Agenda of the 15th, 19 nation *Arab Summit Conference* held in Baghdad between May 28-30, 1990. India reciprocated the Iraqi gesture by sending out the then external affairs minister, I.K. Gujral on a three day visit to Baghdad (June 18-20, 1990). When he met Saddam Hussein, the latter assured him "that Iraq will oppose Pakistan's efforts to raise the Kashmir issue at the Organisation of Islamic Conference meet in Cairo in July 1990". Saddam said "Iraq does not accept the encouragement to terrorism and interference in the neighbour's affairs. If such bilateral issues like Kashmir are to be discussed then the internal affairs of many Muslim states would have to be discussed as well". He also said that "Iraq as always considered India as a special country with whom Baghdad will like to develop "Political, Cultural, Technical and Scientific relations.,,[30] Earlier on June 19, Iraqi Deputy Prime Minister and Foreign Minister Tariq Aziz said that "the politics of religion is not acceptable in a modern society and violence and terrorism had to be opposed whatever their cause and form."

Inder Kumar Gujral offered a fresh buyer's credit of 60 million dollars to Iraq to boost India's commodity exports. In 1988, India had given 50 million dollars buyers credit to Iraq which had been fully utilized.

It is noteworthy that even when India asked Iraq to abide by the resolutions of the United Nations and vacate its occupation of and aggression against Kuwait in 1990, Iraq in no way obstructed the repatriation of 172000 Indian nationals from Kuwait and another 9000 from Iraq itself. The Indian government had to create a special cell to deal with the Gulf War (1990) claims of Indian nationals, Indian Companies and Government of India. The A, B, C, D claims numbering about 140,900 till December 1993 are valued at US Dollars 1874.5 million and about 100 'E' claims of about US Dollars 1360 million have been forwarded to the UN Compensation Commission in Geneva.

At the same time during Iraq's occupation of Kuwait on receiving reports of shortages of food in Kuwait and Iraq, India sent 9775 tonnes of essential food supplies and medicines with the approval of the UN sanctions committee through the Indian ship M.V. Vishva Siddhi, which reached the Iraqi port of Um Qasr on 26 September 1990. 4773 tonnes of these food times were distributed among Indian nationals and others and the rest were off loaded and stored in Iraq and Kuwait on the advice of the UN Sanctions Committee for distribution among nationals of other countries. *This reflects a positive approach on the part of India as far as humanitarian problems in Iraq and West Asia are concerned. India should continue with this policy in the future.*

It is to be emphasized that despite agreeing with and voting for UN resolutions on Iraq and asking Iraq to implement them India has maintained a sustained exchange of high level political visits even when governments have changed in New Delhi. Some examples of such exchanges are worth noting.

An Iraqi delegation led by their Foreign Ministry Permanent Under Secretary for political affairs Mr. Abdul Jabbar Omar al-Daouri paid an official visit to India in September 1993 for exchange of views with the Indian government. This was followed by the visit of the Kuwaiti Deputy Prime Minister.

In 2001, when the BJP led NDA government was in power in New Delhi (it still is), the Iraqi Minister of Transport and Communications, Dr. Ahmed Murtadha, Ahmed Al-Khalil, visited India from 4 - 9 July 2001. During his visit, the Iraqi Minister called on the Minister of External Affairs, Minister of Communications, Minister of Railways, Minister of Law, Justice, Company Affairs and Shipping and Minister of State for Civil Aviation. Two joint working groups were set up in the areas of Communications and Railways during the visit.

A 75–member goodwill delegation headed by Deputy Chairperson, of the Rajya Sabha, Dr. Najma Heptulla accompanied by the Ministers of State for Railways, Commerce and Industry and Shri Digvijay Singh as Deputy Leader visited Iraq on board a special flight from 31 August to 2 September 2001. The delegation included Members of Parliament, businessmen, mediapersons, members of civil society and academicians. The delegation had meetings with the Iraqi Vice-President Taha Yassin Ramadan, Deputy Prime Minister Tariq Aziz, Speaker Sadam Hammadi, Minister of Transport and Communications, Minister of Industry and Minerals, Minister of Trade and the Foreign Minister. The leaders of the delegation was received by President Saddam Hussein. Dr. Heptulla delivered a written message to the Iraqi President from our Prime Minister.

More visits followed in 2001 itself. The Iraqi minister of Electricity Mr. Sahban F Mahjoob accompanied by a 3–member delegation paid an official visit to India from 26 November to 4 December 2001 at the invitation of the Minister of Power. He called on the Minister of Power, Minister of Heavy Industries and Public Enterprises and interacted with businessmen.[31]

The second significant trend in India's policy in the current global situation is to favour multilateral action through the United Nations for a peaceful resolution of disputes. India put up for the consideration of the international community in 1990 a 3–point programme for the peaceful evacuation of Kuwait by Iraq. Again before the Second Gulf War in 2003, India opposed unilateral military action by USA and UK and also a regime change imposed from outside by forces not having proven popular legitimacy. The Union Cabinet officially regretted the start of unilateral military action by USA-UK forces in Iraq on 18th March, 2003. This can only mean as has been stated in the resolution adopted by the Indian Parliament that USA and UK should withdraw their occupation forces from Iraq at the earliest and allow the United Nations to help form a new popular government in Iraq.

In view of the current speculation in the media about US requests for sending Indian troops to Iraq to help in stabilizing the situation, some significant aspects of the situation should be kept in mind. India is being asked to send its troops not as a part of any United Nations Peace keeping Force but to assist forces of occupation of USA/UK and a few of their allies. Not only are none of the other members of the Security Council not willing to accept USA's request, it is not at all clear under whose command will the Indian troops function or what their duties will be. It is noteworthy that Saddam Hussein and his 400,000 strong army have gone underground presumably to fight a long drawn out guerilla war against the occupation forces of USA and UK.

Sending Indian troops to Iraq now will be tantamount to participating in hostile action against political forces otherwise friendly to India. It will be considered a hostile action by most Muslim countries who have also opposed the unilateral military action by USA and UK in Iraq and by Muslims in India and South Asia, hundreds of thousands of whom have sent their family members to live and work in the Gulf region and who are the biggest source of foreign exchange remittances to India. A handful of such troops can hardly ensure peace in this volatile region; it will only drag India into a difficult, delicate and damaging situation.

There are other aspects of the current situation in Iraq which Indian policy makers should keep in mind. Much has been written in the media about the personal connections of the decision making group around President Bush with the American Oil Companies.[32] The haste with which some oil contracts have been given to Exxon and Chevron is in rank bad taste, especially even before an interim government had been formed. It is doubtful whether these contracts which are not legal can be implemented without a legitimate government being in power in Iraq. The reasons given for the dissolution of the Baathist Party by the American representative of the occupation forces - violation of human rights, building weapons of mass destruction - have not been proven. All efforts to set up a legitimate interim government by the occupying forces have failed. The Governing Council setup to administer Iraq and draft a new Constitution is more an American nominated Committee than a legitimate interim government formed voluntarily by the major political parties of Iraq. The danger of religious extremists starting violent action by suicide squads is seen in daily attacks and campaigns against the occupying forces in different parts of Iraq.[33] India should not send any troops to Iraq except as a part of an UN effort also agreed to by a legitimate government in Baghdad, formed with UN and international backing and then ratified by contesting elections.

India before it can become a partner in the reconstruction of Iraq must insist on the installation of a legitimate government in Iraq - under the auspices of the United Nations. The Baathist Party should be allowed to participate in the process of the formation of a popular government. The US–UK forces and Companies can only remain and work in Iraq if a legitimate government in Baghdad agrees to it. The UN can take the lead in calling an international conference of oil producer and consumer countries to fix a range within which oil prices should remain assuring a fair profit to the industry but preventing an arbitrary increase in oil prices globally.

India has to remember that Iraqi nationalism matured in a series of conflicts against the British, the monarchy, Shia religious fundamentalism of Iran and finally two major wars against USA and UK and their coalition allies, not to mention the rigors of the UN imposed sanctions regime which lasted for well over twelve years. Self ownership of national wealth, the desire to persuade other Arab countries to follow a secular and a democratic path and the willingness to fight for these causes on all fronts have made the Iraqi nation a well resolved people who can go through fire and brimstone to have a government of their own. This is not to deny that the Iraqi system had no faults like authoritarianism at the top, corruption in a large bureaucracy holding up further progress and the insistence that only the leadership of the Baathist Party could achieve the goals of Iraqi development and help to solve the Palestinian issue. The Baathist Party in its own imperfect ways supported land reforms, women's education and employment and the building of a secular modern society all of which were set back by the sanctions regime. Hence, a Baathist like regime with or without the Saddam Hussein group, a more moderate Baathist Party with a new name even seems a likely candidate to lead Iraq in the future. Such a political formation is needed to prevent Iraq going the Iran way. Other coalitions like the Iraqi National Congress led by Chalabi do not seem to have the same proven credibility or organic links with the people to be real leaders. At any rate a direct American or British controlled administration looks too much like a nineteenth century British colonial state to be successful in building a real democracy in Iraq in the twentyfirst century.

In recent years India's secular image has taken quite a few knocks with the demolition of the Babri mosque in Ayodhya and the recent communal riots in Gujarat. Sending Indian troops to Iraq to exercise surveillance over nationalist Baathist and even religious Shiite groups would deliver another blow to India's espousal of progressive nationalism and Third World solidarity. Rather, India must work to bring about a peaceful political settlement in Iraq acceptable to all members of the international community and to the representative sections of the Iraqi nation. It must insist first of all on constituting a representative Iraqi national government and then cooperate with it as per mutual agreement.

References

1. Statement (of the Indian Union Cabinet) on the current situation in Iraq, *Strategic Digest,* New Delhi, Vol. 33, Number 4, April, p. 2003, p. 296.

2. Kenneth R Timmerman, the Death Lobby, how the west armed Iraq, Houghton, Mifflin Company, New York, U.S.A. 1991, p. 390.

3. Dilip Hiro, Iraq Granta Books, London, 2003, p. 107.

4. See for example Report on statement by Hans Blix entitled "Iraq dumped WMDs years ago," Hindustan Times, 19/8/2003, p. 12; See also Report entitled "Senate report to call CIA's WMD bluff" Indian Express New Delhi, 25/10/03, p. 9

5. Dilip Hiro, op. cit, p. 180.

6. Report on George Bush's speech to the UN General Assembly, "Iraq needs the help of friends: US", The Hindu, New Delhi, 24/09/03, p.12.

7. Dilip Hiro, op. cit, p. 53.

8. Anthony H Coresman and Ahmed S Hashim, Iraq, Santions and Beyond, Westview Press, Boulder, Colorado, USA, 1997, p. 131.

9. Dilip Hiro, op. cit., pp. 24/25.

10. Ibid, p. 55.

11. Anthony Cordesman and Ahmed Hashim, op. cit., p. 43/p. 56.

12. Report on "Mystery force comes alive at night to strike at the US" by Michael R Gordon, New York Times Service, The Asian Age, New Delhi, 12/6/2003, p. 3; See also Feature on Iraq "Danger Around Every Corner," The Time Magazine, October 27, 2003, New Tork, USA pp. 22-28.

13. Seema Mustafa, "In Iraq, a US soldier dies every day," The Asian Age, New Delhi, 21/6/2003 p. 1.

14. Report on "Rise in US' Iraq costs surprise Democrats" The Asian Age, New Delhi 14/7/2003 p. 7.

15. Report on "2nd Blast hits Iraq–Syria oil pipelines" The Asian Age, New Delhi, 24/6/2003, p. 6.

16. Report on "No Food, No Water, No Ruler," The Times of India, New Delhi, 12/4/2003 p. 4.

17. Raport on "Local Elite in Iraq losing faith in US lead," International Herald Tribune, 10/7/2003, p. 1.

18. Report on "US firms hog almost entire USD 1 billiion Iraq pie" The Asian Age, 24/6/2003, p. 1.

19. Report on "US Iraq project hits roadblocks," The Hindustan Times, New Delhi, 19/9/2003, p. 12.

20. Various relevant Annual reports of the Ministry of External Affairs (MEA) Government of India.

21. Asian Recorded, Vol. 74, 1968, p. 8553.

22. Asian Recorder, Vol. 22, 1976, p. 13038.

23. MEA, Annual Report, 1980–1981, p. 20.

24. Ibid. p. 20.

25. MEA, Annual Report, 1981–1982, p. 15.

26. MEA, Annual Report, 1982–1983, p.14.

27. Rai Singh, New Dimensions to Indo–Iraq relations, Link New Delhi, July 1, 1990.

28. Monthly Foreign Trade Statistics of India, DGCIS, Calcutta, Part II, Imports, March 2000–2001, table on imports.

29. Ibid, PT. I Table on Exports pp. 1515–1522.

30. MEA, Annual Report 1990–91, passim.

31. MEA, Annual Report, 2001–2002, p. 37.

32. See for example Jeffery D Sachs, US Crony capitalists go to war, Economic Times New Delhi, 2/5/2003.

33. See for example, Reports (a) 'New Iraq Mission challenges US 'Spartan Brigade', The Asian Age, 3/06/2003, p.6, (b) 'US troops find few guns in Iraq house searches,' The Asian Age 4/06/2003.

12

Anglo-American Operation Shock and Awe in Iraq March-April, 2003

Reflections on Revolution in Military Affairs

Brig Chandra B Khanduri

The Anglo-American Operation in Iraq in March - April 2003 fashionably called as *Op Shock & Awe* has been characterized by several factors unique to it. First, there was no internationally recognized cause for it, except the American obduracy to oust the Iraqi regime under Saddam Hussein for causes that were clearly embroidered. For, the UN promoted inspection of the so called Weapons of Mass Destruction (WMD), allegedly held by Iraq could never be found; the Iraqis had willingly offered all along their systems of weapons for inspection– and destruction and, above all, the whole international comity of nations represented at the UN had rejected any military action by US and its allies.

Second, in an overt demonstration of its military prowess, the Americans went alone (with the exception of UK and Australia) and in a new kind of *blitzkrieg* trounced the *elite* Iraqi Army in less than three weeks. Combining a massive strike by its Precision Guided Munitions (PGM), Cruise missiles, long and short range stealth airforce, its clandestine CIA and special forces operations, information warfare and an exhaustive psychological warfare besides exploiting the anti-Saddam Iraqis from both inside and outside the country, the result was a foregone conclusion.

The war, as the records show had never ceased after the 1991 Gulf War, when the country had been divided into virtually three parts - the 'no-fly zones' of autonomous Kurds region of the north, the central Iraqi and the southern Shiite Zone. These 'no fly zones' had not only trisected the country but its oil wealth was allowed only for 'oil for food'. It also became an experimental battlefield for the British-Americans when they used new weapons especially new aircraft, the new armament and the various aspects of its information war against Iraq for a full decade.

It was a proverbial war of David versus Goliath that the Iraqis stoutly offered resistance of three weeks in the actually declared war, was creditable. However, a nation like the US which follows the Macaulay dictum that 'moderation in war is an imbecility', saw Iraq bludgeoned into submission.

Middle East has always been regarded as strategically important region by the US. Recall the words of General Eisenhower. He had said in 1951: "As far as sheer value of territory is concerned, there is no more strategically important area in the world than the middle east." The creation of the Baghdad pact, the CENTO, support to Israel, so on, its occupation of Iraq now, stems from this strategic consideration.

One of the important lessons of this war from the militray point of view was a full-fledged demonstration of the RMA. The following part of the text assays to briefly narrate its recent growth and the doctrine the American military has evolved in consonance with the nuances of its strategic perception. Its relevance to the Indian Armed Forces is also deliberated.

RMA Defined

The RMA is another name for military technological revolution and is, in fact, a continuous process of inception of science and technology into the art and science of warfare. The central tenet of the RMA is that advances in technology must lead to significant changes in how the military forces are to be organised, equipped and trained. It also envisages to update tactics (i. e. the art of employment of troops in battles) and overall strategy (i.e., employment of a nation's resources) for a successful conclusion of a conflict. RMA, seen, in modem light, therefore, aims to achieving long range precision strike capabilities by combining *Intelligence, Surveillance, and Reconnaissance (ISR) systems.* Its final goal would thus be to pulverise an enemy system of command and control, and adversely affect its critical decisions and actions. It is afterall, the enemy commander and the nerves of an enemy nation's leadership that eventually become the focal point of decisive military objective.

How have the Americans achieved their RMA Capability?

Taking the lessons from World War II and more recently from the end of the Cold War and the 1991 Gulf War, American military leadership became conscious of its strategic role as the sole superpower with self-acquired leadership of the world. Its economic power gave it a natural superiority. It has always followed the dictum that diplomacy without adequate strength is hollow. Soon after the 1991 War, it began to review its military policy. The 'Basic Force, 1991', the 'Bottom Up' Review, 1993' and the 'Quadrennial Defence Review, 1997', began to provide the 'Regional Defence Strategy' and 'Shape Respond Prepared Strategy'. *All these progressively envisaged transition from an armed force of ' industrial era'* to one of 'information era'. In this process of continued upgradation it so far culminated into the latest, 'The Joint Vision 2002' which gave further impetus to the RMA pertaining to the new weapon systems, defence and doctrinal researches, evaluation and decision.

Already a global armed force with bases all over the world, the 'September 11, 2001' known as '9.11', events afforded it yet another boost to expand its operations against the Islamic fundamentalists of

Taliban and anchor into the Central Asian Republics, Pakistan, besides entrenching into Afghanistan the country that saw RMA practised in full as part of *Operation Enduring Freedom.* As a sequel, USA has also embarked upon overseas interventions such as in the Philippines, Indonesia, Columbia and even threatened the Maoists of Nepal.

One of the major developments following '9.11' has been the strengthening of the 'home security'. It would become evident that the US Government of the day is increasingly getting dependent on the military and using it to achieve its political objectives and redefining the role of the military. Of the latter, noteworthy are the four essential tasks assigned to the military; to defend homeland; to deter aggression and intimidation of crucial areas of the world; to defeat aggression and win decisive victories; and, to undertake limited number of small scale emergent actions. As a result, the US defence budget today is more than treble of the whole of Europe's at $380 billion and it would overshadow the whole of the world's at $ 500 bn in next four years. The Roman march of the US to empire building and hegemony is already in full swing!

Observe another discernible change in the American defence paradigm - the shifting of the *design of defence pattern based on Threat to that of basing it on Capability with emphasis on strategic flexibility.* This implies briefly that the US would, in future, base its own capability on multiple threats rather catering for specific adversaries. Its military significance is enormous in terms of quantum, quality and the nature of the future US Armed Forces. So is the concept of Joint Forces Command and organisation cell "MC-02" tasked to generate knowledge about diplomatic, economic, cultural aspects of the known and imagined adversaries (the so called 'axis of evils') with a view to use them as 'diplomatic tools'. So has a Management 'Crisis Group' been created that envisions likely crises and manages the national resources, coalescing the support from allies and friends.

Out of this, the conceptual emphasis has shifted from what some analysts call *'Rim to Nucleus'*. It's ramification is both defensive and offensive. In the defensive shape it envisages protection of crucial areas and thwarting of attacks on own vital areas. In its offensive role it would combine ISR with C^4 (command, control, communication and computers). The nucleus of the enemy's vital mobile and fixed targets are the objective and annihilation, rather than attrition is to be the future *modus operandi.*

The vastly superior C^4 ISR, had provided Americans 'cakewalks' both in Afghanistan and Iraq (unlike their horrible reverses in Korea and Vietnam) and they continue to transform their weapon systems, organisations including integration and creation of a 'global strike force'.

The outcome is what we saw in Afghanistan and Iraq. Of enduring interest to us are the new weapons systems and the ISR characterized by the high-tech systems. The world was witness to both pilotless aircraft - UAV/AUAV Predators locating and engaging enemy; the long range bombers flying from US and UK; the stealth aircraft such as F -117, striking from sea platforms; light and and heavy tanks rolling over the Iraqi deserts under the American supremacy of the air space. What struck prominently was the increased accuracy of the PGM although some did go astray. The *cyber warfare* striking at the enemy's information and control system proved, at least, experimentally, successful. So was the Psy war (more of propaganda) for the so called battle for the hearts and minds. Its results, however, wore off as the Iraqis saw the ulterior motives of the Anglo-French force that exploitation and not so called 'liberation' was their main motive.

If the ISR has done simply wonders with (long range targets and objectives), the man behind the gun and the soldier on the battlefield especially the *Special Forces* have represented the thus far imagined robotic soldiers. *A private equipped with body armour, hand held communication systems, Vector-VI binoculars, Laser Range Finder, XM-l 07 Long Range Sniper Rifle along with a Lap Top is the pride of the US Army, and is best equipped to do his task, survive and be available for any special task in any battlefield milieu.*

Imagine also the Units, brigades and divisions equipped with *digitised systems* of, on the spot terrain and enemy evaluations enabling them to see some 50 to 100 Km ahead. This is what a dream organisation would be for the Indian Army–or for that matter any army.

To summarise the American RMA is mainly characterized by:

- The PGMs guided by Global Positioning System (GPS) have allowed pulverisation of most vital targets but also encouraged the operability and effectiveness of smaller forces such as Special Forces including parachutists.
- The stealth aircraft (F-117, -22) penetrate deeper and with their ever improving versions with Mach 8 to 10 capability, they may be faster in response than field artillery.
- The satellites UAV s, Electronic counter measures, AWACs the J Stars (Joint Surveillance Target Attack Radar System) help remove the 'fog of war'.
- The tactical and strategic communications help not only control the battle but help improve flexibility.
- Joint doctrines and US Joint Forces commands have been formed for effective and economic battlefield responses.
- Total integration of battlefield resources, command and control system are being achieved through a 'Triad' system of nuclear and conventional forces.

To achieve their objective and maintain their superiority, the American are today prepared to go to any extent. This is best established by what *Washington Post* said on February 2, 2003:

"President Bush in his Directive No. 178 had said that the US reserves the right to respond with overwhelming force including potentially nuclear weapons to the use of WMD against our forces abroad, our friends and allies." So the American willingness to repeat Nagasaki - Hiroshima remains; it remained so in Iraq. So perhaps are its covert plans for anyone that stands upto it.

It need to be also said at this stage that what the American and the British showed in Iraq turned out to be a *super exercise in what the Janes Weekly of.April 20, 2003 called displaying a window of future warfare.* There is no doubt that there is a continuous march of RMA and in not too-distant-a future it would challenge the time and squeeze the space.

What is the larger feeling?

Seeing the recent development the world today has 'sat up' and summoned up the feelings of the world community as it share the view of the *Russian Mirror* of April 2-4 which said: " (After Iraq) not a single state in the world could feel safe and the instability that has now emerged will grow with negative consequences in other regions and areas of the globe." "The American power", it further opined, "has spawned fear even among the one time superpower Russia and the growing superpower China". One only sees with sympathy the Syrian stand on the Iraqi leadership that seemed to have fled into the country and those so called 'rogue states' or the 'axis of evil' who might, someday be receiving its wrath!

Morally, America has failed on all counts; it has failed for what it has all this time stood for–democracy, international consensus and human values. But seen the way the new American Frankenstein has emerged, the American power can not be ignored any more. It will require a conglomeration of countervailing nations to balance a mighty and powerful America hell bent on having its own way.

The Indian Problem

India is making a brave *albeit* hesitant effort to improve its technology and armament industry since mid -1960s. Admittedly, the strides made thus far have yet to inspire full throttled conviction that a breakthrough has been achieved or is likely to achieve in not too distant a future. Our slow progress on LCA, MBT, C4I space and ocean technology projects, have unfortunately been lagging behind the scheduled time frames. However, considerable progress has been made in missilery, nuclear and information technologies. We have also not progressed spectacularly in integrating our national defence resources; nor has the MOD achieved effective results in integrating with the Services or accepting the appointment of Chief of Defence Staff. The Government, it seems, is giving in small concessions most grudgingly, prioritizing its political goals over defence and security– a malady of the Nehruvian era that led to the 1962 debacle.

The doctrinal issues such as a nuclear doctrine or doctrine of joint conventional-nuclear command, the management of national crises, that may suddenly erupt also seems to have taken a backseat to political considerations and contingencies. The result is we have thus far succeeded only partially in developing a strategic culture and ackowledging the need that security is an essential part of national growth and economic prosperity. It is quite certain that unless we integrate defence and national security under one responsible head, unless the professional advice is incorporated into overall national security, there is unlikely to be any real time gain in our overall strategic capability.

One more vital issue warrants our attention. The American imperialistic ambitions and its acquired hegemonism add one more angle to the twin threats India has continually faced from Pakistan and China. If this American hegemonism and unilateralism continue unabated, as it already seems to be doing so, can the possibility ever be ruled out that America might thrust an unequal and unjust solution on India, in so far it relates to the dispute over Jammu & Kashmir with Pakistan. Obviously, we need to learn our lessons from the American operational capability and see that our diplomacy is adequately supported by our military strength which alone could deter such a move.

The American military operation in Iraq may well fail - and one hopes so–to install a governance to its own liking and design, but the formidable military response it was able to generate against Iraq and a brute yet gigantic display of its RMA it made leaves a hard lesson for all countries including India that there is no substitute to maintaining technological and military preparedness. If there is a substitute to it, it is slavery like the mighty Japanese faced after World War II or what the proud Iraqis are facing now.

13
US in Post Saddam Iraq

R. R. Subramanian

The destruction of the UN building in Baghdad and killing of the chief UN Supervisor D'Mello and sixteen others by Syria based militants in Iraq shows fragile is the peace. US President George Walker Bush has failed to grasp the true aspirations of the Iraqi people. The unequal battle won by American military forces and subsequently deposition of Saddam Hussein has not won the peace. Shri AB Vajpayee was wise in not sending Indian military troops to Iraq.

Iraq with a large Shiite population has not welcomed the continued presence of US and other western military troops in Iraq. The Kurdish question is yet to be resolved even as Turkey, an American ally aims to enter Kurdistan in Northern Iraq.

There has been no shred of evidence to indicate that Iraq was in possession of weapons of mass destruction. The Scientific Advisor to the British Ministry of Defense has killed himself under suspicious circumstances. He had debunked Prime Minister Tony Blair's claims that Iraq was in possession of nuclear weapons.

In spite of the US Central Intelligence Agency (CIA) denying that Saddam's Iraq was buying uranium from Niger, President Bush went on to repeat the allegations in a formal speech to the American nation. The US administrator Paul Bremmer who is supervising Iraq has been unable to put together a viable political coalition in Baghdad that can protect American interests.

Iran and Syria are the two "countries of concern" that Washington would like to observe for their terrorist activities and secure Israeli interests, even as the Palestinian problem remains nowhere near to a solution. Israel has possessed nuclear weapons since 1965. Its monopoly over these weapons of mass destruction (WMD) has not worried the US. When Iraq or Iran attempt to procure these weapons the US shows undue concern. The United States by its continual stay in Iraq since the ouster of Saddam Hussein has not endeared itself to the Iraqi population. It is indeed possible that Baghdad like Kabul in Afghanistan may be in control of the US military but in the outlying areas America is facing stiff resistance.

After the fall of Baghdad in March this year and the capitulation of the Iraq Revolutionary Guards (IRG) one had assumed that America would have a free reign in Iraq. It now appears as if the IRG like the Taliban has regrouped to strike at the American military forces. It appears as if the US with its awesome military and technological power has failed to win the peace as the hearts and minds of the Iraqi people are not with it.

Also, the capitulation of the Iraqi revolutionary guards to the US and its allied military forces during the surge on Baghdad has now manifested itself as a regrouped militia that is continually attacking at will the US and British forces.

The Shiite clergy has no intentions of countenancing American occupation. Thomas Freedman of the *New York Times* would have us believe that contrary to reports appearing in other media, especially the Arab TV Al Jazeera, the US is in control and carrying on ably the tasks of reconstruction of Iraq.

Iraq's neighbour, Iran, is in the process of enriching uranium in centifuges at Natanz. These centrifuges have been obtained clandestinely from Pakistan which has also the source for North Korea. The US–Pakistan relations are facing no straim as Washington of Bush sees Islambad as a pivot in its fight against Islamic fundamentalist terror,

US–Russia relations are facing tensions as a result of Iran's quest for nuclear weapons and Moscow's confinuance of supply of nuclear reactors to the Busher Station.

Also the US strategy for Iraq conceived under the guise of destroying Saddam's weapons of mass destruction (WMD) was actually aimed at securing its oil fields. Dick Chenney, Rumsfeld and Conddeeza Rice are strongly tied up with the oil interests of American oil companies. Their pursuit of these interests has given a thrust to a foreign policy that suits the neo conservatives, that surround Bush.

Iraqi oil fields have yet to pump oil wells to reach a level of production that would match the level of imports of the US from Saudi Arabia.

Also the attack on the US on 9/11/2001 only ignited US fears about the origins of Al Qeida and its outfits in Saudi Arabia. US–Saudi relations have not shown any fundamental strains so far. The US attack of Iraq as also on Afghanistan have no doubt consequences for the politics of oil be it for Gulf oil fields or the Caspian sea near Central Asia.

The US war on terrorism puts no pressure on Pakistan which under the leadership of General Musharraf has shown no desire to let up on cross border terrorism in Kashmiri.

The Hamid Karzai government's writ presently extends to Kabul even as the Taliban regroups on the outerlayers of Afghanistan that borders Pakistan. Washington has replaced the American military with troops of the NATO. Turkey is a member of NATO and if this is the subsequent model that is to be followed in Iraq, the Kurdish rebellion in the northern part of Iraq will intensity. Turkey appears presently to be restrained by Washington.

Is the US Pentagon keeping alive the myth of the erstwhile Baathist leader in order to secure popular support at home? The Bush Administration faces re–election in November next year, will it attempt further strikes on Iran or Syria in its confirmation of the war on terror and thus seek brownie points in its struggle for popular legitimacy?

In the earlier Gulf War a decade ago Bush Sr. stopped short of the invasion of Iraq fearing a tilt of the balance of power towards Iran. This allowed Saddam to rapidly reconstruct and even attempt to rebuild weapons of mass destruction (WMD). None of these WMD were found by the UN monitoring agencies. Bush Sr. had obtained UN approval for its intervention in the Gulf War. His son George Walker Bush and his neo con advisors see no need for approval. The UN does not seem to have the clout it once did.

Shri A. B. Vajpayee, the Indian Prime Minister has linked India sending military troops to Iraq, to a UN mandated resolution. Iraq was a traditional friend of India in the Non–Aligned movement and hence any humanitarian intervention by India in the reconstruction of Iraq should be welcomed.

The Iraqi people with their heritage and civilization cannot countenance a foreign occupation. So far there has not been a democratic government put in place in Baghdad. The United States aims to make Iraq an alternative base to Saudi Arabia so as to provide Israel security against the terrorists operating from Iran and Syria. This is a myth as the Palestinians pose the real threat to Isreal, with the Middle East peace nowhere in sight.

If Iran like North Korea were to unleash its nuclear weapons as also misslies, Israel's monopoly in this area will be weakened. The Bush neo cons hope to bring Iran to heel by pressuring Putin's Russia. Moscow is no mood to oblige as it can remain no longer passive after Iraq.

14

The United States Attack on Iraq and the Muslim World

Kalim Bahadur

The 21st century has opened with the emergence of a new colonialism and the first colonial war has been fought in West Asia. It was the invasion of the oil rich but a weak country Iraq by the superpower the United States with all the military weaponry at its command. The colonial wars in the past centuries used to be fought to civilize the primitive natives and to exploit the natural wealth of the colonial countries. The American war against Iraq was aimed at changing a dictatorial regime and to give the Iraqi people a democratic dispensation. The control of the oil resources of Iraq by the United States went with it as a corollary. The Arab countries topped by the Gulf States own three quarters of all Arab and Islamic countries' oil reserves which in turn own two–thirds of the international oil reservoir. Washington had been politically preparing for this war ever since the first Gulf War in the early nineties. The terrorist attacks of the twin trade towers of New York only expedited the preparation for war and provided a reasonable alibi for the war on the oil rich country. The recent reports in the United States and the United Kingdom show that the establishment in Washington and London had suborned the intelligence agencies to provide false reports about Iraq's possession of weapons of mass destruction to justify war against Iraq. In fact both President Bush and Prime Minister Tony Blair were whipping up war hysteria by alleging that President Saddam Hussein could be ready to launch

WMD within 45 minutes. It has been now found the reports which were claimed to be based on 'impeccable intelligence sources' of the United States and the United Kingdom were doctored in many cases and even cooked up to justify the invasion. It was even alleged that Saddam regime had some links with Al Qaeda and terrorist groups. There has as yet been no conclusive evidence against Osama bin Laden or the Taliban linking them to the terrorist attacks in New York on 11th September 2001 yet the United States decided to launch massive attacks on Afghanistan killing thousands of innocent people and destroyed the Taliban regime.

The decision makers in Washington and London believed that the brutal dictatorial regime of Saddam Husain's atrocities were so well known that the people of the world including those in the countries in West Asia would believe anything said about the regime and would support the Anglo–American war. It was calculated that the Shia–Sunni divide in Iraq would be an asset as the Shia community which had been antagonized by Saddam regime's repressive policies of discrimination against the community would also rise up and support the invaders. The Shias had reason for their hostility against the rulers as they comprise the majority of population and yet they had been subjected to persecution and repression by the Sunni rulers. The Saddam regime had also been disliked by the people of the region because the way it had invaded its neighbour Iran in the early eighties, encouraged and supported by Washington, and carried on the war for almost ten years. Soon after the end of the Iran–Iraq war Saddam overran Kuwait in 1990 and inflicted upon the people of that country bloody atrocities.

. It was when Saddam decided to seize Kuwait in early nineties that United States woke up to the autocratic regime's many crimes, violations of human rights etc and swore to destroy it. During the first round of the first Gulf War Washington could not topple Saddam Hussein. United States policy in the Middle East is not merely formulated because Saddam Hussein is a tyrant and he had imposed an autocratic regime over Iraq or even that he was keen to develop nuclear weapons or that he possessed WMD etc. The fact of the matter is that the region has vast oil resources of the world. And not only that but the other rival powers Russia and China are located in the neighbourhood. The region is politically volatile where people are mostly Muslims while most of the regimes lack legitimacy and are prone to cataclysmic changes and coups and counter coups etc. This combined with rising tide of Arab nationalism, Islamic fundamentalism represented by the late Khomeini, and the Al Qaeda led by Osama bin Laden who threaten United States interests. It was soon after the 11th September 2001 terrorist attacks that the United States decided to deal with the Taliban regime in Afghanistan which was hosting Osama bin Laden after that to expand the war against terrorism to war against the so-called evil empire, i.e., Iraq, Syria, Iran, North Korea , etc. Redrawing the political map in the Arab region through planning to topple a number of regimes that oppose American policies. Persuading recalcitrant countries through temptation of economic aid or simply by regime change. One analyst has analysed that the US goal is to convert the Arab region into an American oasis in order to impose their hegemony after getting rid of Arab axis of force and decision–making, which the American administration believes are working against its strategy in the region or does not go in complete harmony with it such as Syria, Saudi Arabia and Lebanon and eventually Egypt. The entire Middle East had to be refashioned. Ever since the opening of the operation against Iraq the American propaganda machinery has been targeting Iran and Syria. The American objective is not merely Oil but hegemony over the entire West Asian region which will extend up to China and India in the East, covering Russia in the North and Africa in the West. This will also secure Israel which can act as the forward defender of the US interests which to some extent it already does. The way the Anglo-American forces overran Iraq shows that there is little to obstruct the United States in achieving its objective.

The very fact that the United Nations was completely immobilized by the United States by misinterpreting the UN resolutions allowing it to take preemptive action against one of its members. True many members of the UNO are dependent on the United States which allows it to pressurize them to turn a blind eye to such blatant acts of aggression against a weak country. The political order created after the Second World War has been destroyed by the United States by sidetracking of the United Nations and the aggression against Iraq. The occupation of the country and the way Iraqi assets have been seized by the United States army remind the re-emergence of the colonial order which ruled large parts of the world in the 19th and the 20th Centuries.

The colonial war imposed on one of the Muslim countries is not something new for the people of the region. Most of the Middle East countries had been under direct or indirect imperialist control during the last two hundred years. After the collapse of the Turkish Empire during the last quarter of 19th century almost all the former colonies of the Turkish Empire were divided among the new European colonial powers. The colonial system weakened and broke down after the First World War though colonial powers retained influence over large parts of Middle East till after the Second World War. Many of the rulers in the Arab countries owed their thrones to the former colonial masters. The rulers of Egypt, Saudi Arabia, Jordan, Iraq, Libya, and Morocco were not only dependent on the colonial powers but even received their doles from them.

The people in these countries did not accept the colonial rule without resistance. In fact the liberation struggles in Algeria, Tunisia, Libya, Palestine, Lebanon, Syria against colonial rule and for democracy in other countries where colonial rulers had imposed monarchies was successful in some of these countries but in the rest of the countries the struggle has continued ever since. The fact that population in most of these countries has been Muslim adds complexity to the situation... The beginning of the domination of the region by the western powers was preceded by the decline of the Muslim power, mainly the Turkish Empire which at one time extended from one end of the North Africa in the West to the Euphrates in the East.

The rise of nationalism in the Arab countries took ethnic and religious form. The overthrow of King Faruk and the emergence of Gamal Abdul Nasser in the fifties and his decision to nationalize the Suez Canal was the high water mark of Arab nationalism. The emergence of Israel as one of the pillars of United States policy in the Middle East, the setting up of the Central Treaty Organization and the Baghdad Pact which later became the Central Treaty Organization (CENTO) were seen as the Western moves to counter the rise of Arab nationalism. It was in the late sixties that the incident at the Al Aqsa Mosque that the Muslim countries decided to form an international organization, though many international organisations were already in existence floated by many Muslim rulers to serve their national interests. The institution that came into being after the Rabat Conference held in the aftermath of the Al Aqsa Mosque incident in late 1969 was called the Organisation of Islamic Conference (OIC). The unity of the Islamic world has been a dream of the Muslims for a long time however, in the modern age when the world is divided into sovereign nation states each of which has its own interests common perceptions of developments and common actions is almost impossible. The OIC is divided between the oil rich Arab states like Saudi and the poor Muslim countries like Bangladesh and Sudan etc., and the former have close linkages with the Western countries. The OIC has not been able to either promote unity of action among the member Muslim states nor resolve any of the major issues facing the Muslim world. Even during the Iraqi action could only content itself with a call for the ceasefire. It could not even persuade some of the Muslim rulers who otherwise pose as guardians of the Muslim Ummah not to cooperate with the American armed forces, for example, Qatar hosted the US Central Command HQ. It was because of this weakness that the United States could use its leverage within the ruling groups of most of the OIC countries and force them to cooperate with its aggression against any country. During the first Gulf war 12 of the 21 Arab countries led by the Saudi Kingdom had joined the United States in bringing Iraq to its knees.

In the aftermath of the 9/11 terrorist attack on the New York Trade Towers the United States had declared war against terrorism with calls to the world that they must join the international coalition against terrorism and President Bush's famous "you are with us or against us". The Taliban leaders in Afghanistan were given ultimatum by Washington to hand over Osama bin Laden who had been declared responsible for the terrorist attacks against the United States. Pakistan's Gen. Musharraf had also been forced to jettison the Taliban and join the American bandwagon against Afghanistan. Within two months the United States launched massive air attacks on Afghanistan. There was little sympathy for the Taliban among the people of the Muslim world. Their rigid and extraordinary orthodox interpretation of Islam relating to religious rituals, atrocious restrictions on the rights of women, ban on music and entertainment of all kinds and lastly the demolition of the rare Bamyan Buddhas in defiance of massive outcry throughout the world had outraged the Muslim world. It was obvious from day one that the Taliban regime was no match against the superpower. However, during the massive air attacks on Afghanistan thousands of the innocent Afghans were also killed and injured who had possibly no hand in the activities of the Taliban and they might as well have been victims of the Taliban's repressive regime. The people in the Muslim world had no sympathy for the Taliban but they could not approve of the killing of innocent people. Many people believed that the guilt of Osama bin Laden in the terrorist attacks in New York had not been proved and, therefore, killing of so many innocent people was nothing but brutal massacre. The American policy in Afghanistan after the destruction of the Taliban regime also has not won much appreciation in the region. Though a formal government headed by Karzai has been placed in Kabul yet it does not have either legitimacy or control over the country. The remnants of the Taliban are regrouping while warlords are back to their old game of perpetual infighting. The United States forces have not been able to apprehend either Osama bin Laden or the Taliban supremo Mulla Omer. Thus, the main objective of international alliance against terrorism of bringing Osama bin Laden to book has not been fulfilled till date.

It was in this background that Washington began to turn its attention to Saddam Hussein. A massive propaganda campaign was unleashed against Saddam Hussein which was joined in by the Prime Minister of Great Britain. The war against terrorism had not been finally won and now President Bush was trying to make the people believe that Saddam regime was also responsible for terrorism, it was claimed that it had some linkages with the Al Qaeda for which no evidence was adduced and none has been found so far.

But this time it was not a replay of the Gulf War in 1990 when Washington was able to put together an alliance of 28 nations to liberate Kuwait from the Iraqi occupation. This time Arab states were reluctant to be seen as a part of any alliance for the US-led military action against Iraq. Unlike 12 years ago, the international alliance against terrorism could expect military support from no more than two or three countries. Analysts said that it was obvious that Kuwait would certainly help but the Turks would go along only if they were given enough reward. Eventually, the major obstacle was the Turkish Parliament which refused to allow 60 thousand of US army to transit through its territory on its way to Northern Iraq. On the other hand also, no Arab leader was willing to lift a finger to help the Iraqi leader, Saddam Hussein. The Arab leaders' dilemma was if they supported the US they would have to go against the sentiments of their own people. They could not also afford to antagonize the Americans either. They all wanted Saddam Husseain to be removed but they themselves wanted no part in that endeavour. In 1990 Iraq's invasion of Kuwait divided the Arab world. More than half of the members of the Arab League had joined the US–led attack on Iraq. Arab contingent against Saddam then was led by the Saudi Armed forces and that of Egypt.

Yemen, Jordan and Tunisia and the PLO had opposed the American-led coalition at that time. King Husain of Jordan and Yasser Arafat had attempted to bring about peaceful and Arab solution of the problem. They were accused then of being pro-Saddam and appeasers by the West and the Arab supporters of the anti-Saddam Arab leaders.

The events of 9/11 have changed the situation in the Arab world since then. Yemen, Jordan, and Mr. Arafat were taking a different approach this time. Yemen had faced an Al Qaeda terrorist attack on a US naval ship in the Aden harbour in 1998.Later it had agreed to the US forces taking action against the Al Qaeda members in its territory. Recently Yemen agreed to allow in some US forces to root out Al Qaeda members from its territory. King Abdullah of Jordan was also opposed to terrorism and supported the US anti-terrorist campaign. But he was against any attack on Iraq because he like many others believed an attack on Iraq would be disastrous for the entire region. According to him it would disturb the security and stability of the region. Most Arabs leaders agreed with him and were apprehensive that an attack on Iraq would fuel anti-American sentiment which was running high because of Washington's failure to curb Israel's attacks against the Palestinians. American diplomacy, they say, should focus on bringing peace to the Middle East rather than attempting to drum up support for a new war against Iraq. Middle East observers pointed out that the situation was different this time as compared to 1990 as Iraq had not invaded any other country but the Arab people saw Iraqi people suffering, the country on its knees. There was widespread anger among the people in the region about the double standards of the US policy particularly in regard to Israel. While Washington was demanding that Iraq comply with all the UN resolutions while Israel for decades has ignored others demanding its withdrawal from occupied Arab lands. It was also alleged the US remained silent on Israel's nuclear stockpile while focusing solely on Iraq's suspected pursuit of weapons of mass destruction. It was clear most Arab leaders would offer grudging support to the US for changing the regime in Iraq and most did not want to be seen as being in any way implicated in it. They wanted it to be done as quickly as possible. Their opposition to the invasion of Iraq by the United States and allies was only meant for public consumption.

Some of the radical Arab countries which had in 1990 sent troops to join the American coalition had now a different view of the situation as they had good relations with Iraq. In any case both Syria and Libya have been accused by Washington of sponsoring terrorism and charged of even being members of the evil empire and they could not now help the US in bringing down an Arab regime. Some of the UAE countries like Bahrain and Qatar, are dependent on the Iraqi oil yet they supported by the US by offering facilities for the American fleet and the U.S. military base in Qatar served as the command center for the US military operations during the war.

There is no doubt that the popular opinion in the Muslim world was overwhelmingly against American aggression against Iraq. This was not necessarily in favour of Saddam Hussein and his autocratic regime. It was reported that in spite of the fact that Turkey's interests lay in supporting the United States and the regime wanted writing off of their US $ 5 billion in return for their support to the US. Later the country's parliament refused to cooperate with American military operations. It was reported that 90 per cent of public opinion in the country was against the American attack on Iraq. A massive rally had been held in Rabat (Morocco) as early as January this year against the possible war in Iraq. Not only that the Al Azhar, one of the great centres of Islamic learning had passed a Fatwa against the war and leading Islamic intellectuals in Cairo had condemned the threats of war against Iraq. There were protest demonstrations in large cities in almost all the countries in the Muslim world against American designs in Iraq. Massive marches had been organised protesting against war against Iraq in Europe and the United States. Once the war had begun the 15th conference of the OIC had condemned the American occupation of Iraq. Earlier, the Secretary General of OIC had called for the immediate cessation of the war against Iraq.

Iraq had no chance of putting up a respectable resistance against the massive gigantic force mobilized by the United States and UK against Saddam Hussein's ramshackle rag tag armed forces. Iraq has been conquered by the Anglo-American armies. All claims that Iraqis were waiting to be liberated have been belied. It was expected that the Shia population would welcome the American has also not materialized. Autocratic repressive regime has been replaced by an equally oppressive foreign regime. Slowly the resistance is gathering momentum. No weapons of mass destruction have been found nor any nuclear weapons discovered which were claimed to be the reason for the pre-emptive military operation. The conquest of Iraq ushers in a new era of neo-colonisation and hegemony of a superpower in the region. The peace and stability of the states in the region which in any case were doubtful has been shattered. New radical forces of extremism and fundamentalism which have been unleashed would be difficult to control.

15

The US Invasion of Iraq and the Muslim World

A K Pasha

Since the end of the II World War the US came to have close ties with a number of Muslim countries like Turkey, Pakistan, Saudi Arabia, Iran, Jordan and many others. When Britain, France and Israel invaded Egypt in 1956, the US opposed the war and later called for Israeli withdrawal from Sinai. The US at the same time came to have conflictual ties with Nasser's Egypt after Suez War. It overthrew the Mossadeq government in Iran in 1953, and supported Israel in the 1967 war which led to the defeat of Egypt, Syria and Jordan. The US could not prevent the division of Pakistan which affected its credibility in the Muslim world. It had to face Arab oil embargo in 1973 for supporting Israel. However the overthrow of the Shah of Iran by Khomeini in 1979 was a turning point in its policy towards the Muslim World. Soon the Soviet military intervention in Afghanistan provided an opportunity to assert its influence in the Muslim world by mobilizing support for Jihad against Moscow with the help of Pakistan, Saudi Arabia and other Muslim states. Soon it also encouraged Iraq's Saddam Hussein to invade Iran and sustained the 8 year Iran-Iraq war. When Israel bombed the Iraqi Osirak nuclear reactor in 1981, it suited US policy which was to weaken both Iran and Iraq. Both UK and US had also disapproved Iraqi nationalization of its oil companies in 1972. Severely weakened due to the terrible losses in its war with Iran, Saddam

Hussein expected the US and GCC states to bail him out of his predicament. Instead the reverse happened. Not only the US abandoned Saddam Hussein but GCC states overproduced oil which hurt Iraq. The result was Iraqi invasion of Kuwait as a bargaining chip to achieve Saddam's demands - the waving of loans and a curb on the GCC oil production.[1] Although US support to Israeli invasion of Lebanon in 1982 and US naval bombardment of Lebanon in 1982-83, US attack on Libya in 1986 and also its efforts to isolate PLO had undermined US position in the Muslim world but with Egypt, Turkey, Morocco, Pakistan, GCC states, Syria and others on its side the US mobilized a coalition to liberate Kuwait from Iraqi occupation in 1990-91. It is well known that the US aborted all peaceful means to get Iraq out of Kuwait. Many Arabs are convinced that US decision to go to war against Iraq in 1991 was in fact a "deliberate choice" aimed at crippling Iraq's military and economic infrastructure. The US had grown apprehensive over the emergence of Iraqi military power coupled with Iraqi efforts at modernization including the creation of an impressive infrastructure and an industrial and technological base. Iraq achieved all this despite its eight year long ruinous war with Iran. Soon after Iraq's invasion of Kuwait, US Secretary of Defense wanted to know from his department about Iraq and its capability. "They are formidable", he was told. "They have a capable military and a developed industrial base. They are modern for a third world country. They are nationalistic. They are dangerous".[2] Saddam Hussein's August 12, 1990 linkage theory which demanded Israel's withdrawal from Occupied Arab Territories not only annoyed the US but it exposed its double standards. No wonder Israel equally feared Iraq and its capability. In fact, the destruction of Iraq's military capability and its advanced infrastructure has clearly served Israeli aims as well as US interests. Iraq's military capability had posed a strategic threat to Israel's domination in the area. It is interesting to remember that the OIC, Arab League and GCC had failed to prevent the Iran-Iraq war, US war on Iraq in 1991 and the UN sanctions on Iraq since 1990.

Since 1991 the USA despite its best efforts, using the UN sanctions, no fly zones in north and south of Iraq, UN inspectors, almost daily bombings, support to Iraqi National Congress and other anti-regimes forces and several failed coup attempts failed to dislodge Saddam Hussein. In October 1998 the US Congress enacted the Iraq Liberation Act to replace Saddam Hussein. A sum of $ 97 million was allocated for carrying out the task through covert operations. Richard Hass - a member of the National Security Council and special assistant to the President under the elder Bush, (soon to be appointed director of policy planning in the State Department of George W. Bush - with additional responsibilities as US coordinator of policy for the future of Afghanistan) pointed out in his book *Intervention,* that regime change often can only be accomplished through a full scale military invasion leaving the conquered nation in ruins and necessitating subsequent "nation-building" . "It is difficult to target specific individuals with military force... US efforts to use force to bring about changes in political leadership failed in the cases of Qaddafi in Libya, Saddam in Iraq and Aideed in Somalia. Force can create a context in which political change is more likely, but without extraordinary intelligence and more than a little good fortune, force by itself is unlikely to bring about specific political changes. The only way to increase the likelihood of such change is through highly intrusive forms of intervention, such as nation-building, which involves first eliminating all opposition and then engaging in an occupation that allows for substantial engineering of another society.[3]

It is interesting to note that an arch imperialist group called the Project for the New American Century (PNAC) was established with Dick Cheney, Donald Rumsfeld, Frank J. Gaffney, Paul Wolfowitz, George W. Bush's younger brother Jeb and Lewis Libby (Cheney's Chief of Staff). This group brought out a document in September 2000 which called for the creation of a 'global Pax Americana' and which also called for an attack on Iraq to secure "regime change" even before Bush took power in January 2001. The group also called for US global military supremacy and the use of pre-emptive military force to defeat any challenges to that supremacy. The September 11, 2001 attacks on WTC and Pentagon enabled the Bush administration to declare war on International Terrorism. The doctrine pushed by Dick Cheney and others in the PNAC had no serious takers, but after September 11, 2001, "Cheney and his supporters and Ariel Sharon, are not being given the war they have desired so passionately, so obsessively over a dozen years to date". The US war on International terrorism led to the attack on Afghanistan and ouster of Taliban government. The Axis of Evil' speech of George W. Bush on January 29, 2002 identifying Iran, Iraq and North Korea, was a clear signal to Baghdad about the impending focus on Iraqi WMD. With legal and moral principles abandoned, the debate focused on US "national interest" and its ability to use force to punish its enemies. The PNAC document supported a blue– print for maintaining global US pre-eminence, precluding the rise of a great power rival and shaping the International security order in line with American principles and interests. This 'American grand strategy must be advanced for 'as far into the future as possible'. It also calls for the US to 'fight and decisively win multiple, simultaneous major theater wars' as a 'core mission'. The Report "Rebuilding America's Defenses": Strategy, Forces and Resources for a New Century" also showed Bush's cabinet intended to take military control of the Gulf region whether or not Saddam Hussein was in power. It said: "The US had for decades sought to play a more permanent role in Gulf regional security. While the unresolved conflict with Iraq provides the immediate justification, the need for a substantial American force presence in the Gulf transcends the issue of the regime of Saddam Hussein."[4] No wonder the US became more strident in its demands for the return of UN inspectors to Iraq. Due to persistent pressure and lobbying from the US, the UNSCR 1441 was adopted in November 2002 allowing for stricter time-bound inspections of Iraq. As Rolf Ekeus admitted: "There is no doubt that the Americans wanted to influence inspections to further certain fundamental US interests".[5] The UN weapons inspections were used as a tool of provocation, spying and assassination. The UN inspectors led by Hans Blix went to Iraq to search for WMD. More than 800 inspections on more than 400 sites were done. They found nothing and this was duly reported to the UNSC in three reports. The US continued to insist that Iraq was not revealing its chemical, biological and other WMD. From the very outset, it was clear the US was not in favour of giving the UN inspectors enough time to peacefully disarm Iraq. Hans Blix and head of IAEA wanted three more months to complete the inspections and certify that if Iraq didn't have weapons - UN sanctions could be lifted.[6]

US interest in prolonging UN sanctions on Iraq was among other reasons to prevent foreign investments in Iraq as also rehabilitation of the country's oil industry. Thus UN sanctions became an important instrument for the US to prevent other powers from getting a foothold in Iraq. As *Business Week Online* in late January 2003 expressed the economic benefits to be derived from a US invasion of Iraq : "Since the US military would control Iraq's oil and gas deposits for some time, US companies could be in line for a lucrative slice of the business. They may snag drilling rights too". Along with Iranian, Libyan oil, the Iraqi oil was outside the influence of the US. The US aim is to make Iraq conform to the dominant requirements of the capitalist world economy, which include opening up its resources to more extensive exploitation.[7] Since the Gulf region is the main energy producing region in the world, for US strategic power Iraq is absolutely central to it. Iraq's oil resources are vast and as cheap to extract as Saudi oil. To control Iraq is to be in a very strong position to determine the price and production levels, not too high, not too low, to split OPEC and to use this power in US global strategy. It is not so much with US access to it as it does have to do with actual physical control of oil. Since no geological survey has been conducted in Iraq since the 1970's, experts believe that the proven resources underestimate the countrys' actual oil wealth, which could be as large as 250 billion barrels. Three decades of political instability and war have kept Iraq from developing 55 of its 70 proven oil fields. Eight of these fields could harbor more than a billion barrels each of "easy oil" which is close to the surface and inexpensive to extract. As Gerald Butt, Gulf editor of *MEES* put it: "There is nothing like it anywhere else in the world. It's the big prize". Thus from the US oil interests point of view, the UN sanctions were seen as double edged sword: even as they kept international competition temporarily at bay, they precluded the exploitation of oil resources with an estimated value of several trillion dollars. The war against Saddam Hussein was intended among other things, to resolve this contradiction.[8] No wonder Ahmed Chalabi in October 2002 told the *Washington Post*: "American Companies will have a big shot at Iraqi oil". The US national energy plan - the Cheney Report–released in early May 2001 calls for a major increase in US engagement in regions such as the Persian Gulf in order to secure future oil to supplies.[9] That is a deeper economic struggle that the US is waging to preserve its economic supremacy in the world. It is war between Euro and US dollar and Iraq has become the military beachhead. As Australian economist Geoffrey Heard, said: "The war in Iraq is actually the US and Europe going head to head on economic leadership of the world". Since Iraq started at France's persuasion to trade in Euros for its oil from 1999 replacing US dollar, other states like Iran, Russia and Venezuela also started thinking of switching over to Euro from dollar for their oil trade. US had to nip this in the bud as the dollars' grip on oil trading and consequently on world trade in general, was under serious threat. Heard observed, "If America did not stamp on this immediately, the economic Bush-fire could rapidly be fanned into a wild fire capable of consuming the US economy and its dominance of world trade". The war over Iraq may be a war for oil but at a deeper level, it is also a war for the defense of the continued control of the world oil economy through the US dollar.[10] Dick Cheney and his supporters persuaded George W. Bush that *Operation Iraqi Freedom* would unleash the "explosion of joy" and Iraqis would greet the US liberating the Iraqi people from the tyrannical regime of Saddam Hussein. Three weeks of "shock and awe" carpet bombing and pushed by nearly 1.5 lakh US soldiers led to massive civilian casualities on the Iraqi side. But majority of Iraqis see US forces as an occupation army rather than as liberators.

The mounting civilian deaths during and after the war is leading to growing opposition world wide especially in the Muslim countries, to continued occupation of Iraq by the US. President Hosni Mubarak of Egypt, Saudi leaders and other pro-US Arab Muslim leaders from Bahrain, Qatar, Kuwait, UAE, Oman, Jordan, Morocco, Pakistan feel vulnerable due to their support to US led invasion of Iraq. Since the US forces have not found WMD so far, this raises a question mark over the motives behind Operation Iraqi Freedom. The US got the UNSC remove sanctions on Iraq without a report from UN inspectors that Iraq was WMD free. The fact of the matter is there are very few buyers for US accusations about WMD in Iraq. Moreover, the US wants to restrict the UN role primarily to humanitarian tasks, while Washington wants to have full say in the new Iraqi set up. However the OIC states would like the UN to play a lead role in the transitional arrangements leading to Iraqi elections and thus circumscribe the role of the occupying power. The US intends to stay longer in Iraq with the help of Iraqi exiles and its military presence. No wonder it is opposed to French calls for immediate transfer of power to the Iraqis.

The fall of Baghdad to US forces on April 9, 2003 with little resistance from the Iraqi forces and the subsequent breakdown of law and order, large scale looting, and burning of ministries, national archives/library, museums, public and private houses and even hospitals, indicates the scale of disorder, which has descended on Iraq. US soldiers were for the most part mute spectators to the widespread loot and arson. Initially the only thing they safeguarded was the oil ministry in Baghdad and the oil fields/installations in Rumailayah area and in Mosul and Kirkuk, clearly revealing their objectives behind the invasion. The lack of electricity (during the peak of summer with day temperatures over 40 degrees C) and water supply, together with severe shortages of food and medicine and inadequate facilities at several hospitals to treat the mounting number of civilians injured in attacks after the war ended, led to widespread demands for withdrawal of US forces from the Baghdad and other areas. In fact there have been daily demonstrations on these issues together with lack of job opportunities. People have been openly opposing the continued presence of American troops in the country and also their control over the oil industry. The Shia ulemas were the first to mobilize masses on the issue of continued presence of US forces. The common slogans were "Leave our country, we want peace", "No Bush, No Saddam, Yes Yes to Islam", "No Shias, No Sunnis, Yes Yes to United Islam". The Imam of Al Aadhamiya mosque in Baghdad, Ahmed at Kubaisi, whose mosque was bombed, said the US invaded Iraq to defend Israel. He led thousands of demonstrators in Baghdad who shouted: "No to America, No to Secular State, Yes to Islamic State", we reject American hegemony", "We are Sunni and Shia brothers, we will not sell this nation". They also shouted "Iraq's oil for the Iraqi people". [11]

Paul Bremer, the US civil administrator has appointed 25–member Iraqi Governing Council (GC) where Iraqi exiles like Ahmad Chalabi, [who promised to recognize Israel in three months] Adnan Paschachi and others including Sunnis, Shias, Kurds, Christians, women have been given representation. One of the women members of the GC was killed in September 2003 revealing the precarious law and order issue in Iraq. This should be seen in conjunction with the attacks on UN headquarters in Baghdad, killing of Ayatollah Hakim Bakr and daily killing of US soldiers and Iraqi civilians. The lack of security and instability in Iraq is not only due to lack of facilities like power, food, jobs, hospitals so on but also due to US policy to purge the system of the Baath Party members and also such Baathist members from policy, paramilitary, bureaucracy, universities and other structures of state. The process of witch hunting has begun with the help of Iraqi exiles, who are now wielding enormous power and influence, leading to widespread domestic resentment. The reconstruction process has been initiated by the US through US companies and this is breeding corruption and tainting the US administration. There are constant reports, which suggest that the US intends to stay in Iraq for several years and will continue to use Iraqi military air bases all over Iraq. The statements from US President George Bush and UK Prime Minister Tony Blair that "the Coalition forces will not stay in Iraq a day longer than necessary", have gone with the wind, although they were quoted in *Washington Times* and *New York Times* recently that US troops would stay in Iraq for an indefinite period. Although due to global pressure, US and UK have been talking about a constitution, elections, transfer of sovereignty to Iraqi people so on, but top US, British diplomats leading reconstruction efforts are of the view that the "US would remain in charge of Iraq for an indefinite period".[12] There are conflicting estimates of the cost of reconstruction of Iraq ranging from $ 20 billion to $ 200 billion out of Iraqi oil revenues. While the US is issuing billions of dollars worth of contracts in favor of US companies and sometimes to companies from the countries of the so-called "coalition of the willing", it has not been able to win the "hearts and minds" of Iraqi people. Throughout the world people have grave doubts about the legitimacy of the US led war and occupation of Iraq. The "liberators" became an occupying force with "Authority", blessed by the UNSC Resolution 1483 since May 22, 2003. Paul Bremer, the American "Pasha" encouraged the Governing Council over which he has the right to veto, to open Iraq and its industries for 100% private ownership/participation except in oil and mineral resources. Even before UNSCR 1483, the invading forces had already signed the ownership charter.[13] Most Iraqis/Arabs look at US as having issued itself a property ownership situation and has become the landlord of Iraq. Oil rich Iraq with a 7000 year old civilization appears to have become an American asset. Appropriating the wealth of Iraq is not as easy as the US believes. As Saudi foreign minister, Prince Saud al Faisal, said, "The Iraqi people should administer and govern their country by themselves and any exploitation of their natural resources should be in conformity with the will of the legitimate Iraqi government and its people. If what they (US) intend is the exploitation of Iraqi oil, it will not have any legitimate basis". [14]

The Iraqi resistance to US occupation has not only intensified since the fall of Baghdad but the US has confirmed that from being sporadic attacks by the remnants of the Old Baathist elements, a full scale guerilla warfare and now a well organized sophisticated resistance is going on against US forces. Despite the arrests and killings of the Baathist leadership, the Iraqi people have not buckled to US dictates and it is unlikely they will meekly surrender to US led occupation of their country. Not only opposition to US forces is widespread but daily attacks and killings of US forces is taking place in villages, towns and the streets of Baghdad and other cities. Not only the Iraqis want the withdrawal of US forces from Iraq immediately, Iraq's neighbours, meeting at the level of foreign ministers in Riyadh, (April 2003) Saudi Arabia, also called for early withdrawal of the occupation forces from Iraq as well as for respecting Iraq's territorial integrity. The states who took part in the meeting were Iran, Turkey, Jordan, Syria, Saudi Arabia, Egypt, Bahrain and others. Flush with quick victory over Iraq the US has started training its guns on Syria and Iran. US Defence Secretary Donald Rumsfeld, accused Syria of sending military equipment to Iraq and Iran of sending military personnel into Iraq. He also warned Syria against meddling in Iraqi affairs. John Bolton recently (September 2003) addressing the US Congress accused Syria of not cooperating in combating terrorism and that it was seeking chemical, biological and other WMD. US secretary of State Colin Powell also confirmed Washington's strict policy toward Syria, before the AIPAC–a Zionist organization. The signals made about the possibility of targeting Syria indicate that American reiterations - about not dividing the region and creating political disorder and chaos in it - are mere lies. They also mean that the battle in Iraq aims at fulfilling Israel's objectives by weakening Syria and leaving the Palestinians to face a deadlock. By these machinations and accusations Israel aims at drawing the British,

Americans and the Arabs into a bloody war while it reaps the gains, concludes Al Watan.[15]

If anti-American sentiments sweeping the Islamic world are not neutralized soon by way of quick US withdrawal from Iraq, then the US invasion and occupation, undoubtedly seen as illegal, unjust and unnecessary, would fuel deeper anti-US feelings and would lead to wider complications for the US. Since the US justified the invasion of Iraq as speaking of the 'will of the people' but the will of the people in Palestine has, for decades, meant little more than the rubble of Palestine.[16] Throughout the Muslim world people know that only the US could apply effective pressure on Israel to withdraw from Palestinian lands so that the injustices against the Palestinians could be rectified. Muslims worldwide are aware of the fact that there are numerous UN resolutions, which clearly define Israel's occupation of the West Bank, Gaza Strip, and East Jerusalem as illegal. Yet the US gives Israel 40 per cent of all US foreign aid–around $ 3.5 billion annually, i.e., roughly $ 500 per Israeli citizen. In addition, the US gives loans to build new Israeli settlements on Palestinian land and also supplies planes and helicopter gunships, which are used to kill Palestinians. Not only the US insisted on UN sanctions against Iraq (which killed millions of Iraqi people) because of alleged violations by Iraq of UNSCR but supports Israel (by aid and veto at UN) when it has violated UNSCR 242 and several other UN resolutions for over 35 years. The war against Afghans, Iraqis and Palestinians and other Muslims is seen as US hatred against Muslims and their own hatred of US emerges from this harsh reality.[17]

Due to non-resolution of the Palestine-Israeli Conflict, the US could become the target of suicide attacks and terrorism on a much larger scale. US double standards, with war and occupation of Iraq and a soft approach towards Israeli occupation and repression on the Palestinians, would hurt US interests. Although Tony Blair and Jack Straw accepted "double standards" on Palestine and understood the Arab concern, only quick progress towards establishing a Palestine state and an end to Israeli oppression is wanted. Straw said: "There is a real concern too that the West has been guilty of double standards - on the one hand saying the UN Security Council Resolutions on Iraq must be implemented, on the other hand, sometimes appearing rather quixotic over the implementation of resolutions about Israel and Palestine."[18] Asked if he would plead guilty to double standards, Straw said, "To a degree yes... and we're going to deal with it. Its our responsibility, yes, to deal with Iraq but also, yes, to deal with the Israel–Palestine crisis". Straw said, citing UN resolutions calling for two independent states, that he felt "angry and upset" at the Israelis. Britain, he told the BBC, is "100 per cent committed" to the establishment of a viable Palestinian state with its capital in Jerusalem, based on UNSCR 242, the 1967 borders, the end of Jewish settlements, and a solution of the Palestinian refugee problem." Although a peace Road Map has been prepared by the Quartet - the UN, US, ED, Russia which calls for the creation of an independent Palestinian state by 2005, but due to Israeli objections and divisions within the Palestinian leadership, the Road Map has become a non-starter. What is required is clear mechanism to implement what is agreed upon unlike the Oslo Accord which was repudiated by Israel as it had called for the creation of a Palestinian state by May 1999. Israel has always refused to implement the agreed provisions as it desires to retain major part of West Bank, Gaza Strip and East Jerusalem. If the US continues to express lack of seriousness on their issues and tolerates Israel's massacre of Palestinians, including wholesale destruction of every vestige of Palestinian statehood, its targeted murders of Palestinian leaders, house demolitions settlements building, by pass roads, closures, curfews and daily humiliation of Palestinians, the world would soon call for sanctions on Israel like the UN did on Iraq. The fence being built by Israel on West Bank encroaching the Palestinian land shows Israeli desire for Palestinian territory. The time has come for US to put pressure on Israel to withdraw from all occupied Arab lands. Anti-American sentiments in the Muslim world have reached dangerous levels. The Muslim world is divided on the issue of Iraq and this has led to turmoil, ferment and uprising in many parts of the Muslin world. But one has also to realize the strange dichotomy in the Muslim world. Most Muslim rulers are pro-US and some are non-aligned. The Palestinians and other affected Muslims in Iraq, Afghanistan elsewhere hate America for not supporting their cause and not restraining Israel but Arab and Muslim rulers from Kuwait, Egypt, Saudi Arabia, Pakistan and others thank the Americans for supporting this cause. In fact such regimes are kept in power with US assistance and have little reason to dislike the US. "It is those who see themselves, for whatever reason, as victims of American power and policies who have real grudge."[19] But the Muslims look upon such rulers as puppets of the US as also anti-democratic in nature. Due to lack of political freedom and authoritarian rule, Islamic groups are growing and are opposed to puppet Muslim rulers who are subservient to US policies. The Muslim rulers promise their citizens democratic reforms, elections and greater role for NGO's and civil society. But the elections are invariably manipulated and rigged so as to ensure the victory of those in power. The other extreme instance is of Algeria where the military prevented the Islamic groups from forming the government. According to one writer: "For too long the USA has supported political and ideological causes and backed authoritarian regimes in Muslim countries which have brought misery, degradation and humiliation to many across the Muslim domain". [20] Although the Saudi Crown Prince Abdullah is credited having made the statement: "It is time for the US and Saudi Arabia to look at their separate interests. Those governments that don't feel the pulse of their people and respond to it will suffer the same fate as the Shah of Iran", but the US occupation of Iraq and Israeli occupation of Palestine has prompted key US allies like Egypt and Saudi Arabia to keep a low profile during the OIC and Arab League deliberations [on Palestine and Iraq] and proceedings in the face of strident calls for Jihad from some quarters. Even though Muslim public opinion would support call for punitive measures against Israel if collectively agreed at OIC meetings but no such measures are suggested due to fear from the US. Even an international protection force for the Palestinians is not taken up seriously with the US.[21]

The Iranian foreign minister, Ali Akbar Velayati, had deep distrust of the OIC when he said: "We do not accept the current configuration of the OIC and have a fundamental objection to the way it works," but Iran's President Khatami reminded the delegates to the eighth OIC summit: "There is no problem which cannot be solved through understanding and fraternity, and the OIC is the most suitable base for friendship, fraternity and resolving of the existing indignation and disputes".[22] It is this contradictory policy and the conflicting pulls and pressures from within the Muslim World the US was able to take advantage and occupy Iraq. If it were not for the silence of Iran, Turkey, Syria and support from Kuwait, Saudi Arabia, Qatar, Bahrain, UAE, Oman, Jordan, Egypt, Morocco and others, it would not have been possible for the US to strangle Iraq under UN sanctions for nearly 13 years and bomb daily under the guise of maintaining no fly zones in the north and south of Iraq and eventually invade and occupy a Muslim country. The UN Humanitarian Coordinator in Iraq resigned in 1998 by saying: "we are in the process of destroying an entire society. It is as simple and terrifying as that. It is illegal and immoral." Two years later as the Iraqi death toll crossed a million he would exclaim: "There's no better word I can think of Genocide is taking place right now, in Iraqi cities. To say it's a passive thing is not correct. It's an active policy".[23]

So if Muslims support the Iraqis and Palestinians against US and Israel, the "Muslim rage" is seen as "nothing short of the age-old Muslim craze". The Jewish scholar Bernard Lewis speaks of an alleged global resuscitation of Islamic confrontation by reference to the generic, or perhaps genetic, aberrance of the "Muslim" psyche. Alerting to the psycho-pathology of the violent Other in all-but-unwholesome formulations, the diagnosis is disturbing: "Today much of the Muslim world is again seized by an intense and violent- resentment of the West... .Why?..It should by now be clear that we are facing a mood and a movement far transcending the level of issues and policies and the governments that pursue them. This is no less than a clash of civilizations–the perhaps irrational but surely historic reaction of an ancient rival against our Judeo-Christian heritage, our secular present, and the worldwide expansion of both."[24] Since September 11, 2001 events in the US and stray attacks on US interests since then, the US-Israeli [partly West and its backers] propaganda machine has targeted Muslims worldwide in the war on terrorism. As Doris Lessing wrote to Granta magazine: the Americans after the events of 11 September, "have become touchy, and ready to break off relations with accusations of hard–heartedness". Gripped by patriotic fever, Americans see themselves "as unique, alone, misunderstood, beleaguered, and they see any criticism as treachery." [25] Harold Pinter, a celebrated playwright and actor was even more scathing. He said the US has "exercised sustained, systematic, remorseless and quite clinical manipulation of power worldwide, while masquerading as a force for universal good. It is arrogant, indifferent, contemptuous of International Law, both dismissive and manipulative of the UN: this is now the most dangerous power the world has ever known- the authentic "rogue state", but a "rogue state" of colossal military and economic might. There is profound revulsion and disgust with the manifestation of US power". [26]

The need and justification to invade Afghanistan, Iraq and the determination to contain terrorism before it repeats September 11 events, the US has launched an unlimited war on terrorism and pre–emptive or preventive war is legitimized and so far Muslim societies have borne the brunt. Under the circumstances threats from Muslims and Islamic world are projected as Islam's international role and that Islam has become a global contender and so on. No wonder Islam's news value has increased. As Edward Said observed: "For the general public in America and Europe today, Islam is "news" of a particularly unpleasant sort. The media, the government, the geopolitical strategists, and - although they are marginal to the culture at large–the academic experts on Islam are all in concert: Islam is a threat to Western civilization". [27]

Those who are familiar with European history would know the background why the US looks at the threats from some Muslim countries which need to be eliminated. European experience of its "hot war" with Islam is one major factor. According to one writer European identity has been shaped and defined in opposition to other people, especially the Muslims, which is seen as vilified and demonized enemy. European experiences with Islam were transferred to America. "These old and familiar assumptions are not history. They operate today in the unthinking reflexes, ideas and attitudes of hyper-imperialism. They are embodied in American rhetoric and policy. They are recycled in every intervention America has made in the affairs of other countries".[28]

The US policy makers had hoped to achieve quick victory over Iraq and then to reorder the map in the strategically important Gulf region, but due to mounting resistance in Iraq, the US is now facing new and entirely unexpected challenges to its objectives. And lack of aid and sniping from France, Germany, Russia and also lack of expected help from others like Turkey, Pakistan, India and others is dragging the US deeper and deeper into the Arabian deserts and the largely unfamiliar terrain. The US had unique and unprecedented goodwill after Sept. 11 events throughout the world including most Islamic states, but this has been dissipated fairly quickly. The US now has to contend with anger and hatred in the Muslim world due to its double standards and dubious policies concerning Iraq and Palestine. Despite worldwide criticism and. growing domestic opposition the shortsighted Bush administration with its war mongers led by Cheney are in no mood to listen to saner voices from any quarter. As Amit Chaudhuri wrote: " Only the American public can put pressure on, and change, the aberrant policy: but the American public's main source of information about its country's foreign policy is Hollywood with its images of terror and frightening rhetoric of 'good' and 'evil'".[29]

The USA may be an open society, but it is also a closed circle. The Americans don't care very much for the rest of the world. They care about themselves and their standard of living. We have to find answers as to why Americans tend towards an insidious distrust of others, and show such neglect for the needs, desires and hopes of the rest of the world?[30] The Iraqis, Palestinians, and Afghans are not the only ones. Others are also on the firing line and unfortunately most are in the Muslim world if we take US threats to Iran and Syria as next on this road to taste American wrath supported eagerly by the Israelis who also tend to benefit greatly from such events.

References

1. A.K. Pasha, *The Gulf in Turmoil* (New Delhi: Lancers Books, 1992) pp. 1-49 and 70-126; see also Douglas A. Borer," Inverse engagement : Lessons from 45-Iraq Relations, 1982-1990. *Parameters* Vol. 33, No.2, Summer, 2003, pp. 51-65

2. A.K. Pasha, *Contemporary Gulf: State Society. Economy and Foreign Policy* (New Delhi: Detente Publications, 1999) pp. 261–263; Jerome Slater, Ideology vs. The national Interest: Bush, Sharon and US Policy in the Israeli - Palestinian Conflict, *Security Studies*. Vol. 12 No. 1, autumn 2002, pp. 164-206.

3. John Bellamy Foster, "Imperial America and War", *Analytical Monthly Review*, Vol. 1, No. 2, May 2003, pp. 8-9, A. Bogaturov, "The Iraqi Crisis and the Imposed Consensus Strategy", *International Affairs* (Moscow), Vol. 49, No. 2, 2003, pp. 83-91.

4 Ibid., p. 49; David Hastings Duna, "Myths, motivations and misunderestimations : The Bush Administration and Iraq", *International Affairs* (London), Vol. 79, No.2, 2003, pp. 279-97.

5. Ibid., p. 45; Michael J. Glennon, "Why the Security Council Failed", *Foreign Affairs*, May-June 2003, Vo1.82, No. 3, p. 16-35.

6. A.K. Pasha, *Iraq: Sanctions and Wars* (New Delhi: Sterling Publishers, 2003) p. 120.

7. Foster, no. 3, p. 8; see also Daniel Neep, "The Impact of War in Iraq", *Rusi Journal,* April 2003.

8. Ibid., p. 47; see also Adeed Dawisha and Karen Dawisha, "How to build a democratic Iraq", *Foreign Affairs,* May-June, Vol. 82, No. 3, 2003, pp. 36-50.

9. Ibid., p. 49; Sukumar Muralidharan, "Iraq and Crisis of the US Imperium: of dollars hegemony, deft and the English language", *Social Scientist,* Vol. 31, No. 53-54, March-April 2003, pp. 74-89.

10. Pasha, No. 6, p. 132; see also Faleh Abdul Jafar and Hoshan Daurd.

11. Ibid., p. 137. *Tribes and Power : Nationalism and Ethnicity in the Middle East* (London : Safi, 2003) pp. 69-135.

12. *Gulf News* (Dubai) April 4 and 7, 2003 (Ahmed Janabi, Liberators, Occupiers or owners?)

13. Pasha, no. 6, p. 138; see also Amir Taheri, "Time Running Out for Iraqi Shiites to join mainstream" *Gulf News,* 9/7/2003.

14. Amit Choudhary, *London Review of Books,* 4 October 2001, p. 21, in Ziauddin Sardar, Merryl Wyn Davies, *Why do People hate America?* (London: Faber and Faber, 2002) p. 34; see also martin Indyk, "A Trusteeship for Palestine?", *Foreign Affairs,* May - June 2003, Vol. 82, no. 3, pp. 51-66.

15. A.K. Pasha, *Arab - Israeli Peace Process: An Indian Perspective* (New Delhi: Manas Publications, 2000) pp. 206-225 and 241-269.

16. Mustapha Karkouti, "A Road Map without proper Directions", *Gulf News,* 1 April, 2003; see also Richard Crockett, *America Embattled : September 11, anti–Americanism and the global Order,* (New Delhi: Roli Books, 2003) pp. 88- 98.

17. Pasha, no.6, p. 141, "Do not trust Israel," *Gulf News* 1 April 2003.

18. Sardar, no. 14, pp. 54-55; see Marc Lynch, "Beyond the Arab Street : Iraq and the Arab Public Sphere", *Politics and Society,* Vol. 31, No. 1, March 2003, pp. 55- 91.

19. Quoted in P. Ulph," Saudi Arabia: Feeling the Heat", *Janies Islamic Affairs Analyst,* December 2001, p. 7, cited in Naveed S. Sheikh. *The New Politics of Islam: Pan-Islamic Foreign Policy in a world of states* (London: Rontledge Curzon, 2003) p. 60.

20. *Amin Saikal, Islam and the West: Conflict or Cooperation* (London: Palgrove, Macmillan, 2003) p. 130.

21. Sheikh, No. 19, pp. 65, 72; see also Noor Ahmed Baba. *OIC : Theory and Practice of Pan-Islamic Conference* (New Delhi: Sterling, 1994) p. 171.

22. Ibid., p. 80; see also Anthony Arnove, ed; *Iraq under siege: The Deadly Impact of sanctions and war* (New Delhi: Viva Books, 2003, p. 45. In early 2000 Hans Von Sponeck, his successor or a humanitarian Coordinator in Iraq and Jutta Burghart, Lead of UN World food program in Baghdad also resigned in protest against the sanctions. See also K.P. Fabian, *The Commonsense on the war on Iraq* (New Delhi: Somaiya Publications, 2003) p. 86-87.

23. The USA will not succeed in fighting terrorism or in widening and safeguarding its interests in the Muslim world on a long term basis unless it behaves in a way that wins the minds and hearts of the Muslim people, Saikal, no. 20, p. 130.

24. Sheikh, no. 19, p. 8; Bernard Leuris, "The Roots of Muslim Rage", *The Atlantic Monthly*, Vol. 266, No. 3, 1990, pp. 47-60.

25. Sardar, No.14, p. 35; see also Faleh Abdul Jabar, ed: *Ayatollahs, Sufis and Ideologues : state, religion and social movement in Iraq* (London: Safi Books, 2002) pp. 149 - 161.

26. *Ibid.* Fred Halliday. *Islam & the Myth of confrontation* (London, Tauris, 2003) pp. 107-132.

27. Edward W. Said, *Covering Islam* (New York: Vintage Books, 1997) p.144.

28. Sardar, no. 14, p. 160; Muslims feel that the Bush Administration and its allies are definitely out to pursue an agenda well beyond combating international terrorism - namely to secure a geopolitical marginalization of political Islam and to restructure Central Asian and the Middle East from Afghanistan to Morocco. The purpose is to ensure that never again can a force. whether religious or secular, be able to achieve a position whereby it could challenge US dominance in the region or threaten the interests of Israel. Saikal, no. 20, p. 132.

29. *Ibid.*, p. 34.

30. *Ibid.*, p. 200; see also Milan Rai, War Plan: Iraq: Ten Reasons against war on Iraq (London: Verro, 2002) pp. 45-56.

16

The American Invasion of Iraq : Implications for Arab and Afro-Asian World

Jagdish P. Sharma

The American led war against Iraq which started on March 20, 2003 was the bloodiest and most brutal of all armed conflicts since the Second World War. The United States along with United Kingdom launched their invasion of Iraq in blatant defiance of international public opinion and of the United Nations Security Council. The war has not only resulted in all round destruction of humanity in Iraq but has social, political, economic, military, strategic, psychological and emotional effects of far reaching consequences. This act of unprovoked aggression is aimed at subduing with overwhelming military force a country and its innocent people who stand in the way of its naked imperalist and neo-colonialist designs. It is also aimed at striking terror in the hearts of the Afro-Arab-Asian people as a whole, by demonstrating the awesome firepower and arrogant military might of the US. In terms of human losses if has been estimated that thousands of innocent Iraqi people were killed. On the other side the Americans and the British are happy about the fact that the war has been won at a low cost sacrificing only 128 American and 31 British soldiers. The unjustness of the war is that the innocent civilian Iraqi population was bombed in the name of liberation, democracy, human rights and peace. The cities were razed to dust, food, water supply and electricity were cut off and medical aid denied. Never in the history of wars in the world has any city suffered such horrendously heavy bombardment as Baghdad during America's terroristic "Operation Shock and Awe". Never have so many civilians been slain, so many buildings blown to rubble and the significant Mesopotamian civilization's cultural centers destroyed and many hospitals strewn with casualties because of the barbaric cluster bombs and murderous missiles sprayed with killer appetite.

The American war against Iraq has been one of the most protracted and most devastating conflicts in terms of social and human casualties and economic damage. It has also been a highly intense conflict in terms of sophisticated arms consumption and use, particularly of technologically advanced weapons systems. The war against Iraq has been fought not only on the ground, with infantry, tanks and artillery but also with devastating air and naval battles. There is general chaos and confusion throughout the country. Large scale looting is still taking place right in front of the US marines, with not even hospitals and cultural institutions spared. The American forces have behaved in the same manner as medieval invaders and colonial conquerors who looted and subdued defeated countries. The world has witnessed hapless Iraqi women and children face an immediate tragedy: their society has been ravaged by aggressors who were all along speaking untruths about Iraq's possession of weapons of mass destruction. An analysis of America's illegal, unnecessary and illegitimate war against the innocent people of Iraq has led to bitter feelings among the people in Afro-Arab-Asian world. The principal reason for the war was Iraqi disarmament. Yet weapons of mass destruction were not used by President Saddam Hussein's regime, nor have any been found. The ten weeks of searches, based on US intelligence, failed to turn up any chemical, biological or nuclear weapons in Iraq. More than twelve years ago, President George Bush (Sr.) ordered US troops into the Gulf in response to Iraq's intrusion into Kuwait. At the end of the Kuwaiti-Iraq war in 1991, the United Nations imposed sanctions under Iraq-

UN Security Council Resolution (UNSCR) 661— which were to remain in place until the provisions of UNSCR 687 were complied with, mainly the certification that Iraq had destroyed all of its weapons of mass destruction. The comprehensive sanctions of UNSCR 661 were some of the strictest sanctions ever imposed upon a nation. A large number of Iraqi civilians, including women and children have died as a result of the economic sanctions. The UN and other international agencies have estimated that the sanctions against Iraq have contributed to hundreds of thousands of deaths. But 1998, Iraqi infant mortality had reportedly risen from Pre-Gulf war rate of 3.7 per cent to 12 per cent.

However, in major policy change, the United Nations Security Council (May 22, 2003) overwhelmingly voted for the lifting of sanctions against Iraq and endorsed the idea of a US-led administration in Baghdad. The resolution essentially legitimised that the US and Britain as occupying powers will remain such time as an "internationally recognized representative government is established". France, Russia and Germany wanted a higher profile for the UN but had to settle for something less.[1]

One of the major attractions for the Americans and the West in Iraq and Gulf region, of course, is oil, another, the natural resources and the strategic location of the region. They view oil, as well as other Gulf resources as extremely precious. The US attaches major importance to the oil resources of the Gulf and North African region. It wants to ensure US oil interests the continued supply of oil from the Arab African world on a scale satisfying the needs of the Americans and at prices "acceptable" to them. Between 1972 and 1981, the US oil imports from the West Asian, Gulf and African countries rose 29 times in monetary terms and 2.9 times in volume. Until early 1982 the African countries were the main area from which the US imported its oil. In 1981 they provided 47.3 per cent of the oil from the Muslim African states. Nigeria, Libya and Algeria were the largest oil exporters to the US. However, in view of the Reagan Administration's toughline towards Libya, the Americans stopped their oil imports from that country in

March 1982 and shifted their attention to the Gulf provided 41.4 per cent of US imports with Saudi Arabia chalking up about 35 per cent of that.[2]

From the US perspective, any Russian or European access to these resources, is troublesome. America actively strives to keep these resources, as well as economic potential of the region and its market of 250 million people within its sphere of influence. All these plans, however, could be easily sabotaged if the Iraqi state under President Saddam Hussein was not properly contained or destroyed. America's oil-related commercial motives can be served only if a puppet regime is constituted from among the list of CIA favourities. After conquering Iraq, the Americans have begun their malicious propaganda campaign against Syria and Iran. A notice has been served on every country big or small to conform to an American code of conduct.

The US Secretary of State Colin Powell warned Syria in mid-April that Syria would find itself "on the wrong side of history" if it tried to destabilize post-war Iraq or continue harbouring radical Palestinian groups. Britain warned Syria that it must quickly answer charges that it has acquired chemical weapons and is harbouring fugitives from the ousted regime in neighbouring Iraq. It also accused Damascus of promoting international terrorism as well as obstructing the Arab-Israeli peace process.[3] If it was Syria last month, it is Iran now, receiving threats from the Bush Administration. Going by the present indications, the pressure is on to make both countries "behave". The Bush Administration has cut off contacts with Tehran and is considering "public and private actions" to destabilize the Iranian government, according to a report published on Sunday, May 25, 2003 by the *Washington Post*. The report said that Pentagon officials were advocating efforts to foment a popular uprising that would topple Iran's government. American intelligence reports have suggested that Al Qaeda operatives in Iran played a role in the deadly bombings of May 12, in Saudi-Arabia.[4] The British Prime Minister, Tony Blair also warned Iran against harbouring Al-Qaeda suspects saying this was "unacceptable". The US severed ties with Iran after the 1979 Islamic revolution. Last year Bush branded Iran as part of an 'axis of evil' trying to develop banned nuclear weapons. The official Iranian press agency, IRNA, however, refused the US allegations as false and based on faulty intelligence. But the Iranian officials vowed to arrest any militants who might have slipped into their country.

The US adminsitration is panicky about Iran's nuclear programme. Some neo-conservatives in US would like Israel to take out Iran's nuclear reactor, as it did Iraq's nuclear reactor in 1981; but Israel wants America share persistent concerns being expressed by the US that Iran was harbouring Al Qaeda elements and interfering in Iraq by supporting Shia resurgence in the war-torn country.

"Our own reading is not quite the same" the Foreign Secretary, Kanwal Sibal said, adding that Teheran has told India that the Iranian model did not apply to Iraq. Though India is very much part and parcel of the US-led "coalition" against terrorism, New Delhi clearly differs from Washington as far as Iran is concerned–a point that has clearly been made by India.[5]

The US-led war in Iraq has weakened the United Nations, the former Indian Prime Minister, I.K. Gujral, said recently. He asked the Indian Government to take note of the increasing US presence in South and South-West Asia. A sharp debate has broken out among Russian military experts and policy–makers over the meaning for Russia of the rapid US victory in Iraq.

There are about 1.2 billion Muslims in the world, and 300 million in West Asia, North Africa and Gulf region. American Enterprise Institute's Michael Ledeen espouses a revolutionary mission that "will successfully transform the lives of hundreds of millions of people throughout the Arab-African World". Leden argues that the key is subverting and toppling regimes that sponsor terrorists. His list includes Iraq along with Iran, Syria and Saudi Arabia. Another list contains half a dozen countries and also includes the Palestinian Authority of President Yasser Arafat. The animosity toward the US is on the rise in the Arab and Afro-Asian World. In spring 2002, Zogby International polled 10 countries, 8 of which were Muslim, and found remarkably similar opinion. While many expressed admiration for the American institutions and culture, US policy in the Arab World fared poorly, with approval ratings well below 10 per cent. In the region, America's policy is seen as skewed to the gross disadvantage of the Palestinians. Even in Morocco, only 38 per cent of the public opinion viewed the US favourably. In Egypt only 15 per cent of the public had a positive view. In a massive December 2000 global poll that included the Arab World, PEW Foundation researchers described Arab opinion toward the US as "overwhelmingly negative".[6]

The Arab neighbours of Iraq told the US recently to get out of the country as soon as possible. Foreign ministers of Iraq's immediate neighbours Turkey, Iran–Kuwait, Saudi Arabia, Jordan, Syria, as well as Egypt and Bahrain issued a joint statement at a meeting in Riyadh saying the Iraqi people must run their own country and control their oil wealth. The Arab ministers said they wanted the UN to play a central role in Post-War Iraq, echoing similar demands made by European Union leaders at their summit in Athens. Libya under President Muammar Gaddafi threatened to withdraw from the 22–member Arab League in protest over the groups' inability to take "a firm and strong position" toward the US-led invasion of Iraq. The Libyan leader has several times in the past threatened to quit the Cairo-based Arab League over its impotence," notably in relation to the Israeli-Palestinian conflict.[7]

Most of Iraq's neighbours are worried about America's singular bid to redraw the map of Arab and Afro-Asian region and redesign the world order through its military hegemony. They also want the Bush administration to be careful when it talks about democracy and reforms in Arab-African world. America does not seem to realize what bitter memories the Arabs and Africans have of foreign democracies trying to shape and dominate the region. It is dismaying to watch

America, which long ago rejected the notion of colonialism, trying to repeat the mistakes of an old Europe whose past attempts to dominate the region by force led to more than a million Arab deaths. America is also mimicking the preemptive war doctrine and policies and strategies of Israel, which have failed utterly to being peace and security. It is also important to realize that the issue of Iraq gained urgency in the White House not for Iraqis' sake, but because September 11, 2001 destabilised America's security and stability. The Bush administration's attempt to lump together secular Saddam Hussein and fanatic Osama bin Laden, which is inconvincing to most people around the world, has scared the hell out of the American people. Arab-African democrats only hope that democratic America will restrain Washington's imperial and neo-colonial ambitions. Otherwise no one will be able to deter the radical politics of religious fanatics and those of American's neo-conservative right.

Most Arab and Afro-Asian and European states are concerned that the US might monopolise the economic opportunities in the post-Saddam Iraq. The international community is worried about the United Nations being by passed again by the US in the reconstruction phase as in the case of launching the invasion of Iraq. Even Britain which is the staunchest ally of US in the military operation against Iraq has started talking of greater UN involvement. Fears of the US exploiting Iraq and its precious resources has increased. After the self-styled liberators, the American are behaving like an occupying power. This is the crux of the problem. In this process they are getting into problems with other powers and Arab-Persian neighbours of Iraq. So far as OPEC nations are concerned they feel the US will command the big Iraqi oil production and belittle their importance. If the oil prices collapse, that will have a major impact on Arab-African oil producing states. From the security angle, there is a large American military presence of US troops in the area. The Americans are thinking in terms of having four military bases in Iraq. This will give them a dominating status in the entire region. The US warnings to Syria and

Iran have also increased fears of deliberate American interference and loss of sovereignty by the countries in the Arab-African and Asian region. The Iraqi story has not ended. And the nations have to be on guard against the US, flushed with military victory, riding rough-shod over their interests.

Reference

1. *The Pioneer* (New Delhi), 23 May, 2003.
2. A. Kislov and R. Zimenkow, *USA and the Islamic World*, New Delhi, Sterling Publishers, 1984, p. 15.
3. K. R. Singh, "Gulf Crisis 1991 and 2003 and changing World Orders", *Defence Watch* (New Delhi), pp. 32-35.
4. *International Herald Tribune*, 26 May 2003.
5. *The Hindu* (Delhi), 31 May 2003.
6. Augustus Richard Norton, "America in the Middle East : Statesmanship Versus Politics" *Current History* (Philadelphia) Vol. 102, No. 660, January 2003, pp. 3-4.
7. *East African* (Nairobi), 4 April 2003

17

Economic Impact of Gulf War on India

R K Wadhwa

In the wake of oil crisis of 1973, the Gulf Region assumed worldwide importance with the growing per capita income and continued dependence on imports. Oil being the main source of revenue for most of the countries, the Region heavily relied on imports of machinery and equipment for oil exploration, construction activity, and consumer goods. The three wars experienced by the Gulf in the last two decades slowed down the economic activity of the region. The longest war being the Iran-Iraq war which lasted for eight years (1980-88), followed by Iraq's invasion of Kuwait in 1990 and the recent US-UK Military Action against Iraq in 2003. Incidentally, Iraq has been involved in all the three Gulf wars.

As is known that the entire industrial and economic development of a nation rests on the oil, it became the most scarce commodity by various economies of the world. The emergence of oil in the Gulf Region made the OPEC countries the nerve centre for supplies of oil to the world. Some people believe that Iraq being the second largest producer of oil, next to Saudi Arabia, in the world perhaps intended to control and be the super oil power. This lust for super oil power, it is said, led to the Iraq-Iran War in 1980s which lasted for eight years, followed by its invasion of Kuwait in 1990. Though its dream was not fulfilled yet it had to pay heavy price in terms of confronting huge amount of financial problems, depletion of foreign exchange reserves, and damage to oil export facilities - the sole foreign exchange earner

- due to the war in eighties. Subsequently, after the invasion of Kuwait, Iraq had to face UN economic sanctions and damage from military action by international coalition, beginning in January 1991, which led to severe reduction in the economic activity thereafter.

Iraq's Dependence on Oil

Were it not for its wealth of mineral resources, Iraq would not have been in its current sociopolitical predicament as huge reserves of oil and natural gas gave it great wealth and influence disproportionate to its relatively smaller population. The country's main oil fields are located near Basrah, not far from the Persian Gulf in the north-central part of the country, around Mosul and Kirkuk; and in the east-central Iraq, near Khanaqin. Iraq also has brown coal deposits and various metals, along with gypsum, phosphates, salt, and sulphur.

Oil revenue has been the mainstay of government income since the 1950s. In 1968 the oil-based nature of the economy was reinforced by the introduction of command management, with the government regulating all economic activity other than peripheral agriculture, personal services and trade. The dominance of the state sector has gone hand-in-hand with the concentration of activities in the main lowland cities, leading to a decline in agriculture's contribution to GDP (5.1 per cent in 1989) and in its importance as an employer of labour. Since the imposition of UN sanctions, the government has made a number of unsuccessful attempts to increase agricultural output.

Economic expansion during the 1970s was driven by the oil sector. However, the 4.4 per cent average annual growth in GDP from 1965 to 1973 was low in comparison with the other oil-based economies in the region. This relatively low growth was in part explained by the poor performance of the non-oil sector; land reform introduced after the revolution in 1958 adversely affected the private sector. The oil sector also suffered, as a result of disputes over participation, and then nationalization, between the government and the Iraq Petroleum Company. The surge in GDP growth in the mid- and late 1970s, at an average rate of 10.4 per cent per year in 1974-80, was halted by the Iran-Iraq war, as all available resources were diverted to the war effort. Although economies are sometimes stimulated by wars, in Iraq's case the military build-up was almost entirely composed of imported equipment.

Oil Industry in Iraq

Iraq's oil industry was built up by foreign-controlled companies, including Iraq Petroleum Co. owned by BP, Exxon, Mobil, Partex, and Shell, which operated in the north, and Basra Petroleum Co. operating in the south–east. By 1975, these operations had been nationalized by the government and two new companies formed, Iraq National Oil Co and the Northern Petroleum Organization.

Maintaining oil exports to feed its 23-mil people presented Iraq with a major challenge as oil wells, particularly in the northern Kirkuk oil producing area, have suffered in the absence of badly needed spare parts. Production from the giant Kirkuk oilfield, discovered in 1927 and containing 10-bil in reserves and, from Rumaila in the south is in decline as the fields have matured, making it vital for Iraq to revisit idle oilfields and explore in the Western desert.

Iraq has the world's second biggest reserves after Saudi Arabia with proven reserves of 112-bil bbl and probable reserves of 214-bil bbl. But the country has not been able to expand its exploration program in the last 20 years, first as a result of the 1980-88 Iran-Iraq war and later because of UN sanctions in place since 1990.

The then Senior Deputy Oil Minister in an interview said: "The figure we reached and which is widely known, is that we could discover 214-bil bbl of oil in addition to the present proven reserve. We are sure of this figure as all available indications and scientific standards say. This means that we will exceed the 300-bil bbl when all Iraq's regions are explored".

"We have also said on many occasions that we have indications of oil structures—these are only primary indications—estimated to be more than 560 reservoirs that could be oil fields that need digging, appraisal and which we believe have a high potential oil presence," he added. "We believe that when we prove all this, Iraq will be the number one holder of oil reserves in the world. We are highly confident of this."

The latest available report by experts from oil Services Company Saybolt International submitted to the UN in March 2000 said a production level of 3-mil bd of crude oil was achieved without the technical resources to apply " good oil field practices. " The report said that without prompt action, production would continue to decline. Iraq has plans to raise its oil production from around 3-mil bd currently to 6-mil bd by 2010. Iraq is also hoping to be a major gas exporter but negotiations with neighboring Turkey on building a gas pipeline have not reached a conclusion.

International Trade

Iraq's economy is dominated by the oil sector, which has traditionally provided about 95 per cent of foreign exchange earnings. In the 1980s financial problems caused by massive expenditures in the eight-year war with Iran and damage to oil export facilities by Iran led the government to implement austerity measures, borrow heavily, and later reschedule foreign debt payments; Iraq suffered economic losses from the war of at least $100 billion. After hostilities ended in 1988, oil exports gradually increased with the construction of new pipelines and restoration of damaged facilities. Iraq's seizure of Kuwait in August 1990, subsequent international economic sanctions, and damage from military action by an international coalition beginning in January 1991 drastically reduced economic activity.

The UN sanctions on exports of crude oil resulted into deficit in the balance of trade and the imports surged to USD 665 million against exports of USD 425 million in the year 1995. However, the restoration of crude exports on the implementation of the UN's Oil-for-Food Programme in December 1996 led to a decline in the trade deficit from USD 240 million in 1995 to USD 65 million in 1996. In the following years Iraq has experienced a favourable balance of trade registering three and a half times increase in 2001 at USD 6339 million from USD 1763 million in 1997, - a decline of 42 per cent from the peak level of USD 10959 million during 2000. While the exports grew by 2600 times, imports witnessed an increase of 614 per cent during the period 1995-2001. Details of the trend in international trade of Iraq during 1995–2001 are given as under:

Table 1.

Trend in International Trade of Iraq (USD Million)

Year	*Exports*	*Imports*	*Total*	*Balance of Trade*
1995	425	665	1090	-240
1996	503	568	1071	-65
1997	2904	1141	4045	1763
1998	5108	1833	6941	3275
1999	9672	2072	11744	7600
2000	14289	3330	17619	10959
2001	11087	4748	15838	6339

Source: Direction of Trade Statistics, IMF, 2002.

Although government policies supporting large military and internal security forces and allocating resources to key supporters of the regime have hurt the economy, implementation of the UN's oil-for-food programme in December 1996 has helped improve conditions for the average Iraqi citizen. For the first six, six-month phases of the program, Iraq was allowed to export limited amounts of oil in exchange for food, medicine, and some infrastructure spare parts. In December 1999 the UN Security Council authorized Iraq to export under the programme as much oil as required to meet humanitarian needs. (The status of Humanitarian Contracts approved, on hold, and arrived as at 30th April 2002, since start of Oil-for-Food Programme in December

1996 is given in Annexure 1). Oil exports are now more than three-quarters pre–war level. However, 28 per cent of Iraq's export revenues under the programme are deducted to meet UN Compensation Fund and UN administrative expenses. The drop in GDP in 2001 was largely the result of the global economic slowdown and lower oil prices. Per capita food imports have increased significantly, while medical supplies and health care services are steadily improving. Per capita output and living standards are still well below the pre–war level, but any estimates have a wide range of error. Details of Crude Exports under the Oil-for-Food Programme are given below:

Table 2

Crude Export under the Oil-for-Food Programme

Phase	*Volume of oil (millions of barrels)*	*Value of oil exported ($-mil)*
One	120.0	2,150
Two	127.0	2,125
Three	182.0	2,085
Four	308.0	3,027
Five	360.8	3,947
Six	389.6	7,402
Seven	343.4	8,302
Eight	375.7	9,564
Total	**2,206.5**	**$ 38,602**
Phase	*Volume of oil (millions of barrels)*	*Value of oil exported (€-mil)*
Nine	293	€ 6,668 (or $5,638)
Ten	300.2	€ 6,004 (or $ 5,350)
Eleven	213.9	€ 4,540 (or $ 4,155)
Twelve	10.9	€ 251 (or $ 237)
Total	**3,036.5**	**€ 17,809 (or $ 15,814)**

Source : The Office of the Iraq Programme (OIP).

Despite the sanctions, the US is the biggest single market for Iraqi crude oil through indirect sales by traders who buy Iraqi crude oil and sell it on.

Unofficial Exports through Syria

Considering the inadequacy of export revenues under Oil-for-Food Programme to meet the economy's import requirement, unofficial exports of crude oil started in 2001 - outside the UN control - through Syria using a leaky old pipeline running from northern Iraq to the Syrian Mediterranean port of Banias. The unofficial export of crude oil was estimated to the tune of 200,000 bd. However, Iraq and Syria have denied this practice. According to Western diplomats Iraq was also smuggling crude oil through the Persian Gulf on "rust bucket" vessels that did not meet international maritime standards while truckloads of smuggled fuel oil crossed into Turkey with their contraband cargoes daily.

Pricing Mechanism of Iraqi Crude Oil

The Oil-for-Food programme has always been dependent on global oil prices. In the first three phases, Iraq's exports were limited by ceiling set by the UN Security Council. When the ceiling was raised in mid-1998, the price of oil was moving down and it was only from mid-1999 onwards that Iraq was able to take advantage of better prices and raised ceilings with exports averaging around 2-mil bd and revenues of more than $20/bbl.

Secure supply of Iraqi crude grades grew into a major issue because of the complex politics surrounding Iraq and the UN oil-for-food framework under which Iraq exported its crude oil.

The UN/Iraq oil-for-food programme faced a potential financial crisis due to a substantial drop in revenues generated by Iraqi oil exports. The reduced level of Iraqi crude exports under the programme was blamed primarily on uncertainties surrounding the mechanism of pricing Iraqi oil. A key determinant in this procedure was the level the official selling prices (OSPs) for the two main Iraqi grades–Kirkuk and Basrah Light - were set.

The OSPs were proposed by Iraq's State Oil Marketing Organization (SOMO) to the UN's oil overseers and were fixed according to destination.

The UN's oil overseers then decided whether or not to recommend the OSPs to the UN Sanctions Committee. The Committee then had 24-48 hours to accept or reject the OSP as a fair market value. If the price was rejected by the Committee, SOMO had to make a new proposal.

In September 2001, it is reported SOMO was demanding an extra payment, imposing a surcharge, for lifters to be paid outside the framework of the UN oil-for-food programme, in contravention of UN sanctions. This resulted in more frequent rejections of OSPs, with the UN Sanctions Committee invariably asking SOMO to raise its price. To combat SOMO's illegal surcharge, the UN Sanctions Committee in October 2001 imposed a retroactive pricing mechanism that led to the substantial decline in surcharge of only 15 cts/bbl from the traders. However, a dispute emerged between Baghdad, on the one hand, and the US and UK, on the other hand, over the time-period of the pricing window, which currently varies depending on the destination. The three main destinations are Europe, the US and Asia.

US War on Iraq

In spite of considerable opposition and lack of support in United Nations, the US took a unilateral decision along with UK to take military action against Iraq in March 2003. The reasons behind this avoidable adventure could be many and their intended consequences even more obscure. Different opinions have been expressed by political leaders, defence experts and economists all over the world on this issue. Some of the opinions are reproduced below.

Was the Iraq crisis principally about removing a despot from power or was the underlying reality more to do with asserting US global hegemony?

The US position hardened against Iraq especially after 9/11 attack and Mr Bush asserted that Iraq had links with Al Qaeda and "continues to support terror" and that it had been "plotting to develop anthrax and nerve gas and nuclear weapons for over a decade".

For many, including officials in the Middle East, the real motive behind the US attack was the global hegemony. By taking and controlling Iraq, the clique believes, a clear message is sent to the region and to the world about the US's global supremacy, regardless of the costs in terms of human lives and damage to international law, international institutions and US reputation abroad.

Former US President Jimmy Carter, however, was opposed to the US military action against Iraq. He said "Profound changes have been taking place in American foreign policy, reversing consistent bipartisan commitments that for more than two centuries have earned our nation greatness. These commitments have been predicated on basic religious principles, respect for international law and alliances that resulted in wise decisions and mutual restraint. Our apparent determination to launch a war against Iraq, without international support, is a violation of these premises."

Similar views have been expressed by Wesley Clark the retired US general and former NATO commander. While expressing his concern on the US war on Iraq, he said: "They picked war over law. They picked a unilateralist approach over a multilateral approach. They picked conventional forces over special-operations forces. And they picked Saddam Hussein as a target over Osama bin Laden".

It seems Bush Administration was so much obsessed by the idea of regime change in Iraq that it took a unilateral action of imposing war against a strong public opinion within US and elsewhere which did not see any threat from Saddam using of weapons of mass destruction against US troops. In fact, no weapons of mass destruction have been found after the war.

A key part of the right-wing vision in the Administration was that the US as the sole superpower, should tolerate no rivals and should use its military dominance to enforce this new world order.

Some of the supporters of war in the Administration stated: "The US is not just interested in oil from Iraq, it is concerned to maintain political dominance over all the oil-producing countries of the region" - Peter Dale Scott, US Commander.

Secretary of State Colin Powell while addressing the Senate Foreign Relations Committee on February 6 said: "Success in the Iraq war could fundamentally reshape that region in a powerful, positive way that will enhance US interests". He further stated that "while stationing the US troop in occupied Iraq, the US is serving notice to Iran and Saudi Arabia (both of which were once secure bases for US troops but are no longer so) that the US will reassert its presence as the dominant military power in the region".

From the above statements, it can be construed that the US attack on Iraq was not against the use of weapons for mass destruction or removing Saddam from power but it was more to do with asserting US global hegemony in the region.

Game of Oil

Some experts believe that other issues besides global hegemony for raging a war were US interests in terms of oil, petrodollars, and the OPEC euro question. While views were expressed repeatedly that the war has nothing to do with oil, one cannot discount the importance of oil.

It was opined that Iraq being the second largest reservoir, next to Saudi Arabia, and constituting 11 per cent of the world oil reserves may increase its oil production and diminish the market pressure on oil-importing countries like the US. The increase in Iraqi oil production will weaken the power of OPEC to influence oil markets by decision to restrict output. Besides, the Iraqi oil production to expand to near its capacity, the quotas established by OPEC would cease to be honoured in today's markets. Viewed from this angle perhaps the Bush Administration intended to topple Saddam in a pre-emptive attempt to initiate massive Iraqi oil production far in excess of OPEC quotas, to reduce global oil prices and thereby dismantle OPEC's price controls. The end-goal of the neo-conservatives is incredibly bold yet simple in purpose: to use the 'war on terror' as the premise to finally dissolve OPEC's decision-making process, thus ultimately preventing the cartel's inevitable switch to pricing oil in euros.

Euro as an alternative oil transaction currency perhaps was another issue. Nevertheless, the euro gained considerable strength against the dollar in the previous year in the build-up to the war and traders are of the opinion that this trend may continue. One analyst suggested: "The Federal Reserve's worst nightmare was that OPEC may switch its international transactions from a dollar standard to a euro standard". Whether this would happen in the medium term is to be seen and watched but by installing a puppet government in Baghdad the US was ensuring that OPEC momentum to the Euro gets vetoed not only for Iraq (which was using the euro for oil sales - as could be seen from the table on exports of crude oil under Food-for-Oil programme) but also for Iran, which is also considering a switch to the euro.

Some of the other reasons why countries like France, Russia, and China did not support the US-UK Military Action against Iraq could be related to their vested interests in exploration of oil in Iraq.

Iraq was producing 3.I-mil bd of crude oil before its forces invaded Kuwait in August 1990, making it the second biggest oil exporter after Saudi Arabia within OPEC. Saudi Arabia made up the bulk of the shortage on oil markets when Iraqi oil disappeared from markets and prices shot up to $30/bbl.

Iraq was hoping to return to its pre-Gulf War production capacity and to increase the same it would need USD 40 billion of investment. The government therefore invited Russian and Chinese oil companies to help develop its northern and southern oilfields, many of which were mothballed or suffered water damage.

France and Russian companies interests were at stake and were not interested to hand over oil management to the US - deals signed with Saddam Government. It is felt France, Russia and China may even oppose lifting of UN sanctions proposed by US after war.

Russian Oil Company - LUKOIL - said "from a legal point of view the reserves in Qurma field are theirs -potentially a USD 20 billion investment - if LUKOIL is squeezed out we will go to the Arbitration Court in Geneva, which will then immediately freeze the reserves." It was stated that if LUKOIL does not get the rights, the development of Iraq's most important field may get delayed by four to six years.

It is felt that the US attack on Iraq was a game of oil as could be observed from the statement given by Colin Powell immediately after the war "countries which did not support US-UK Military Action against Iraq may have to pay a price".

Economic Impact of War on India

Ever since war clouds shrouded the Gulf, government officials and the Reserve Bank had put up a bold face and said the country is prepared for any exigency. It had piled up an oil reserve while the RBI boasted its USD 75 billion of foreign exchange reserve. But the leading credit rating agencies sounded a note of caution saying if war gets stretched and oil prices surge over USD 30 a barrel, the economy may witness higher inflation and slower manufacturing growth which may pull down the prospects of achieving near 6 per cent GDP growth.

All these observations would have proved to be true had the war continued for a longer stretch. The main factors were that "India is the highest recipient of remittances from Gulf amounting to USD 10 billion per annum had the war continued for a longer duration the country would have witnessed a decline in the remittances as the professionals would have kept more dollars as reserve fund to meet exigencies". Besides, US and Gulf are coincidentally the two sensitive areas that were someway or the other engaged in the war.

Secondly, India imports 70 per cent of its petroleum consumption and around 60 per cent of imports come from countries in or near the war zone. The supplies of oil would have got affected resulting in the slowdown of economic activity.

On the eve of war, World Bank also gave the warning bell for India and the global economy saying that there may be a surge in oil prices that may hit countries like India which are net importer of oil. Besides, the prolonged war may dampen the investor and consumer confidence worldwide. As regards India's trade with Iraq, it enjoys a favourable balance of trade with regard to non-POL items. India's export which was of the order of USD 26 million in 1990 got a setback on the imposition of UN sanctions in 1991. However, from 1996 onwards it has witnessed a phenomenal growth from USD 0.65 million in 1995-96 to USD 207 million in 2001-02. Major items of exports include machinery and instruments, manufactures of metals, tea, oil meals, wheat, drugs and pharmaceuticals, electronic goods etc. In terms of imports, India is a net importer of oil from Iraq. The trend in India's exports to Iraq during 1995-96 to 2001-02 is given in Table 3.

Table 3

Trend in India's Exports to Iraq (USD Million)

Year	*Total India*	*Iraq*	*% Share*
1995-96	31,842	0.65	0.002
1996-97	33,498	2.17	0.006
1997 -98	35,049	11.21	0.032
1998-99	33,211	36.29	0.109
1999-00	36,760	49.44	0.134
2000-01	44,147	82.71	0.187
2001-02	43,708	206.83	0.473

Source: CMIE.

It is expected that India's exports will get a boost after the lifting of UN sanctions in the post-war Iraq especially in the reconstruction activity.

To conclude the US war on Iraq did not have any significant impact on India. However, had the war prolonged for a longer stretch, it would have certainly the adverse impact on the Indian economy.

References

1. Country Profile on Iraq, 2002, Economist Intelligence Unit, London.
2. *The Financial Times*, London (www.ft.com).
3. US Department of State.
4. *The Economic Times*, New Delhi.
5. *PTI Economic Service*, New Delhi.
6. Direction of Trade Statistics, *IMF Yearbook 2002.*
7. Foreign Trade Statistics, Centre for Monitoring Indian Economy, Mumbai.

Annexure 1

Status of Humanitarian Contracts

Status of Humanitarian Contracts*

(USD Million)

Sector	*Contracts Approved*	*Contracts on Hold*	*Contracts Arrived*
Food@	5,760	0	9,212
Food-handling	2,554	455	1,567
Health@	1,924	453	1,822
Oil-spares	2.014	732	1,356
Electricity	3,059	938	1,502
Water/Sanitation	1,487	652	926
Agriculture	2,614	787	1,744
Education	683	279	385
Telecommunication & transport	1,685	542	622
Housing	2,092	188	1,159
Special allocation#	26	164	0
Northern governorates	1,294	29	1,326^
Total	**25190**	**5,219**	**21,620**

* As as 30th April 2002; since start of oil-for-food programme in December 1996.

@ Includes food and health-sector supplied bulk-purchased by the Iraqi government for the three northern governorates.

^ Excludes food and health-sector supplies included above.

\# For the needs of Iraq's most vulnerable social groups as established by the UN Secretary-General's 29th November 2000 report.

18
Post-War Iraq Situation: Economic Implications

Girish Mishra

The military victory of the United States over a small developing country like Iraq with a population of just 24 million was never in doubt. That it would humble, with its massive military and technological power and economic might, an already emanciated and starved nation by more than a decade long application of economic sanctions was a foregone conclusion. If there was any doubt, it was about the capacity of the USA to fashion a new Iraq after its own image of a democratic and economically vibrant country. History testifies that the USA has seldom been successful at the latter task.

If the USA fails in its mission of rebuilding Iraq, history will certainly decree that the invasion was futile and America will be held guilty of bringing unnecessary devastation and loss of lives to innocent people. "The stakes are particularly high in Iraq because, if history is any guide, occupation and reconstruction will shape US relations with the Arab world—and perhaps the whole Muslim world–for decades."[1]

Ever since its foundation, the USA has indulged in more than 200 foreign military interventions, but only in 16 cases or about 8 per cent its declared aim was nation-building. America's foreign interventions have exhibited three attributes: (a) change or strengthen the existing regime, (b) attempt nation–building efforts which require deployment of troops to ensure security and provision of basic services, and (c) continue supporting post-conflict by stationing US troops and civilians.

Out of the 16 attempts at nation-building, only 4 could create durable democratic regimes after the US troops left. They included Japan and Germany after the Second World War, Panama in 1989, and Grenada in 1983. "In these four countries, democracy, as measured by the widely used Polity Democracy Index maintained at the University of Maryland, was sustained 10 years after US troops left. In the other 11 countries (excluding Afghanistan where the final judgment has not yet been pronounced), democracy failed to emerge or endure during the same time frame. Worse, in the countries where US nation-building efforts floundered, brutal dictatorships and corrupt, autocratic regimes gained power after the US exit. This record implies a success rate of 26 per cent (four out of 15 attempts).[2]

The factors responsible for the failure of nation-building attempts included some like socio-economic situation, historical background and governing capacities of the countries where the US intervention took place. It is needless to say that they were beyond the power of the US to alter. They were in the nature of the given data. Another factor was the decision to go alone in pursuing the task of nation-building. Out of the 12 cases where US efforts at nation-building were without the collaboration from others, 10 were unsuccessful. "The key variable in failed unilateral nation-building attempts seems to be the type of interim administration deployed immediately following military intervention. Of the 16 cases, seven saw interim rule by US–supported surrogate regimes-governments that were almost totally dependent on Washington. ... In the 10 years following US troops withdrawals, none of the target countries ruled by such governments had made the transition to democracy.[3]

A big question that always faced the US was as to what form political transition in nation-building should take. Ideally, power should be transferred to elected representatives of local people. But it is easier said than done because only in very few cases there was a functioning electoral system or some sort of national cohesion. So far as Iraq is concerned, it is feared that a full-fledged electoral process may aggravate ethnic and religious differences and dormant prejudices. It may lead to some sort of a civil war situation. It is proposed that, to begin with, some kind of interim administration based on multilateralism should be established under the aegis of the UN. This approach has been tried in four of the 16 cases of US nation building. Though a multilateral approach does not always succeed, yet its success rate has been greater than any other approach. In the case of its failure, the blame does not solely rest on the US shoulders. A powerful section in the US holds: "The poor record of past unilateral nation building leaves a UN–led approach as the least risky alternative. In addition to bringing legitimacy, experience in managing post-conflict societies, and economic and military contradictions from its members, a UN–led interim administration of Iraq will help discredit popular conspiracy theories deriding Washington's intention toward Iraq. Since the Bush administration has publicly disavowed an intent to establish long-term military bases in Iraq or to take advantage of its vast oil resources, having the United Nations as the lead partner would give the administration instance credibility.[4]

It seems while toying with the idea of bringing in multilateralism by involving the UN, it has begun the process of getting an interim government of its own choice and liking to be established. It, however, appears that most Iraqis are either hostile or indifferent to American endeavour. It is reflected in daily attacks on American forces and other acts of sabotage. Till now no important section has come forward to declare that Americans are liberators, not colonizers or occupiers. "The United States enjoys no clear advantage in trying to develop a new political system for Iraq. It has no historical ties to the country and little understanding of Iraqi culture and society. Many Iraqis resent the United States as an occupying power. And the factor that made .the war so successful–reliance on a relatively small, mobile force whose strength lay in technological superiority rather than manpower–is a serious liability to reconstruction. Stabilizing a country requires a large, visible presence on the ground, not sophisticated weapons."[5]

The United States did formulate plans for Iraq. To begin with Saddam Hussein was to be removed and the character of the Iraqi state and the social structure were to be radically altered. Leading members of the Saddam regime and active members of the Baath Party were to be excluded. The USAID (the US Agency for International Development) had come out with its blue-print for reconstruction. It was entitled "Vision for Post-Conflict Iraq." American contractors were to implement it. They were to help restore physical infrastructure and public utilities. Health services were to be restored to at least one fourth of the population within two months after the conflict was over and to 50 per cent including cent per cent women and children in six months. A new school curriculum was to be introduced in a year's time. Roads and electrical grids were to be repaired and made fully functional as early as possible. Iraq was to be turned into a model of participatory democracy where the central government was to be entrusted only with defence, internal security, currency and finance, foreign affairs, law and justice, and strategic natural resources such as oil and gas. Everything else was to be the domain of local government. It soon turned out that this scheme of things was unrealistic and this became obvious as soon as the coalition forces formally declared their victory over the forces of Saddam Hussein. Yet in the middle of April, the USAID gave a $7.9 million contract (which was to increase to $167.9 million in a year's time) to the Research Triangle Institute, a North Carolina contractor for strengthening "management skills and capacity of local administrations and civic institutions to improve delivery of essential municipal services such as water, health, public sanitation and economic governance; includes training programmes in communications, conflict resolution, leadership skills and political analysis.[6] A few days earlier, the USAID had invited contractors to bid on a 12-month, $70 million Iraq Community Action Program, which was to organize community committees for identifying community needs and mobilizing people for fulfilling them. Commenting on them, Marina S. Ottaway said: "Thus, consciously or not, the United States is simultaneously applying two contradictory reconstruction policies in Iraq. Each has a separate logic and coherence, but combining the two renders both illogical and incoherent. Where the United States has little control, invasive projects of social and political transformation cannot succeed. US contractors cannot channel political participation through the new structures they are supposed to create unless there is an occupying force large enough to curb the influence of religious and tribal leaders. Hoping that a light occupation and a quick transfer of power will result in the democracy the United States promised the world is either deeply cynical or excessively optimistic. Hiding a heavy–handed American occupation behind the facade of a quickly formed Iraqi interim authority could theoretically reconcile the two approaches. Yet Iraqis are likely to notice the strings and turn on both the puppets and the puppeteers.[7]

Both Bush and Blair have declared that now onwards the natural and other resources of Iraq will be used for the benefit of its people, not for enrichment of a very tiny section of the society as in the days of Saddam Hussein. Accordipg to them, there will be no place for bribery or under-the-table-deals in oil and gas. To begin with, oil production will be 2 million barrels a day and for this necessary repairs and arrangements for safe restart of production, refining, distribution and export will have to be undertaken. American companies will execute this responsibility. Experts do not seem to be very optimistic about this. According to them, 2 million barrels a day will bring in only about $15 billion a year. It will not yield any financial surplus because most of it will have to be spent on modernization and upgradation of facilities damaged as a result of the wars with Iran and Kuwait, economic sanctions and recent invasion by the United States-led coalition forces. Before the Gulf War of 1991, Iraq's oil production capacity was around 3.5 million barrels per day, but now it is between 2.6 and 2.8 million barrels per day. It will take, if everything goes well, at least three years to regain its pre-1990 production levels. Iraq possesses 74 explored and evaluated oilfields. Of them only 15 oilfields have been developed. Thus while it has enormous possibilities, it lacks capital and technology to benefit by them. At the existing level of production Iraq may supply only 2 per cent of oil needs of the world, but adequate investments and conducive economic and political climate is ensured this may rise to 4 per cent in three years and to 7 per cent in next ten years.

It is estimated that reviving and sustaining a capacity to produce 2 to 3 million barrels of oil per day needs an investment at least to the tune of $30 to $40 billion. According to Edward C. Chow, an expert in the matters relating to oil: "The longer term goal is more challenging-to reach and sustain production of 5 million barrels per day (or more). Iraq has the second-largest known reserves in the world–over a hundred billion barrels of oil. But to raise production Iraq must not only revitalize existing fields but also explore and develop new fields and construct new installations for processing and export. Such risky megaprojects can easily cost tens of billion dollars each.[8] It is not possible to finance repair, modernization and expansion of such large projects by existing oil revenues. One way out suggested is inviting international oil companies to undertake them. They may be offered attractive terms and conditions. The snag here is that no foreign company will dare come to Iraq unless its safety and security is guaranteed and there is sufficient assurance of political stability in the country.

If the experiences of countries like Russia, Kuwait and Saudi Arabia are any guide, it will take many years before foreign companies of repute will begin investing in the oil sector on any significant scale. It is said that if everything goes well, it will take at least ten years for oil production to reach 5 to 6 million barrels per day.

In the meantime the situation in Iraq does not seem to be improving. There is a great deal of insecurity among the people. Economic future looks bleak with almost 60 per cent of labour force unemployed. Both the police and army are in the state of demobilization. This has added to increasing lawlessness. Basic services like water, electricity, medical and sanitation facilities, education system, etc. are not functional. It has been estimated that it will take $1.5 billion a year for 5 years to satisfy electricity needs of the people.

Paul D. Wolfowitz, UN States deputy secretary of defence and a leading member of the neocons fraternity has admitted that some of the key assumptions underlying American occupation of Iraq were wrong. They were :

(a) removal of Saddam Hussein will remove the threat posed by the Baath Party,

(b) Iraqi army units and police would come over the American side in significant numbers, and

(c) Iraqi population would welcome American troops as liberators.[9]

There is no denying the fact that the Iraqi regime, headed by Saddam Hussein was repressive and dictatorial. But it was wrong to conclude that the Iraqis would ipso facto prefer an alien power to come and "liberate" them. Americans forgot that Iraq was an ancient nation, but with a most modern population, in the Arab world. Iraqi nationalism had been not only strong but had also cut across religious and ethnic divisions.[10]

At no stage before the invasion, the Americans bothered either to reveal their real intent or to take any sizable section of the Iraqi population into confidence or secured its support. All through, only some rootless Iraqis propped up and funded by the CIA went on making some feeble noise in the Western press. In view of this, it should surprise nobody if the Iraqis at large take the invasion and occupation of their country as an affront to their national pride. Ordinary Iraqis feel insulted and angered by frequent searches, roadblocks and rude behaviour of the occupation army. In view of this, there is all the possibility that a perpetual low intensity conflict continues and certain groups continue to indulge in hit and run tactics. All this shows the failure of the Americans to build goodwill among the Iraqis and it is needless to say that without this no national economic reconstruction is possible. The Americans must assuage the feelings of the Iraqis at large who have not forgotten their decade-long sufferings due to sanctions and the killings of thousands of civilians and the destruction of infrastructure worth $170 billion in 1991. These civilians were in no way responsible for the Iraqi invasion of Kuwait nor did the infrastructure form part of the personal estate of Saddam Hussein.

In 1999, a UN panel had reported to the Security Council of "increase in juvenile delinquency, begging and prostitution, anxiety about the future and a lack of motivation, a rising sense of isolation bred by absence of contact with the outside world, the development of a parallel economy replete with profiteering and criminality, cultural and scientific impoverishment, and disruption of family life.[11]

Iraq's agricultural production had declined by 50 per cent since 1990, its industrial sector had collapsed and infrastructure almost disintegrated. Its GDP came down to just $40 billion last year from $130 billion in 1979. Medical and sanitation facilities had become very meagre. Schools and universities were barely functional. At present, America is spending $1 billion a week (or $25,000 a month per soldier, which is equal to the annual income of 10 average Iraqi families).

The invasion and conquest of Iraq is going to have grave and far-reaching implications for the United States. As Keynes warned in his famous book *The Economic Consequences of the Peace*, published soon after the First World War and the conclusion of the Treaty of Versailles, the victors too would have to suffer harmful after-effects. In fact, it was the victors who prepared the ground for the rise of Hitler and Nazism, which menaced Germany and the rest of the world for many years and ultimately led to the Second World War. Felix Rohatyn, a former American ambassador to France, is not wrong when he says: "Times now call for a new Keynes to do so again–but this time to write about the economic consequences of the war for the winners."[12]

Not only politically and militarily but economically also it was foolish on the part of America to pursue unilateralism in dealing with Iraq. It is bound to have disastrous consequences for its economy. Unlike old imperialist countries, it is dependent on import of capital, energy and technical know-how. Its foreign trade is always in the red. It is burdened with an ageing population and the consequences it entails. In this situation it is not easy to bear the rising costs of military occupation and nation-building in Iraq. Its global military commitments are also no less. The American economy does not show any firm signs of revival. The fact that the rate of economic growth in the second quarter (April-June) of 2003 reached 2.4 per cent per annum as against the forecast of 1.5 per cent per annum does not arouse much optimism. The rate of unemployment marginally declined from 6.4 per cent to 6.2 per cent and consumer confidence has not been significantly revived. The budgetary deficit has increased thanks to tax cuts for the rich.

The revival of economic growth has been largely due to increased military spending. It shot up to 44.1 per cent per annum during the second quarter, the largest increase in any quarter since the third quarter of 1951 when America fought the Korean War. In the first quarter of 2003, military spending declined by 3.3 per cent. Thanks to the increased military expenditure federal spending rose and created conditions of temporary revival of the economy.

During the present Bush administration, the United States economy seems to have landed itself in great difficulties. The much-trumpeted "New Economy" appears to have lost its potential to accelerate the rate of growth and make the economy immune to business cycle fluctuations. A large number of American companies have, in recent months, put in their applications under bankruptcy provisions. Heading the list has been Enron not unknown to the Indian people. A number of large companies of information technology sector have downed their shutters. It has come to light that a number of them had resorted to corrupt practices like falsifying their accounts with the help of accounting firms like Arthur Andersen, banks and politicians. Joblessness has reached a very high level. Now, a number of companies have started transferring jobs to developing countries like India in order to cut costs and boost profitability. This, however, has intensified social tensions in America. Thus America is beset with both economic and social difficulties. In this situation, if it does not solve the Iraq problem, which is of its own making, it is going to have far-reaching political, economic and social consequences. Felix Rohatyn has rightly remarked: "The Iraq war, the recession and stock market losses, together with the tax cuts proposed by the Bush administration have transformed the US budget outlook. Three years after the budget ran a surplus of $240bn, this year's deficit could rise to $400bn. The President's recent request for $80bn for the Iraq war and reconstruction is likely to be a first instalment, more realistic estimates run to $200bn or more over the next five years in the long run, the picture is dismal. Instead of the $5,000bn-6,000bn surplus once estimated for the decade ending 2013, the present outlook is for a $1,800bn deficit, according to the Congressional Budget Office. Estimates of economists outside the government reach as high as $4,000bn. There are hopes that Iraq's oil revenues will offset most of the reconstruction costs. But it will take several years and billions of dollars to bring production to its full potential." [13]

At present there are 160,000 coalition troops are deployed in Iraq. Of them around 148,000 are American soldiers. They cost the United States exchequer $3.9 billion a month.

Britain is a very junior member of the coalition. It has contributed only 11,000 troops. Even then the cost to British taxpayers will be far in excess of £5 billion with £ 1 billion spent before the actual engagement. This exceeds the size of the special "war chest" provided by the Treasury. The cost of maintaining the British troops in Iraq is estimated at £ 150 million a month. In two years the total cost will not be less than £3.6 billion. The total estimated pre- and post-war costs will come to £4.6 billion besides the expenses incurred on 6-week war including ammunition, lost equipment, accidents, and fuel are yet-to be calculated. This is bound to increase the extent of budgetary deficit, estimated at £27 billion before the war.

The initial enthusiasm among the prospective investors in Iraq seems to be dying down. The following report in a prestigious British financial paper is revealing: "David Posten, a furniture dealer from Maryland, was intrigued by the idea of doing business in post-war Iraq–so keen in fact that he paid $475 to attend a conference in Washington on the country's reconstruction.

"Crowded into a hotel ballroom with 500 other delegates, Mr Posten listened attentively as panelists outlined the historic opportunities in an oil-rich country halfway across the world.

"They spoke in breathless tones of Iraq's ancient commercial tradition, and how life was gradually returning to normal on Baghdad's streets. And then the subject turned to security.

"You better wear a bullet-proof everything," was the lesson Mr Posten came away with, almost certainly to the chagrin of the conference organisers. "Just when you're comfortable doing your job, someone's liable to come shoot you in the head."

"That disturbing revelation has been dawning across the business community after months of excited buzz about the billions of dollars to rebuilding Iraq.[14]

The hope that the removal of Saddam Hussein, leading to a regime change would open immense possibilities of securing contracts for construction works has started evaporating in view of the continued daily killings of American soldiers and acts of sabotage. The number of American casualties since the war was formally declared to be over has crossed 50. There is a continuing threat even to infrastructure facilities recently repaired and made functional. With the waning enthusiasm on the part of the private sector, the problem of getting adequate investment is becoming every day difficult. A British security consultant in Iraq has painted a grim picture and is of the view that even under a best-case scenario, US forces will have to remain in Iraq for at least two to three years to maintain stability. He thinks, the situation is fraught with danger that any inapt handling may lead to widespread insurrection.[15]

The following report underlines the seriousness of the situation: "The security burden has fallen heavily on Halliburton and Bechtel, the US construction and engineering giants that have won the largest contracts to repair Iraq's oil industry and other infrastructure. "Security is our greatest concern," says Bechtel spokesperson Alison Abbott. The company's workers in Iraq are under 24-hour protection by Fards, and regularly consult the US military to find out where they can operate."[16]

Obviously, in the prevailing conditions, costs of running business will go up. While these big and experienced companies may stay put, others–medium and small companies–may not survive. This has been worrying the Bush administration. Besides, the danger of a third Gulf War can also not be ruled out. This danger may arise if the US stays put for a longer period than 12-14 months, tries to impose its own model of economic and political reconstruction, the burden of reparations and debts continues on the back of Iraq and the security situation deteriorates.[17] The *Washington Post* warned about militants getting bolder and more daring with every passing day. It was not certain that they were working under the command of Saddam Hussein. "The danger is that they will succeed in triggering a broader guerrilla war against US troops fed not just by loyalty to the Baath Party but also by popular discontent with American occupation–a war that could destabilize Iraq and the region around it." What is the way out? "The first step toward regaining the initiative would be full acceptance by the administration of the fact that more resources are needed–more money, more civilian administrators and more troops.[18]

It is obvious that a great deal of uncertainty accompanies the situation in Iraq. One is not sure whether the Americans along with other members of the coalition will be able to accomplish their intended task of reconstruction. Already doubts are being expressed in many quarters. Some say that Iraq may go the Vietnam way even though apparently suitable terrain does not seem to be available for successful conduct of guerrilla warfare. The Bush administration, dominated by the neo-conservatives, too is not interested in involving the UN in the task. [19] It wants other countries to deploy peacekeeping forces to work under its command.

Let us conclude our discussion with the following apt observations from Edward W. Said: "I wish I would say that general understanding of the Middle East, the Arabs and Islam US has improved, but alas, it really hasn't. For all kinds of reasons, the situation in Europe seems to be considerably better. What American leaders and their intellectual lackeys seem incapable of understanding is that history cannot be swept clean like a blackboard, so that "we" might inscribe our own future there and impose our own forms of life for these lesser people to follow. It is quite common to hear high officials in Washington and elsewhere speak of changing the map of the Middle East, as if ancient societies and myriad peoples can be shaken up like so many peanuts in a jar. But this has often happened with the "orient", that semi-mythical construct which since Napoleon's invasion of Egypt in the late 18th century has been made and remade countless times. In the process the uncountable sediments of history, a dizzying variety of peoples, languages, experiences, and cultures, are swept aside or ignored, relegated to the sandheap along with the treasures ground into meaningless fragments that were taken out of Baghdad.[20]

References

1. Carnegie Endowment for International Peace, *From Victory of Success: Afterward Policy in Iraq*.
2. *Ibid.*
3. *Ibid.*

4. *Ibid.*

5. *Ibid.*

6. Quoted in *Ibid.*

7. *Ibid.*

8. *Ibid.*

9. Peter Slevin and Dara Priest, "Wolfowitz Concedes Iraq Errors," *The Washington Post,* July 24, 2003.

10. Max Rodenbeck, "The Occupation," *The New York Reviewof Books,* Vol. 50, No. 13.

11. *UN Document S/1999/356.* Annex II.

12. Felix Rohatyn, " The unbearable expense of global dominance", *Financial Times,* June 9, 2003.

13. *Ibid.*

14. Joshua Chaffin, "Iraq's streets spell fear for potential investors", *Financial Times,* July 9, 2003.

15. *Ibid.*

16. *Ibid.*

17. Anthony Cordesman, "How to slide into a third Gulf War," Financial Times, July 30, 2003.

18. "Facing Reality in Iraq," *The Washhington Post,* July 8, 2003.

19. *The Washington Post,* August 2, 2003.

20. Edward W. Said, "A window on the world", adapted from the introduction to a new edition of Orientalism, Published by Penuin, *The Guardian,* August 2, 2003.

19

Iraq–Down the Memory Lane

Manorma Dewan

It was a freezing cold December, 1957 night. The station wagon stopped in front of a huge beautiful mosque. Ahmad Mustafa, the driver of the vehicle which brought us from Tehran said in his broken Urdu HUM BAGHDAD MEIN HAI" (We are in Baghdad). The long journey from the Iranian capital was extremely interesting though tiring.

We were in the old part of Baghdad where famous Kadhmain mosque is situated. Thousands of pilgrims visit this mosque every year for spiritual sustenance. I found the whole atmosphere awe inspiring. The place looked like a painting depicting a typical old street of Baghdad. People were seen wearing long robes.

Since Childhood Baghdad had fascinated me. I have read and enjoyed the Arabian Nights written by Richard Burton and various other stories about the wisdom of Khalifa Haroon- Al- Rashid who roamed round the streets of Baghdad incognito to ascertain the real condition of the people. He used to punish the guilty officials who neglected their duties and indulged in corruption and oppression of the poor.

It was my first visit to Iraq, and I did not feel a stranger. Walking across the streets of Baghdad, Basra and other cities of Iraq. I came across many scenes which remain imprinted on my mind till today. They relate to many objects, which are both mundane and spiritual.

The Shorja Bazar, in the old Baghdad looked very much like the bylanes of Delhi's Chandni Chowk. Walking through the covered Bazar, I was reminded of markets in Lucknow and Hyderabad where one can buy anything from expensive perfumes to pumpkins and watermelons. Wares at the shops gave me a nostalgic feeling of homesickness.

This was Baghdad, the capital of Iraq in December 1957 - January 1958, only six month before the Historic Revolution of 14th July 1958 which opened new vistas of her destiny and its role in the Arab world, the Afro–Asian Community, and International affairs. I could feel lull before the storm. The atmosphere was tense. One could talk of old cultural relations between India and Iraq, could discuss similarities in food habits and social attitudes but could not openly discuss political situation in Iraq and the Arab world with anyone.

I had the opportunity to visit Iraq and many other Arab countries a number of times from 1958 onwards. My last visit to Iraq was in November 2001. I have witnessed the glorious period of India–Iraq cooperation in trade, political, economic, and cultural fields. It goes without saying that the greatest turning point in the Indo–Iraq relations was the Republican Revolution in 1958. This revolution had a special significance for the Afro–Asian countries. It's biggest contribution was that the notorious Baghdad Pact was made to die an ignoble death. The building, which housed the offices of the Baghdad Pact organization symbolically turned into an orphanage, a fact very humorously hailed by Jawahar Lal Nehru in Indian Parliament. Nehru had hailed the revolution in Iraq "as a turning point in Arab people's struggle for national liberation and social progress."

India's relations with Iraq were close not only because of cultural, spiritual religious and geographical ties, but also due to the fact that both the countries were part of the same imperialist system, the British empire. The philosophy of Arab Nationalism strongly propounded by the Iraqi leadership and which is very similar to Indian nationalism further strengthened these bonds.

Talking about the historical, cultural, religious and spiritual links of India and Iraq we are reminded of the great ruler of ancient Iraq - Khalifa Harun Al- Rashid.

The reign of Harun–al–Rashid is not the history of a county far away from India. India and Iraq had very close links at that time. Jawahar Lal Nehru in his immortal work on Indian History *The Discovery of India* has written the study of Indian learning and science in Baghdad was greatly encouraged by the powerful Barmak family (the Bermicides) which gave viziers to Harun Rashid. This family had probably been converted from Buddhism. During an illness of Harun–al–Rashid, a physician named Manak was sent from India. Manak settled down in Baghdad and was appointed the head of a large hospital there. Arab writers mention six others Indian physicians living in Baghdad at the time besides Manak.

After the advent of Islam, contacts between India and Iraq received a new fillip. The Abbasid period known popularly as the golden age not only in Iraq, but for the whole medieval world saw a great deal of contacts between the two lands. The political contact between the Arabs and the people of sub–continent was only of a comparatively short duration and started and ended with the conquest of Sind in 712 A D by Mohammad Bin Qasim. But there is clear evidence that much more powerful contacts were made through channels of philosophy, religion and commerce.

The first contacts between the Arabs and Indians after the advent of Islam go back to nearly 1,300 years. When the Arabs came to India for the first time, they found here an ancient and brilliant civilization ftom which they were able to learn a great deal.

The desire for the Arab learning was manifested in the great interest shown by the Abbasid court in Iraq in the translations of Indian works on science, religion, astronomy, astrology medicine and mathematics. There is an evidence that the tales of Panchtantra were translated from Sanskrit into Arabic. It was from this Arabic translation that the book was translated into Greek, Latin, Hebrew, French, Spanish Turkish, English and Persian.

The tragic end to the brilliant page in Iraqi history came with Haluku Khan's entry into Baghdad in 1258 A.D. His mongol hordes ransacked the capital Baghdad and rest of the country turning it into a virtual wasteland. The famous library of Baghdad was completely destroyed by Halaku. His Mongal hordes put the valuable books and rare manuscripts in the river Tigris and constructed a makeshift bridge. A complete disruption of the economic and social life of Baghdad followed the vast and highly developed system of irrigation of Iraq which was destroyed completely. For 300 years Iraq was ruled by foreign dynasties. Around 1534, it became a province in the newly established Ottoman Empire. The Ottoman rule came to an end in Iraq when they were defeated by the allies at the end of World War in 1917.

Baghdad continued to hold a great deal of charm for the men of knowledge and learning in India. For example, it is well known that the great saint Mansur - al – Halaj with whom is associated the famous mystic saying "ANAL HAQ" (I am the truth) had spent a number of years in India. In fact this saying is directly attributed to the Vedantic dictum" AHAM SATYAM (I am the truth). In Baghdad, the orthodoxy reacted to this saying with violence and fury which had been common with the religious bigotry in most parts of Asia and Africa in the later middle ages including India. Though it was in Baghdad that Mansur was stoned to death.

But in the Indian Sufi circles MANSUR is revered as a great martyr to the cause of spiritual ecstacy. Study of Urdu poetry will reveal that Mansur.is used as a symbol of truthfulness, fearlessness and revolt against the orthodoxy. Hazarat Sarmad Shahid, the greatest of Indian mystic martyrs had proudly and openly proclaimed MANSUR–AL–HALAJ of Baghdad to be his teacher or Murshid. So the chords that tied India and Iraq and the entire Arab world over a great many centuries until the dark age of political slavery fell over a large part of Asia and Africa.

The names of places like Baghdad and Basra recur quite often in the holy scriptures of the Sikhs and also in the folk–lore of Punjab. The affinity with the land of Sindbad the sailor and the locale of the stories of the Arabian Nights has with India is also reflected in a common habit of naming pretty girls in Iraq as Hind.

When I am writing my impressions of various visits to Iraq in a span of forty three years during which I witnessed Iraq emerging as a major power in the Arab world and India cooperating with Iraq in it's gigantic task of economic reconstruction, I am always reminded of the fact that India had closest of relations and contacts with West Asian region termed commonly as the Middle–East. But a fact which is not fully grasped is that it was only through Mesopotamia (the ancient Iraq) the land of the twin rivers of Tigris and Eupheaters that these contacts were maintained and sustained. The contacts between India and Iraq were both through land and sea. The caravans of Indian and Arab traders are known to have travelled thousands of miles between Baghdad and Banaras (Varanasi) in northern India. The Indian silks were considered literally worth their weight in gold by Aristocracy in Baghdad. More than five thousand Indian traders settled in Baghdad, Basra, Mosul and other parts of Iraq. They represented the centuries old traditions of those bygone days when the products of Banaras and Murshidabad were considered as much a symbol of status as garments from Paris and London are today.

Indian folklore is abundant with the stories of sea–faring sailors who used to fend for fortunes in the Arabian Sea and had maintained a regular service between Basra and various parts of India.

The earliest historical evidence of Indo–Iraqi contacts goes back to a period of about 3000 B.C. Trade with India was very important and began at least as early as 2400 B.C. principally through the cities of Babylonia. At Ur and other places Indian seals and special instruments have been found.

India and Iraq also share strong spiritual and religious bonds. A large number of Indians, both Muslims and Non–Muslims owe spiritual allegiance to Hazarat–Ghause–Azam whose Mosoleum in Baghdad was very well maintained. I was really surprised to know that my husband late Dewan Berindernath's family in the princely Kapurthala state of Panjab held Ghaus–e–Aazam in great esteem and would send Nazarana (religious offering) to it regularly.

Another place in Baghdad the 'Guru Nanak Asthan' has greatly helped in strengthening Indo–Iraqi relations. This is the place where Guru Nanak stayed for forty days on his way back from Mecca and had long spiritual interactions with great Iraqi thinker and philosopher Hazarat Bahlul. In 1958, it was a job to locate this place. A simple room an enclosure of mud in a cluster of palm trees was situated near the old Baghdad railway station. The keeper, of the place, a middle aged Iraqi asked us in broken Urdu "HINDUSTAN–PAKISTAN SE AAYA–NANAK PIR KI ZIYARAT KAREGA?" (Have you come from India - Pakistan? for pilgrimage of Nanak pir?" He took us inside the room where on a mud platform were kept a pair of wooden slippers, one Japuji Sahib, a hand woven Chattai and a TASBEEH of Beeds. On the mud platform hung a tin plate on which was written in Gurumukhi, Urdu and Arabic letters, Hazarat Baba Nanak Prayed and meditated here for full forty days as a guest of Hazarat Behalool.

The 'Guru Nanak Asthan' transformed into a beautiful Gurudwara in a period of two decades. The Indian companies engaged in the massive reconstruction work in Iraq, virtually took charge of the place. The mud courtyard was replaced by beautiful tiles. Carpets adorned the totally renovated room. The outside courtyard had water coolers installed there. All this work was done under the dynamic initiative and guidance of Indian Ambassador to Iraq at that time, Shri K.N. Bakshi. Every Friday, there used to be KIRTAN and LANGAR, where hundreds of Indians participated who were working in various cities of Iraq. Every time I visited Baghdad, I visited the Guru Nanak Gurudwara and many a time participated in the Friday Kirtan and Langar. It is on record that thousands of Shia Muslims from India visited the Holy Shia Shrines in Karbala, Najaf and Baghdad as pilgrims.

Secularism—Arab Nationalism

It was at the holy shrine of Karbala that I was asked for the first time in Iraq whether I was a Muslim? What surprised and impressed me in Iraq was that no one ever asked me my religion. I worked for a long period of thirty years with Iraqi News Agency as Head of it's Bureau in India and interacted with large number of journalists and technical staff but no one ever asked me to which religion I belonged.

For a foreigner, in Iraq it became difficult to distinguish one citizen from another on the basis of religion. Besides, the people belonging to the two main sects of Islam, the Shias and Sunnis, who between themselves constitute a preponderant majority, there are sizable number of Christians belonging to various denominations as well as some smaller pantheistic sects. So strong has been the pull of Arabism that it becomes difficult to make out whether one is talking to a Muslim or Christian. Incidentally, members of the Christian minority form a very important segment of Iraqi Society, occupying many an important position in the Government and also in trade and commerce.

It was difficult to understand the secular character of a country, like Iraq. It was not the secularism as we define and understand in India. But definitely it was an expression of Arab Nationalism. To understand it, it was necessary to know the philosophy of Arab Baath socialist party, which ruled Iraq for a long period. I talked to a large number of writers, political ideologues, journalists and teachers of political thought and read a lot of literature on the ideology of Arab Baath socialism. I understood that it will be wrong to think that Arab Baath socialism is a combination of various trends like the Arab Nationalism, Islam Revivalism, western Liberalism and Marxism. It seems ideologues of Arab Baath Socialist movement have undoubtedly taken cognizance of all such trends and have imbibed the best and the most relevant part of such philosophies. Hence I would define the Arab Baath movement as on ideological representation of the Arab ethos.

What is this Arab Ethos? Arab countries which have given three of the greatest religions of the world, Christianity, Islam and Judaism, have for the last more than half a century been beset with tremendous process of ideological ferment. The Arabs stretching from western most tip of Morocco to the furthest point comprising 23 countries the Arabian Gulf have been experimenting with four major trends of thought, the Islamic fundamentalism, Marxism, Arab Nationalism and western liberalism trying to find an answer to the problems facing them.

The Arab nations, like most of the developing nations, face problems, which are basically a product of long colonial domination which has led to backwardness. The political subjugation under foreign rulers had resulted in an all round impoverishment of the masses showing itself in economic backwardness as well as cultural and economic poverty.

But such strong has been the pull of the factors, which unite the Arab nation in spite of the geographical divisions and political barriers created through artificial carved political entities by the colonial power, there has always remained what can be termed as Arab Ethos.

Whatever might have been the differences among rulers and leaders of various regions of the Arab world, while travelling from Oman in the Arabian Gulf to more than seven thousand miles away to Morrocco and Algeria would find a very essential unity in cultural moorings, linguistic affinity and an awareness of oneness of all the Arabic speaking people.

It was quite a revelation to me that Arab Baath Socialist Party had been making it pointedly clear as preface to all its publications that when the Baathists talk of the Nation it should not be confused with any single Arab country. To them the nation means, both in cultural and spiritual sense, entirety a people's history, culture, language and aspirations. Arabs as being part of one nation both in the cultural and spiritual sense. The different countries in which they live, make up a politically and economically united fatherland. In the Party's documents, the Arab fatherland means all the Arab countries.

Often a practical application of these highest principles of Arab nationalism create rather a confusing situation for foreigners. In Iraqi diplomatic missions, for example, it is not quite uncommon to find that while the Ambassador is a Lebanese Christian, his second in Command is a Jordanian, Syrian or a Palestinian.

But the Arab Baath socialist party had gone even further that merely providing complete equality to their comrades and colleagues from Arab countries in the party organization or diplomatic missions. This approach of Arab unity was also reflected in the citizenship laws in Iraq. Any citizen of an Arab county, including those whose rulers are following policies hostile to the revolutionary Government, can enter Iraq without a visa, or any type of prior permission. Sufficient for him would be to produce a satisfactory proof of his being an Arab national. While in Iraq any Arab national belonging to any Arab country was entitled to same rights and privileges as enjoyed by the Iraqis. It was even open for him to ask for Iraqi citizenship if he so desired.

When I returned to India after my first long tour of West Asia, which included a number of Arab countries and Iran, I was asked a number of questions about the social life in their countries, especially the status of women and spread of literacy.

The Feminine Revolution

Talking about women in Iraq, I have witnessed a real 'FEMININE REVOLUTION' in Iraq in a period of four decades. In December 1957 and January 1958. I roamed round in various parts of Baghdad and had long walks on the beautiful and fascinating Abu Niwas street on the right bank of river Tigris along with my writer/ Journalist husband late Dewan Berindernath. Quite a few eye brows were raised when they saw a woman eating MASGOUF, the world famous Iraqi fish delicacy on the river bank or entering a popular restaurant. At that time all eating places and entertainment places were considered solely for men only. Even an innocent stroll by young couples was restricted to foreign visitors.

But during my subsequent visits to Iraq, I saw a complete change in Iraqi social attitudes. Dozens of popular restaurants, eating shops and entertainment centres looked jam packed with families on the same Abu Niwas street after the sun set.

Transformation of social relationship in tradition bound societies in a country like Iraq assumes real importance. Iraq had neither a tradition of a westernized feminist movement as was the case of Egypt nor it had the benefit of a bourgeois process of Industrialisation and urbanization as has been seen in many countries of South and South East Asia. Yet barring perhaps Egypt, there is no other Arab country, which has a larger number of working women than Iraq.

In Iraq, one could find women working at the most unlikely of places. It was a common experience to meet women heading various departments in ministries like those of Education, Social Welfare, Foreign Affairs, Information, Youth Affairs and even Industries and Agriculture. The chief Engineer, the Head of the Accounts Department and of Public Relations Department in the Iraqi News Agency were women. The Head of the Iraqi Airways was a young energetic woman. Needless for me to say that as an Indian I was really impressed by it. Some of the professions appear to be predominantly represented by women such as education, medicine and social welfare. In fields of Communication, including Mass Media, predominant participation of women could be marked by any casual visitor to the office of any Newspaper, Radio and television station and the telephone exchange.

This is of course common to many third world countries, but one was quite surprised to find women managing traffic at a busy square in Baghdad or driving tractors on a collective farm, a woman as a chief statisticion at a major commercial institution, a woman incharge of drilling operations at an oil field and women engaged in security duties both as officers and members of other ranks in the popular army, the national militia.

Since women were working in large numbers outside their homes, a new social reality emerged in Iraq, which gave respect and status to the old people in the family. Since they were needed by the young working couples, and they were not considered a liability to be suffered grudgingly by the young couples.

During visits to many a homes of my Iraqi friends, I could personally see and feel the status of the old parents. One heard innumerable number of jokes and anecdotes regarding splitting the parents by young working couples.

Today, thanks to a new social reality, older people are virtually being cajoled by numerous claimants for their affection and attention. It was really a pleasure meeting and talking to a pretty petroleum engineer, Khalida, who not only represented the first generation of the working women, but also of the first crop of young women to go to schools and colleges leave alone institutes of higher training and learning equally unknown a few years back, was the right of a woman driving an automobile.

In Iraq, especially, the capital Baghdad, I could not see the dearth of modern fashions. The veil, which was once considered a symbol of the Arab female has completely vanished. Yet it could be difficult to find any woman in Baghdad indecently or inadequately dressed. This is in spite of the fact that traditional inhibitions against mixing of sexes were fast disappearing and men and women could work, talk and lie uninhibitedly as friends, colleagues and friends, colleagues and comades. But so strong has been the emphasis on basic values of decent family life that evils like prostitution and venereal diseases were mentioned only as nightmare of the past.

In Iraq, when came across a healthy outlook on life where modernity has been evenly balanced with basic human values and Arab cultural moorings. Crimes against women such as rape, abduction and eveteasing were almost extinct.

During my various visits to Baghdad, I was often struck by the fact that one could find women walking and driving alone back home after serving late hours on duty, without any fear.

I was quite surprised and impressed from the fact that none of my female Iraqi friends ever liked to talk about problems like eve - teasing, sadness or mis-behaviour towards the fair sex in Iraq. They did talk of other problems and difficulties like scarcity of domestic help, rise in cost of living, increasing demand for more and more luxuries of life. I as on Indian working woman also faced similar problems but I also feel highly insecure while driving alone at night.

In India and other developing countries working women suffered sexual harassment at places of work. In a city like Delhi, one daily hears and reads reports about eveteasing and serious crimes like rape in educational institutions and elsewhere, I never heard about such crimes during my various visits to Baghdad and other Iraqi cities. Was it the strict enforcement of anti - eve teasing law in Iraq or it was due to the social awakening about the status of women? When I discussed this question with my Iraqi friends, I was happy to know that the women in Iraq were really happy with the laws enforced in their country about providing respect and status to them.

In this connection the efforts made by women's organization in Iraq, General Federation of Iraqi Women need some mention. This organization which represented women from all fields of life had become the nucleus not only for the welfare activities for women like running of creches for children of working mothers and involvement of women in various political and social campaigns, but emancipation in national life. The foreigners are amazed that unlike the western countries, where emancipation of women has been turned into a cheap commercialization of sex, vulgarity and obscenity were conspicuous by their absence in Iraq. While there were hundreds of restaurants, cinemas, theatre halls and other places of entertainment full of both men and women, there was a complete ban on any vulgar display of sex or any advertisement using women's body as a sales gimmick.

The custom prevailing in many Islamic and Arab countries of a man having four legally wedded wives seemed to be fading away in Iraq. A legislation enacted in 1977 provided various safeguards to the marital status of women. One of the most important provisions of the social reform law had been the enforcement of severe restriction on bigamy and polygamy. Iraq already had on adverse sex ratio of having 117 males to 100 females. It was in any case not easy for anyone to marry more than once. Since like most of the Arab countries, in Iraq also it is the husband who had to pay a sizable amount of dowry. Age of marriage has been progressively increasing putting a natural stop to bigamous and polygamous practices.

Yet it was considered essential that the legislative support should also be given to the general interplay of socio–economic factors. Reform law made it extremely difficult for husbands to marry more than one wife, since so many restrictions have been stipulated that it becomes almost impossible. Women are also provided a major safeguard by way of placing important restrictions on the right of man to divorce his wife at will. There existed a greater equality between men and women both in the matter of right to divorce and the custody of children in case of broken marriages.

Detailed provisions have been made, making divorced women eligible in many cases to claim custody of their children–a prerogative which was earlier considered the sole preserve of husbands. Yet another legislative landmark in the struggle for social emancipation has been the law banning forced marriages, and marriages pre–arranged by persons other than the prospective husband and wife.

Iraqi laws had at the same time been accompanied by a massive campaign for strict enforcement of provisions of equal pay for equal work by men and women. It was offence under Iraqi law to pay women less than men for any work she was doing. The significance of this provision becomes obvious when one realizes that even in many developed countries women have yet to attain such a stage of development. Sustained and systematic efforts were made to provide more avenues of employment for women. It was an important decision of the Iraqi government taken in 1977 that women would be provided employment in the armed forces. On a broader spectrum, steps have been taken to involve women in national campaigns like eradication of illiteracy, women were also to play a key role in the campaign for compulsory primary education.

While talking about the progress made by Iraq in various fields, it is very necessary to talk about tremendous strides made in the field of education. To Iraq goes the credit of enacting a law in 1978 making it compulsory for parents to get their children educated. In the history of Middle–East it was perhaps for the first time a law had been passed making it an offence for any parent to keep his child outside the school. Parents were persuaded to send their children to school. The law specifically said that if the parents refuse to send their child to school they would be fined in the first instance 100 Iraqi Dinars or a prison term up to one month. The law said that the punishment would be progressively enhanced in case the offence is repeated.

Even the United Nations Statistical Book published in 1978 clearly said that Iraq comes next to Egypt in the entire Arab world in the matter of having the highest number of doctors, engineers and highly technically qualified personnel both in absolute and in per capita terms.

Education in Iraq was not only compulsory but absolutely free at all levels including professional courses like medicine, engineering, commerce and technology. A large number of Iraqi students received training in various branches of higher learning in scientific and technical field at postgraduate and doctorate levels in Universities abroad. Iraqi students were studying in various courses in different Indian

Universities. Almost all the Iraqi students received the training abroad at the state expense.

I was really happy and impressed to know that private educational institutions did not exist in Iraq. This was done with a view to abolish class differences among the students going to various educational institutions and also to provide a uniform system of humanitarian education. While talking about education in Iraq, I would like to make a mention on the Arabicisation of education and all activities connected with the youth students and school going children. What is this Arabicisation? After abolishing the privately–run educational institutions and eliminating dangers of brain washing of the young through alien cultural and intellectual influence and providing a great leveler in eliminating class distinction in the field of education, a very conscious effort was made to imbibe the Iraqi children and youth with all that is best in Arab heritage.

When I came to know about it, immediately the question which came to my mind was that does Arabicisation in educational and intellectual fields aims at excluding teaching of foreign languages thus leading to isolationism in it's approach?

But this was not the case. Teaching in English had become compulsory at the secondary school level, while French was taught in high schools. There was a manifold increase among the number of youth who were well conversant with foreign languages like English, French, German and Russian. That was the reason that a foreigner did not find himself stranded in Baghdad if he lost his way. One would readily come forward to help a foreigner with at least a smattering of English if he found him in difficulty.

As an Indian, I was interested to know how the youth power is being taken care of. The Iraqi regime gave practical shape to the famous dictum of Saddam Hussein "capture the youth and secure the future." The Iraqi rulers realized that the energies of the youth are too precious and potential to be neglected after they finish their work in schools and colleges. To channelise the youth energies into constructive and healthy chanels, youth clubs, youth centres and sports clubs were set up all over the country. Sports were given importance. Sports were not only compulsory in every school and college, the children and youth were inculcated the interest in sports activities. This pertained to both boys and girls.

Besides sports, importance was given to cultural activities like theatre, drama, painting and sculpturing. The Indian artists who visited Iraq were really impressed by the talent of the Iraqi children and youth in the various fields of art and culture.

The Ministry of Youth Affairs in Iraq had to do quite a bit of hard concentrated work to organize the youth activities in Iraq. Special emphasis was laid to enrich the youth mind with all that is best in the realm of ideas throughout human history, particularly the Arab Heritage. The planners of education in Iraq laid special emphasis on Arabicisation, not only of education but all activities connected with the youth, college students and school going children.

I was fortunate enough to have many Iraqi friends and visit their homes. This provided me an opportunity to understand the family relationships and social attitudes in Iraq. When I visited house of one of my very good Iraqi friends Suad, I found the entire family waiting to welcome me.

Suad was not married and was living with his mother, two elder brothers, their wives, children and a younger brother who was studying in the University. While talking to me he showed deep interest in Buddhism, Gandhian philosophy of non–violence and Indian paintings. He was very keen to visit India and study in an Indian University.

Like all Arabs, Iraqis too are very good and generous hosts. I found a feast waiting for me. I also realized that there existed a great similarity in Indian and Iraqi social attitudes, their customs and family relationships. The joint family system still existed in Iraq. One found three generations living together. As I have written earlier the working daughter–in–laws considered their mother–in–laws as an asset and tried to pamper them and keep them in good humour. They were not unwanted.

The family had really worked hard to prepare the food. Leaving aside a few specialities, I found a great similarity between the Indian and the Iraqi food. The *BIRYANI* (Rice and meat cooked together) tasted almost like the one cooked in the Indian homes. Similar was the taste of DAAL (pulse) and *BHINDI* (ladies finger) '*HALWA*' and '*JALEBI*' not only looked but tasted similar to the Indian '*Halwa'* and '*Jalebi'*.

While talking to the family, I came to know that Suad's mother suffered from heart ailment and elder brother's wife had to take regular physio- therapy treatment. Both the ailments required expensive medicines and medical care. I told them how expensive was the medical aid in India and how the private medical practitioners minted money in India.

But I was really happy and surprised to know that all Iraqi citizens are provided free medical aid. This includes supply of modern medicines and treatment by competent doctors and care by trained nurses. Health Insurance laws were made very comprehensive providing for protection and therapeutic health services for all Iraqi population. The Iraqi law and health Insurance also provided free medical treatment abroad to it's citizens.

When I sit down to write my memories of Iraq, covering a long journey of four and half decades, my mind wanders from Baghdad to Basra to Babylon, from Mosul, Tikrit, Najaf and Karbala, from Sammarra, Habboniya lake to the Iraq Museum - from old Shorja Bazar, four kilometre long Rashid street to the posh markets in Al–Mansur, from a small inn near Kadhmlya mosque to the AI- Rashid hotel, from Abu Niwas street to the Saddam Art Centre and from Guru Nanak Gurudwara to the Ghause - Azam Mazar. The names are too many to make a mention.

I stayed in Iraq for four weeks before the July 1958 Revolution, and I have seen Iraq making rapid progress in various fields during my subsequent visits to Iraq. I am also a witness to the massive Indian participation in the Iraqi economic reconstruction.

I was distressed to see Iraqi destruction during the Gulf War in 1990 and the impact of long drawn economic sanctions resulting in hardships for the Iraqi people. But I never found Iraqis demoralised. I found them in a fighting spirit. It seems to be in their genes. Fighting the invaders and reconstructing their devasted country is in their blood.

History stands a witness that when Halaku, the grandson of Changez Khan invaded Iraq he faithfully followed his grand father's tradition and indulged in savage devastation of Iraq. Changez Khan had devastated Iran. He killed one million people in the famous city of Mashed. Only one cat was left alive. Halaku wanted to do one up on Changez Khan.

On entering Baghdad Halaku's soldiers burnt the boat bridge on the river Tigris. He ordered that the new bridge should be constructed of an unusual material. His evil eye fell on the huge Baghdad library spread in three hundred rooms in thirteen big buildings. The books were used to construct the bridge.

The bridge was ready but the books still remained in a big number. This angered Halaku. He ordered that the other side of Baghdad should be burnt with the remaining books. Baghdad was reduced to ashes and it's population was reduced from seven Lakhs to seven thousand.

The heavy US bombardment during the Gulf War had badly damaged the bridges over river Tigris in Baghdad. Iraqis reconstructed them. How Iraq is going to do it's reconstruction now after the American invasion of March 2003 is not easy to predict.

I can visualize the deserted and sad Abu Niwas Street on the bank of river Tigris in Baghdad. I have always seen this beautiful street with well-kept trees and gardens full of people. Most of the restaurants and Tea Houses CHAE KHANAS are also located on the Abu Niwas Street.

Abu Niwas was Omar Khayyam of the Arabs. He was considered a vagabond poet. The Kazis of Baghdad had three times ordered that Abu Niwas be stoned to death or burnt alive. He used to roam around on this very street. He was heard shouting "human beings have a better image than their God, God purposely did not flow wine in the River Tigris for He knew that the religious people will keep on drinking and will join the sacred Mehfil of genuine wine lovers."

The rulers of Baghdad ordered that Abu Niwas should be drowned in a tub full of wine. Hearing the sentence, Abu Niwas praised and thanked the ruler and said, "May God give this kind of death to every artist."

20
Post-Saddam Hussein Period

V.D. Chopra

Saddam Hussein was captured from a hideout in Tikrit on December 14, 2003 in mysterious circumstances. This marked the beginning of a new phase in the struggle of the Iraqi people against US–UK occupation forces. The Pentagon's capture of unharmed Saddam Hussein had wide scale repercussions not only in Iraq and the US but also in the rest of the Arab world as well as the Third World. The fall out of this development will have both long–term and short–term repercussions.

This brings into sharp focus that now there is no ground for occupation forces to remain in Iraq.

Saddam's arrest has provided an opportunity to narrow down differences between the United States on one hand and France and Germany on the other over military action in Iraq. President Bush now can seek reconciliation with France, Germany and Russia by inviting them to participate in reconstructing Iraq instead of excluding them. He can now also work with the UN Security Council to obtain its unequivocal endorsement of the sovereignty transfer to the Iraqis in June, 2004. There are clear indications to this effect. In fact U.N. Secretary General Koffi Annan has already given signals in this direction.

In the final analysis will this development influence political future of Bush is anybody's guess.

President Bush and British Prime Minister Tony Blair as well as the US appointed Iraqi Governing Council (IGC) maintain that the prospect of Saddam's return to power has been completely eliminated beyond any doubt. However, nobody can predict at this stage as to how far Arab Ba'ath Socialist Party will continue to remain a political factor in the life of the Iraqi people.

Nevertheless, it will be naive to minimise nationalistic and patriotic aspirations of Iraqi people Shias, Sunnis and Kurdish.

It is significant to mention here that Shias have already raised the slogan "No, no to Saddam; No, no to America". They have been organising demonstrations against the American occupation forces. Besides this 'suicide squads' are busy in violent activities. According to one estimates till the end of 2003 suicide bombs have killed more than five hundred American soldiers. In fact, guerrilla warfare of the urban style has been going on after the overthrow of the Ba'ath Socialist Party regime.

Shias, constituting three-fifths of the national population, have generally been demanding that in the new democratic set up of Iraq the principle of one person, one vote should be followed. If this principle is accepted Shias will be a leading political force in the country. This implies that Shias want to be a dominant force in the post-Saddam Iraq. But this is not the whole reality. There are democratic and leftist's forces, both Ba'athists and communists and a section of Kurdish people who want a constitution, which represents all ethnic-religious and political forces in the country. Recently, a meeting of twenty-one political parties was held to evolve a consensus on the future political set up of Iraq.

To the dismay of Washington and the IGC and the delight of democrats around the world, the "town hall" selection is unacceptable to Grand Ali Husseini Al Sistani, the popular and seniormost religious figure of the Shia community. It runs counter to the *fatwa* (religious decree) he issued in June. According to this *fatwa* only an elected assembly can assume power to administer Iraq or frame its constitution. Resisting pressure from IGC, Al Sistani has stood his grounds.

It is significant to mention here that the main objective of the US during the next few months is to establish a credible Iraqi government over which it can exercise sufficient control. The Americans are keen to avoid a direct election. This may sweep the Shias to power and establish a theocratic state. That could destroy the secular fabric of the nation and result in a major civil war. However, American policy makers have yet to come to grip with internal situation in the sense that Arab Ba'ath Socialist Party, the Communists Party, Kurdish Democratic Party and influential liberal democrats are important political factors. This is a dilemma, which Washington is facing today.

Mohammed Ghani, a respected 74 years old sculptor, is concerned about such a development. "I am Shia, my wife is Sunni and many of our best friends are Christians," he says. To separate the Iraqis into different ethnic and religious groups will be a big mistake by the Americans and foreign politicians. "We have lived together for generations, for hundreds of years. Only political interests try to tear us apart."[1]

Ironically, it is from these concrete realities that Washington's Iraq policy in the post-Saddam Hussein period is caught in a vicious circle. America fears that Shias would try to engineer an Iranian-style theocracy. On the other hand it does not trust Ba'athists, Communists, Kurdish Democrats and Liberals. Its main reliance is on those individuals who do not have any mass base in the country.

Mr. Bremer, America's administrator in Iraq, was in Washington on 16 January, 04. He met members of the National Security and Mr. Bush and discussed the future political set up in Iraq. On the other hand, the Ayatollah has called for direct popular elections and rejected the American plan of regional caucuses selecting a transitional assembly which will set up an interim government.

questions on the kind of material he had prior to making critical presentation to the United Nations February, 2003.[7]

This shows that the United States administration's defence of its military action in Iraq to destroy its weapons of mass destruction had no justification for Iraq did not possess these weapons.

On the other hand the fallout of military action in Iraq has destroyed both the economy and political structures of this strategic state. David Kay, who headed the Central intelligence agency's team of weapons inspectors until recently, has confirmed that Iraq did not possess a non– conventional capability. In the team's assessment the weapons of mass destruction capability, which Iraq possessed up to 1990, was destroyed years before the invasion, either on the initiative of the former Ba'ath regime or under the pressure of international inspections. While Dr. Kay tried to provide the administration with two avenues of escape, it might not be able to avail of them. It cannot explore the possibility that remnants of the Iraqi programme could have been smuggled out to Syria, since it lacks the domestic and international credibility to pressure the Damascus regime in the way it did the former regime in Baghdad. The administration also cannot take shelter behind the CIA official's statement that errors in judgment should be attributed to the intelligence services rather than to the political echelon.[8]

This establishes that military action in Iraq had political objectives rather than destruction of weapons of mass destruction. These facts show that Iraq did not possess these weapons. This implies that the military action was directed to dislodge from power Arab Ba'ath Socialist Party headed by Saddam Hussein. In the final analysis the military action was undertaken to change the internal political system and control its oil resources.

In this sense Iraq is on the cross roads and the international community cannot afford to "sit and watch". The situation demands that international community the developing countries and non-aligned movement should assert themselves through the United Nations and allow the Iraqi people to determine their own destiny. The way out is that Iraqi people should be given an opportunity to mould their future themselves. Their fate should not be determined by the most powerful nations of the world, the United States and Great Britain. This is need of the hour.

References

1. Ethnic Cauldron: *India Today,* December 29, 03, p. 33.
2. *The Hindu,* January 25, 2004.
3. *The Hindustan Times,* January 25, 2004.
4. *The Hindustan Times,* January 29, 2004.
5. *The Hindu,* January 31, 2004.
6. *The Hindu,* January 28, 2004.
7. *The Hindustan Times,* January 26,2004.
8. *The Hindu,* January 28, 2004.

Index

C